TRUTH ABOUT THE SECURITIES
SCAM 1992

PRAHALAD RAO

BLUEROSE PUBLISHERS
India | U.K.

Copyright © Prahalad Rao 2023

All rights reserved by author. No part of this publication may be reproduced, stored in a retrieval system or transmitted in any form or by any means, electronic, mechanical, photocopying, recording or otherwise, without the prior permission of the author. Although every precaution has been taken to verify the accuracy of the information contained herein, the publisher assume no responsibility for any errors or omissions. No liability is assumed for damages that may result from the use of information contained within.

BlueRose Publishers takes no responsibility for any damages, losses, or liabilities that may arise from the use or misuse of the information, products, or services provided in this publication.

For permissions requests or inquiries regarding this publication, please contact:

BLUEROSE PUBLISHERS
www.BlueRoseONE.com
info@bluerosepublishers.com
+91 8882 898 898
+4407342408967

ISBN: 978-93-5819-167-7

Cover design: Tahira
Typesetting: Tanya Raj Upadhyay

First Edition: August 2023

DEDICATION

This Book is dedicated to Mahalingam Ravi, my Office Associate who passed away in the middle age of His Life in May 2019 in New Delhi due to Covid-19.

DISCLAIMER

Views expressed by the author in this book are based on his personal understanding of the past and perception of the present. This book neither intends nor suggests any attribution of whatsoever nature to anyone or to any policy or program or system existing or envisaged nor this book intends or suggests to hurt sentiments of any person or state or political bodies or religious bodies or political or religious leaders or body of any other nature or defame any of them whatsoever and any construction of the writings in this book otherwise is sole to the person so construing. The author or the publisher will not be liable for any civil or criminal proceedings under the laws of the country.

GRATITUDES

My gratitude to Dr. Sharda, K.Ananth Raman, Royal Hotel, Hyderabad, V.Laxma Reddy, T.S.Murthy, A.R.Venkataraman, P.P.S.Puri, A.S.Dhupia, R.B. Mathur and Lalit Chand, whose guidance, benevolence and humanism in my initial years of service will shine in my heart for ever, C.V.Nair, D. Sankaraguruswamy, Dr. Uddesh Kohli, B.M. Pant, M. Prasad, T.N. Thakur, A.A. Khan, Dr. K. K. Govil and Raji Phillips who gave confidence and lent support to me during my most testing time of life.

My gratitude to senior Indian Administrative Officers (IAS) who headed the organizations, account and audit service officers, eminent engineers, eminent finance & legal experts with whom I had the opportunity to work in one capacity or the other during my thirty years of service in public sector Financial Institutions. Gratitudes to A.K.Sah and Shahzad Bahadur for giving me opportunity to develop my career as a consultant post retirement. My gratitude and special thanks to Dr.J.T.Verghese who offered me chance for continuity of my consultancy job with continued guidance and advice. My association with all of them helped imbibe in me their direction, dedication to the cause of economic development, virtues, values, compassion and affection that became bedrock of my life.

My gratitude to Scholars, Journalists, Thinkers, Philosophers, Historians, Bankers, Economists, Professionals, Socialists and Environmentalists within and outside the country whose writings on Google website helped me to understand the width and depth of subjects selected for this book. Author has disclosed the sources of valuable writings relied upon under "References", also stated in the book at some places. No copyright infringement is intended. Author reiterates his grateful thanks to all of them.

My special thanks to Google for providing inspiration with invaluable sources of information that helped me in completing this book.

In particular, my gratitude to Arun Kumar Sarna who gave me strong standing support during my association with him in service in multi-national consultancy Services Company as well as throughout thereafter.

My gratitude to K. G. Dewan, Sadiq Shafiq and Boben Anto whose ever helping hand remained a sustainable strength to me.

Grateful thanks to M/s BLUE ROSE PUBLISHESERS PRIVATE LIMITED, the Publishers without whose cooperation, guidance and advice, this book wouldn't have reached the readers.

Thanks to my friends, relatives and my family members for their continued encouragement. Their suggestions and support were a great strength for me in completing this book.

11th March, 2023 Prahalad Rao

Table of Contents

DISCLAIMER iv

GRATITUDES v

PART 01 HOW THE SCAM ORIGINATED? 1

PART 02 JANIKIRAMAN & JOINT PARLIAMENTARY COMMITTEES 119

PART 03 BANK RECEIPT - LEGALITY 261

PART 04 SUMMATION 289

REFERENCES 325

ABOUT THE AUTHOR 335

PART 01
HOW THE SCAM ORIGINATED?

"DISASTER IS A SUDDEN CALAMITOUS EVENT BRINGING GREAT DAMAGE, LOSS, OR DESTRUCTION. DISASTERS CAN BE CLASSIFIED INTO TWO BASIC CATEGORIES BASED ON THEIR CAUSE. NATURAL DISASTERS AND MANMADE DISASTERS ARE THESE TWO BASIC CATEGORIES. NATURAL DISASTERS ARE THE DISASTERS CAUSED BY NATURAL FORCES WHEREAS MANMADE DISASTERS ARE CAUSED BY ACTIVITIES OF HUMAN BEINGS. THIS IS THE MAIN DIFFERENCE BETWEEN NATURAL AND MANMADE DISASTER." - HASA – IE PEDIAA WEBSITE.

This Part deals with two aspects, firstly, whether the scam was a system failure or human made? And secondly, how the scam originated? In other words, whether it landed on the earth out of the blue like rain or thunderstorm or lightning or it travelled according to a laid down path to facilitate the scam? Laying of path used here means facilitating the scam through policies framework and other means, that is, the policies and other means undergoing changes in an unusual speed and in seriatim. It may be awkward to look or read so but when these are based on official records, one has to accept them as straightforward. The official records cannot be considered as biased or prejudiced which are attributable to the humans. Both the above aspects have been considered unbiased. The readers may think how it would have helped in prevention of the scam. It could have rather it is affirmable from the available information on records that the scam could have been prevented much before taking its shape. Other than the end results of the scam greatly focused as a centralized point as the headlight of a railway engine, the backup developments never surfaced. One cannot see what is happening in the back until one looks back.

About the system failure: The Securities Scam 1992 was undeniably manmade and men who made it have to bear the burden of it first before passing it on to others as comes out from the reports of the Janakiraman Committee and of the Joint Parliamentary Committee [JPC] that pointedly noted the serious human lapses and deficiencies committed by the commercial banks, foreign banks and the regulatory body. A peep into such lapses and deficiencies cannot be called as a system failure.

The securities scam 1992 was not a system failure as attributed by the then Finance Minister before the JPC but the handiwork of the humans in the process who had the knowledge of it at all levels in the government, RBI and the commercial banks. Findings of the Joint Parliamentary Committee and Janakiraman Committee found the system failure was due to policy pressures and unusual operational human deficiencies. Things happened when they were made to happen and those who made them to happen find 'blame game' as the best self-excuse. [Recent research has emphasized the effectiveness of excuses in protecting the self from the implications of failures and transgressions. The disadvantages of excuses have been relatively neglected. The triangle model of responsibility provides a conceptual framework to analyse how excuses disengage the self from events and the conditions under which advantages and disadvantages accrue. On the disadvantage side, excuse-makers risk being seen as deceptive, self-absorbed, and ineffectual; they are viewed as unreliable social participants with flawed character These undesired consequences result when excuses are used in ways that lower credibility (e.g., fail to receive corroboration), lower goodwill (e.g., blame failures on team members), and produce long-term disengagement (e.g., lead to failures to correct personal deficiencies]. This is what could be attributed to those who excused themselves from their own blames.

The system failure happens in mechanical and IT systems. The proverb 'To err is human' was not the case here. The system failure in this case was ignoring the guidelines and instructions of the RBI to the commercial banks and the RBI's failure to monitor the implementation of those guidelines and instructions for want of which they would have lost their essence. This resulted in free hand to the commercial banks and long hand to the brokers in the interbank securities transactions and, among the brokers, one who had built up good rapport and understanding with the banks made the most fortune. What one could see was excessive greediness was the temptation on all sides, the bankers, the brokers, bureaucrats, politicians and the ministers. That is the crux of the scam. The blame games that followed were to save one and search for scapegoats.

Blame game is to ceaselessly search the opportunities or one or the other excuse on how to trap someone when oneself committed the blame but does not want to own it. That gives a perfumery smell for the person but what is also necessary to know is that the perfume dries up sooner as it doesn't have its permanent character in its contents. So also the blame games are momentary pleasures for one's own comfort but when the Truth is confronted, the blame game starts burning within itself and the reality starts staring. Those who play such blame games cannot absolve themselves nor can escape from the Self-Conscience that is bound to chase, may not be immediately but ultimately in the process of one's life.

The time when it comes before oneself, the Truth laughs at such person and false drives him into a state of deep depression. This also what happens in financial frauds and scams? The blame games once explode, the person starts sinking from confidence, courage and conviction within, the worst that could ever happen to a human. This equally applies to those who played blame games in the securities scam 1992 who have become subjects for in-depth analysis, assessment and conclusion. These have come out from the findings of the JPC which made no reservations to record them. The investigating agency in such cases distances itself from such people and put the ordinary citizens into play in the criminal proceedings. This fact has now started coming into the public domain because of the unceasing and strenuous efforts of the journalists who believe in chasing and not in giving up. I find fit to salute some of the newspapers and new magazines that have done invaluable contribution in digging out the truth.

This book is written by me after more than thirty years of the scam broke out. That needs an explanation on my part. The film series on the same subject were made and released after around the same period. Film series are short scrips that focus on the areas that are more alluring and exciting for the viewers, without which the series lose their very essence. These series, no doubt, gave a best view of the scam as far as they could do.

If you tell a half story to a child, it gets more anxious to know the rest of the story and persists for that until the whole story was told. That is the natural instinct of the child. That is the honest purpose and object of this book that tells behind the scenes story of the scam as much as it was knowable. It is difficult for one to tell precisely details about behind the scam and its hidden beneficiaries, those having been hidden remain beyond one's reach for ever.

I have traced in this book based on research from the information and material available on the Google Website, whom I gratefully thank, in order to throw up also what happened behind and before at the government and regulatory levels that lead to the formation of the scam similar to what happens in the formation of the cyclones. . The cyclones form in the ocean while the scams form on the earth.

Factors that contribute to the eruption of the cyclone in the ocean are known to the IMD that finds out through highly complex technological applications. That kind of complex technological applications are not developed as yet to know the early warnings of formation of the scams on the earth. The factors that evolve into cyclone including the behind the scenes become known to the IMD that enables it to be precise in its prediction. That is not so in scams on the earth for; the behind scenes never surface on the ground rather remain fainted unless and until extraordinary efforts are made by the parliamentary committees, judiciary, financial, legal experts and journalists to revive them.

I have submitted in this book the backup scenario to the extent available that unfolds the factors that spurred up the evolution and formation of the securities scam 1992; it is so because these factors were not officially admitted but compulsively admitted when the JPC started its proceedings. Till then, they were all hidden that placed more focusing attention on the consequential effects of the scam and the roles played by the different people than the factors that were responsible for creation of the scam.

The floppies and magnetic tapes which were seized by investigating agency during its raids on the offices and residential premises of the leading brokers while investigating the securities scam 1992 would have thrown some light on the beneficiaries which stated to have contained such information. These were not presented in the proceedings of the JPC thereby their whereabouts remain unknown.

Does it mean that no bureaucrat or no politician either directly or through their closely associated persons was not benefited from the unearned wealth of the scam? That couldn't have been so. Because, one incidence that supports this view is the association of some stock market pundits and influential people with the ministers, politicians and the bureaucrats, as could be seen from what is submitted in the latter part of this book. There is also information available on record that the brokers, especially Harshad Mehta and other brokers of the same repute stated to have frequent interactions with some Swamiji who had knit the thread closely with the ministers and politicians. Given that, can we rule out that the politicians and bureaucrats were not benefitted from the illegal wealth earned by the brokers including Harshad Mehta and other reputed brokers? That could be said so because the basic evidential records that stated to have contained the names of the beneficiaries, the floppies and magnetic tapes which, the investigating agency lost no time to seize them from the brokers overnight of the scam came to light still remains concealed. This impulsively points to the possibility of the ministers, politicians and the bureaucrats having made hay when sun shined. The line of defence taken by these persons during their questioning as accused by the JPC in its capacity as a court as well as the verdicts recorded by it are also suggestive of what is submitted before.

The Origin: Multimillion financial frauds and scams are not the acts of one or two person[s] but are made through illicit relationship and collusion built among the Interest Groups over a period of time that include political leaders, bureaucrats, Bankers' Bank, Banks and Brokers secretly & systematically until blown up making innocents the victims and the indicted the victorious. The Interest Groups sit silently and watch the developments to safeguard themselves against any accusations; yet they having killed their Conscience having done wrong things hardly feel the upheavals within because that is passed on to the scapegoats. That is the sum of the scam.

Let me place before the readers few words about the Interest Groups:

The book "LAW AND PUBLIC CHOICE-A Critical Introduction" authored by Daniel A. Farber and Philip P. Frickey makes critical analysis of legislative characters and public choice, some of which are reproduced below:

"……..Public choice models often treat the legislative process as a microeconomic system in which "actual political choices are determined by the efforts of individuals and groups to further their own interests, efforts that have been labelled "rent-seeking". Thus, "the basic assumption is that taxes, subsidies, regulations, and other political instruments are used to raise the welfare of more influential group." Although this assumption is obviously simplistic, its very simplicity creates the possibility of constructing powerful formal models. The similarity between pluralism and these economic models is obvious.

Several leading legal scholars have been influenced by this vision of the role of the special interests. The economic theory of legislation recounted by William Landes and Ricdhard Posner is firmly grounded in that tradition:

"In the economists' version of the interest-group theory of government, legislation is supplied to groups or coalitions that outbid rival seekers of favourable legislation. The price that the winning group bids is determined both by the value of legislative protection to the group's members and the group's ability to overcome the free-rider problems that plague coalitions. Payments take the form of campaign contributions, votes, and implicit promises of future favors, and sometime outright bribes. In short, legislation is "sold" by the legislature and "bought" by the beneficiaries of the legislation."...............

Few of us know the factors that facilitated the Security Scam 1992 for; it was where the readily made available facilitations created enticement. Those enticements were visible only to those who had the enticing eyes to capture them for self-flourishing though these were also there for others who were on the other side of the river scam. Almost all of us know that the scam caused tremors in the Bombay Stock Exchange shocking and sucking overnight the investors' investments who had invested their hard earned money into the stock market hoping to make their fortunes. Why and how it happened could be gathered from the stockpile of information, documents and software built by the Investigating agencies, RBI and the Committee [Janakiraman Committee] appointed by it and the Parliamentary Fact Finding Committee [Joint Parliamentary Committee] appointed by the Parliament or JPC spread over a period of about three years to cover the vastness and magnitude of the scam. The scenario that was visible during that period was similar to sounds of continual blasting of stone quarries.

    The sky of the scam was clouded with the financial crisis the country was undergoing in 1991 when the honour of the country was at stake. The then Finance Minister and the Prime Minister had sleepless nights and were abounded with anxious moments in the financial history of the country. The newspapers reported unseemly discussions between the governing system lead by the bureaucrats, the financial pundits and the leading brokers in the country to find a plausible way out to avoid the crisis. It is a different matter how it was allowed to be built up by the preceding governing system but that was not a substitute to the serious problem then in hand. It needs to be appreciated that the scam of the scale that shook the country also suggested involvement of politicians, the bureaucrats, the bankers' bank, the bankers, financial institutions, the opportunists and the brokers' community. It doesn't look so on the face of it but it calls for efforts of a diver who dives into the deep sea to find Organic gemstones that are found in the ocean such as coral, calcite, aragonite, and pearls, mollusks, inorganic gemstones, diamonds etc.

Wikipedia notes "The **1991 Indian economic crisis** was an economic crisis in India resulting from a balance of payments deficit due to excess reliance on imports and other external factors.[*citation needed*] India's economic problems started worsening in 1985 as imports swelled, leaving the country in a twin deficit: the Indian trade balance was in deficit at a time when the government was running on a huge fiscal deficit.[1]

The fall of the Eastern Bloc, which had trade relations with India and allowed for rupee exchange, posed significant issues. Towards the end of 1990, leading up to the Gulf War, the situation became dire. India's foreign exchange reserves were not enough to finance three weeks' worth of imports. Additionally, the Iraq-Kuwait conflict caused a significant shift in the trade deficit as India relied on these nations for crude oil. The surge in crude oil prices further exacerbated the imbalance in India's balance of payments. Meanwhile, the government was on the brink of defaulting on its financial obligations. In July of that year, the rupee experienced a sharp depreciation/devaluation due to the low reserves, which further worsened the twin deficit problem.[2]

In February 1991, the Chandrasekhar government was unable to pass the budget after Moody's downgraded India's bond ratings.[3] The ratings declined further due to the unsuccessful passage of the budget, making it increasingly challenging and expensive for India to borrow money from international capital markets. This placed additional pressure on the country's economy.[4] The International Monetary Fund (IMF) suspended its loan program to India, and the World Bank also discontinued its assistance. These actions limited the government's options to address the crisis and forced it to take drastic measures to avoid defaulting on its payments.[5][6][7]

To address the economic crisis, the government implemented various measures, including the pledge of a significant portion of India's gold reserves to the Bank of England and the Union Bank of Switzerland as collateral. The aim of this move was to secure much-needed foreign exchange to meet India's debt obligations and stabilize the economy. However, this decision was not without controversy and was seen by some as a drastic and desperate move. Critics viewed the decision to mortgage the country's gold as a sign of the government's limited options and inability to manage the crisis effectively.[8]

The economic crisis created a situation where India had to accept the conditions imposed by the World Bank and IMF loan, which included structural reforms. As a result, the Indian economy was opened up to foreign participation in various sectors, including state-owned enterprises. This move towards liberalization was seen by some as necessary to secure much-needed funds and prevent default on loan payments. However, it also led to concerns about the impact of foreign entities on India's economy and the potential loss of control over vital industries.[9][10]

India's liberalization policies since 1991 have led to significant economic growth and integration into the global economy, but have also faced criticism for uneven distribution of benefits, increased inequality, and negative impacts on the environment.[11]

Causes and conscious [edit]

The crisis was caused by currency overvaluation;[2] the current account deficit, and investor confidence played significant role in the sharp exchange rate depreciation.[12][13][14]

The economic crisis was primarily due to the large and growing fiscal imbalances over the 1980s. During the mid-eighties, India started having the balance of payments problems. Precipitated by the Gulf War, India's oil import bill swelled, exports slumped, credit dried up, and investors took their money out.[15] Large fiscal deficits, over time, had a spillover effect on the trade deficit culminating in an external payments crisis. By the end of the 1980s, India was in serious economic trouble.

External debt of India (1970-2020)

One of the main causes of the crisis was the accumulation of foreign debt. In the 1980s, India had borrowed heavily from international lenders, in part to finance infrastructure projects and industrialization. However, by 1991, the country was facing a severe balance of payments crisis, as it was unable to service its debt and was running out of foreign exchange reserves.[16]There were also structural problems in the Indian economy that contributed to the crisis, including a high fiscal deficit, low savings and investment rates, and inadequate export growth.

The gross fiscal deficit of the government (centre and states) rose from 9.0 percent of Gross Domestic Product (GDP) in 1980-81 to 10.4 percent in 1985-86 and to 12.7 percent in 1990-91. For the centre alone, the gross fiscal deficit rose from 6.1 percent of GDP in 1980-81 to 8.3 percent in 1985-86 and to 8.4 percent in 1990-91. Since these deficits had to be financed by borrowings, the internal debt of the government accumulated rapidly, rising from 35 percent of GDP at the end of 1980-81 to 53 percent of GDP at the end of 1990-91. The foreign exchange reserves had dried up to the point that India could barely finance three weeks worth of imports.[17]

In mid-1991, India's exchange rate was subjected to a severe adjustment. This event began with a slide in the value of the Indian rupee leading up to mid-1991. The authorities at the Reserve Bank of India took partial action, defending the currency by expanding international reserves and slowing the decline in value. However, in mid-1991, with foreign reserves nearly depleted, the Indian government permitted a sharp devaluation that took place in two steps within three days (1 July and 3 July 1991) against major currencies.

Recovery [edit]

Further information: Economic liberalisation in India

With India's foreign exchange reserves at $1.2 billion in January 1991[18][19][20] and depleted by half by June,[20] barely enough to last for roughly 3 weeks of essential imports,[19][21] India was only weeks away from defaulting on its external balance of payment obligations.[19][20]

Government of India's immediate response was to secure an emergency loan of $2.2 billion[22][23][24] from the International Monetary Fund by pledging 67 tons of India's gold reserves as collateral security.[8][23] The Reserve Bank of India had to airlift 47 tons of gold to the Bank of England[15][18] and 20 tons of gold to the Union Bank of Switzerland to raise $600 million.[15][18][25] During the transport of the gold reserves to the airport, the van experienced a tyre burst and caused panic.[26][27][8] The government, in the midst of the 1991 Indian General Elections, conducted the airlift with secrecy.[28] The news of the government pledging the entire gold reserves against the loan outraged national sentiments and caused a public outcry.[15][21] The gold was transported to London via a chartered plane from May 21 to May 31, 1991.[15] The Chandra Shekhar government, which authorised the airlift, had collapsed a few months later.[15] This move was seen as prioritising the balance of payment crisis over the welfare of the Indian people and kick-started P.V. Narasimha Rao's economic reform process.[18]

Under Narsimha Rao Government [edit]

P. V. Narasimha Rao took over as Prime Minister in June, and appointed Manmohan Singh as Finance Minister.[15] The Narasimha Rao government ushered in several reforms that are collectively referred to as liberalisation in the Indian media.

The reforms formally began on 1 July 1991 when RBI devalued Indian Rupee by 9% and by a further 11% on 3 July. It was done in two doses to test the reaction of the market first by making a smaller depreciation of 9%.[29] The economic reforms pushed by Prime Minister Rao were met with significant opposition from those who believed that they were an interference with India's autonomy. The speech made by then Prime Minister Rao, a week after taking office, emphasized the need for these reforms. As reported by the New York Times, "Mr. Rao, who was sworn in as Prime Minister last week, has already sent a signal to the nation—as well as the I.M.F.—that India faced no "soft options" and must open the door to foreign investment, reduce the bureaucratic red tape that stifles initiative, and streamline industrial policy."[30]

Aftermath [edit]

Since the implementation of economic reforms in 1991, India has experienced substantial economic growth and has emerged as a prominent participant in the global economy. The liberalization policies of the Indian government have facilitated this growth by attracting foreign investments, increasing trade relations, and promoting domestic economic reforms.

However, while some argue that these policies have benefited India, there are criticisms that suggest otherwise. Some experts argue that the growth has been uneven, and the benefits of liberalization policies have not been equally distributed across the country. Inequality has increased as the divide between the rich and poor has widened, and marginalized communities have been left behind. Additionally, some have argued that liberalization policies have had negative impacts on the environment and have not addressed issues related to sustainability and social justice.[31]

Despite these criticisms, the Indian government continues to promote liberalization policies and seeks to further integrate into the global economy. The success of these policies remains a subject of debate and continues to be a significant point of discussion among policymakers, economists, and civil society groups.

India's gross domestic product (GDP), adjusted for inflation, increased from $266 billion in 1991 to $3 trillion in 2019, while its purchasing power parity increased from $1 trillion in 1991 to $12 trillion in 2019. However, India continues to face several significant challenges, including poverty, malnutrition, and unemployment.

Poverty remains a persistent issue in India, with a substantial proportion of the population living below the poverty line. Despite the economic growth and development, access to basic necessities such as food, shelter, and healthcare remains limited for many people in India. Additionally, low life expectancy continues to be a persistent challenge, with the average life expectancy in India being lower than the global average.

These challenges are not unique to India and are present in many developing countries. The Indian government has implemented various policies to address these issues, such as poverty alleviation programs, healthcare initiatives, and education reforms. However, progress has been slow, and more needs to be done to address these challenges and promote sustainable development in India.[32]"

Against the background of financial crisis the country was in, the government had to cut substantial budgetary support to the PSUs which, in order to meet the financial resource gap, they were asked for finding alternative ways and means to fund their envisaged development programs. To facilitate this, Government of India issued Guidelines by the erstwhile Controller of Capital Issues [CCI] in 1986 allowing the PSUs to mobilize resources through issue of tax free bonds from the open market/private placement. Using this facility, the PSUs raised huge funds from the financial market during the period 1986 to 1991. Besides, the oil producing PSUs were also permitted to raise additional financial resources from the multilateral financing agencies. Both together built up huge funds in the hands of the PSUs. The government stated to have reviewed this situation.

The Government of India [GOI] realized this urgency and issued instructions to PSUs sometime in December,

1987 through the Ministry of Finance, Department of Expenditure providing, inter-alia, that the Public Sector Undertakings should invest funds available with them which are surplus to their immediate requirements in public sector bonds, Government Treasury Bills or as Deposits with the Government as against the Term Deposits that were required to be made according earlier policy. Term Deposits kept with the banks, as and when mature, should also be invested in the above manner. The Department further clarified sometime in February, 1988 that the instructions contained in the letter referred to above apply only to the funds which are not required for a period exceeding 6 months. However, as far as possible surplus funds of public sector undertakings should be invested in the public sector bonds or 182 days treasury bills for which secondary markets are available. These instructions, however, did not define or clarify about what is the secondary market and how to go about the investments.[Emphasis added].

The instructions so issued, however, did not provide for the operational framework to the PSUs for operation in the secondary market into which they were entering for the first time. This gap made the PSUs to make their own assumptions to act upon those instructions. The circumstances under which these instructions were considered necessary at that time when the surplus funds were being placed in the Fixed Deposits with the nationalized banks under the extant instructions of the government prior to the changes effected in the instructions noted before are not available in the public domain. The instructions issued through the second letter referred to above was treated as confidential and immediate. It is not clear why the government treated the second letter as 'confidential' and 'immediate' while it was not so in the case of first letter referred to above.

There was no such element of confidentiality when the instructions related to investment of surplus funds by the PSUs. The first letter specified type of instruments for investment while the second letter further amplified what amounted to surplus funds and availing of the secondary market facilities. 'If the intention was so, it was expected of the government to also have laid down the contours of operational mechanism to be adhered to by the PSUs. One presumption for treating the second letter as 'confidential' could have been to prevent speculation. This didn't serve the intended purpose as the PSUs, in the absence of clear cut operational guidelines on the operations in the secondary market to PSUs, had no choice but to deal through the commercial banks which became a conduit by itself to the brokers who had already been dealing with the commercial banks. The instructions were to have included or fresh set of instructions containing the operational guidelines to PSUs in the secondary market would have been issued, that would have become a forewarning to the PSUs not to deal through the commercial banks or the brokers in order to avoid speculation, if any, the secondary market being dominantly occupied by the brokers.

That was not done being aware that the PSUs had no operational experience in the secondary market. Why the government did not issue the operational guidelines mentioned before is a matter not ascertainable but implied that the PSUs would have to go through the commercial banks. This was where the PSUs were by compulsion had to route the surplus funds through the commercial banks which indirectly meant through brokers who had by then well-established relationship with the commercial banks. This by itself opened the gate for speculation in trading of the government securities and public sector bonds using the PSUs surplus funds. For reasons stated before, this was inescapable for the PSUs. Once the ministers, politicians and bureaucrats sensed the presence of the brokers in the investment of PSUs surplus funds, the gates were opened both ways, one the need for establishing linkage with brokers and the second the brokers waiting at the power corridors to reach the ministers and politicians, especially when the PSUs were resisting to deal with dealers through the commercial banks. The middlemen such as Chandraswami became a convenient tool to be used for establishing contacts with the leading brokers including Harshad Mehta. Given the above circumstances, it cannot be said that the PSUs wantonly or deliberately went through the commercial banks and their brokers. <u>The government instructions stated before played a disguising role in this process whereby they neither issued specific operational guidelines to PSUs for operation in the secondary market nor instructed the PSUs expressly to go through the commercial banks in that matter, the onus thus being shifted on the PSUs for going through the commercial banks and brokers, as if done of their own accord. This is where the PSUs were made to be self-guided that opened up the scope for the scam.</u>

The SECURITIES CONTRACTS (REGULATION) ACT, 1956 [42 OF 1956] defines 'securities' as "a security derived from a debt instrument, share, loan, whether secured or unsecured, risk instrument or contract for differences or any other form of security;" It, however, does not define the 'secondary market' though it was defined later by the Securities and Exchange Board of India [SEBI] established on April 12, 1992 in accordance with the provisions of the Securities and Exchange Board of India Act, 1992. Thus, there was no definition of secondary market during the securities scam period. The New Palgrave Dictionary of Money & Finance considered to be authoritative worldwide defines 'secondary markets': "the marketplace for buyers and sellers of existing securities is called secondary market. The secondary markets are organized to provide liquidity and can take the form of broker, dealer or auction markets." This was defined in legal terms by Securities and Exchange Board of India [SEBI] after it was established in 1992. It is called a market where second-hand securities are sold. It includes both equity and debt market. Securities and Exchange Board of India as a regulatory authority was established under section 3 of SEBI Act 1992 in order to protect interests of investors in securities and to promote the development of securities market.

Let us now consider how the securities market operational system was on the eve of the scam. It is seen that around the same period when the central government changed the policy regarding investment of surplus funds of PSUs, stated before, RBI also issued fresh instructions to the commercial banks in December, 1987 through its master circular that embraced several changes including Ready Forward Deals [RFD], sale and purchase of securities and other operational guidelines. Thus the instructions from the government on investment of surplus funds to PSUs and fresh guidelines of RBI to the commercial banks coincided at the relevant time.

"The regulatory framework is the threat in the country," said the head of a major foreign bank's merchant banking division in a pep talk to his staffers, while fixing annual targets for the different divisions in 1989-90. "We have to learn how to circumvent the rules and regulations. The person who makes money is the person whom the bank wants."

Considering this has been the attitude and philosophy of foreign banks, it isn't surprising to see how the scam happened. The brokers may have erred, but the banks had shown willingness. This is where the line stands drawn on the perforce need for PSUs enter into the secondary market. The interest rate on bonds and investment return rate through the secondary market was an illusion floated for the policy and public consumption. The expectations of the policy makers, the bureaucrats, the politicians and the ministers were much beyond as soon as the connectivity established among them and leading brokers including Harshad Mehta. They had already at the doors of the power corridors as the subsequent developments revealed. Three more banks, namely, Axis, HDFC and ICICI lined up to provide the PMS facility to their customers.

In their over-zealousness to gilt-edge annual reports, not only were regulations deftly side-stepped but even prudent banking norms were jettisoned. The third Janakiraman Committee report which takes a look at the working of Citibank and Bank of America, along-with six other nationalised banks, makes some startling revelations about the modus Operandi of foreign banks. But nothing, it seems, beats the way Standard Chartered went about the business.

The genesis of the scam, say insiders, began in 1988-89. At this time, a London headquarters recruit, Ranjit Mathrani, was made in charge of the fledgling merchant banking division of the bank in India - then controlled directly by London. Adopting highly aggressive methods, the executive set daunting targets for the division.

Willing to risk exposure, the division even at that time was believed to be lending clean - jargon for lending without adequate securities - funds from portfolio management schemes (PMS) to corporate clients.

While PMS clients were offered yields ranging between 11 and 11.5 per cent, lending was done at spreads varying between 6 and 7 per cent. The initial risk exposure which was limited to small sums varying from Rs 3 crore to Rs 5 crore slowly increased to sums ranging between Rs 50 crore and Rs 55 crore.

In some instances, sums were said to have been lent to companies which had earlier been refused money by the bank. "This is not and has never been the regular practice of the bank," says Will Manser, Stanchart's Group Public Affairs Manager in London.

Soon, internal audit started cautioning them. "They were breaking controls, precautions even a street lender would not fail to take," comments a former Stanchart executive. Incidentally, the CBI, investigating the Standard Chartered transactions, had asked, in writing, one month ago for the internal audit report which recorded irregularities by the merchant banking division. Confirming the bank activities, Manser says the scheme has since been discontinued.

Obviously, it's too late. When no corrective action was taken, an internal audit report was prepared in

September 1990, pointing out a series of irregularities in the merchant banking division, and sent to both Mathrani and the head office. Scrutiny of the account books by a team of inspectors sent by London vindicated the audit results. Surprisingly no action was taken against Mathrani.

It was around this time that R. Kannan joined Stanchart from Canara Bank and took over the division. By 1991, when recently sacked India Chief Executive Pesi Nat took over the merged division, the situation had worsened.

In December 1991, the RBI inspected the audit done till the first quarter of the year, commented on the frequent bouncing of the Security General Ledger (SGL) transfer forms and the growing abuse of bank receipts (BR) and violation of norms.

Most bankers feel that it was the level of unwarranted risks taken by Standard Chartered which led it into the eye of the scam, CBI officials say Stanchart investigations - the bank has over Rs 900 crore to account for, as dealings with false receipts - will take another six months to wind up.

The agency has nothing yet to pin on Nat and Kannan - who has also been fired - but are moving along the lines that Stanchart security dealers such as Arvind Lal and Jaideep Pathak who were picked up for interrogation, could not have "exceeded their limits" without guidance from the top.

Despite the Stanchart plea of being caught in a situation where "the bank's own internal policies and guidelines were flouted," and senior management "deliberately misled", bankers and brokers in the money market say things differently.

They feel that the dealers have been unnecessarily victimised to enable the bank to get the fidelity insurance and avoid embarrassment to top management. Sources point out that when the problems were brought to the notice of the top management, most recently in the last week of April, no attempt was made to take internal stock of the situation, or reconcile the securities.

Even in a mid-May meeting with a top RBI official, Nat refused to acknowledge any irregularities in the bank. This happened a fortnight after news of the Harshad Mehta-SBI bank receipt tangle hit the headlines.

Normally, the internal control mechanism would have scanned-the deals on a daily basis and a daily report - and later, a weekly one - would be sent to the management commenting on any possible irregularities. Apparently the system had been abandoned a few years ago.

No arrests or complaints have so far been lodged against the back-office security room or the internal audit control department. Once the dealer puts through the deal, the entire work of collecting securities or making payments is done by the operations department in - banking parlance: the back-office. "We had a situation," admits a senior Stanchart official, "where the front-office colluded with the back-office to defraud the bank."

At the same time, Stanchart officials are at pains to say that their books are in order and cite the report prepared by yet another London team of inspectors which had come in late 1991 and gave a high rating to the front and back-office. Ironically, it was in this month that there were more than 150 deals worth Rs 4,000 crore with the Bank of Karad - now under liquidation.

Stanchart also received BRS from the Metropolitan Cooperative Bank, also under liquidation, which had no authority to issue them. Some of the BRS are believed to have been issued only days after the scam broke.

Even as the renewed investigation of Stanchart is under way the working of two other foreign banks, Citibank N.A. and the Bank of America, is detailed in the third Janakiraman report.

Ranging from minor technical lapses such as issuing BRS with single signatures, to bouncing of bank receipts and not exchanging them with securities within the stipulated 90-day period, there are serious allegations like not holding contracts and delivery orders, mismatches of rates with counter parties and issuing BRS allegedly to raise funds for brokers.

Citibank, for one, denies any wrong doing, especially about benefiting brokers. Says A.S. Thiyagarajan, chief executive officer of Citibank's India operations: "We have at no time parked profits with brokers." That point is still under investigation and Thiyagarajan doesn't have the answers to other RBI allegation.

Bank Am is as tight-lipped. In spite of Stanchart's irregular activities, BankaAm had a lot of dealings with it. Bank Am accepted fresh forms and BRS against bounced SGL forms. Bank Am is also alleged to have issued BRS in excess of its actual security holdings.

In many cases, the Janakiraman Committee has reported that the transactions were tailor-made, done solely with the view of transferring funds by the banks to the brokers. This was either for consideration received in the past or to be received in the future.

The report also says that Bank Am has deliberately violated directives relating to PMS. Money was accepted from clients who were assured a fixed rate of returns. Also, clients were sometimes given dummy contracts which were reversed by adding the amount of interest at the time of maturity.

Basically, it means that in case of short-term funds accepted from clients - in clear violation of RBI guidelines on PMS which prohibit banks from accepting funds for a period less than a year - the bank in its books of accounts would show spot sales of securities through issue of the bank's BRS.

The same securities would then be shown as purchases effected with another party, the dummy. On the date of maturity, the transaction would be reversed with the interest charge payable to the client added in the purchase transaction.

In effect this would be a ready-forward deal with a non-existent party on one hand, and client on the other. The dummy deal would thus be squared off and meanwhile, the bank would allegedly use the funds for its own treasury operations.

For dummy contracts, the parties recorded are UCO Bank, Canfina, the merchant banking arm of Canara Bank, and Canara Bank itself. Bank Am also allegedly transferred BRS even though they are not transferable.

Bank Am's country manager Vikram Talwar says: "Every bank's SGL bounces at some time or the other." On other allegations, his response is either "the bank is studying the report" or "I don't wish to comment at this point of time".

The Janakiraman Committee is interpreting transactions. And the CBI is tracking down the offenders, which could take a while. But the RBI is in a position to take action if it wishes, considering the committee is essentially an RBI exercise. "If there is a violation, action shall be taken," says RBI Governor S. Venkitaramanan.

"But we do want to ensure that foreign banks continue to operate, subject to the laws and regulations of India." The point is: it didn't work the first time, and the RBI didn't accept the truth till it was forced to." [Source: INDIA TODAY - DAKSESH PARIKH - ISSUE DATE: Sep 30, 1992 | UPDATED: Aug 21, 2013 13:59 IST]

PLAYING THE GAME: SCAMS & FRAUDS – POSTED SUMMARY READS.COM WEBSITE - 14 NOV. 2020 [EXCERPTS]:

"In school, the more you know about the subject the better you get in predicting the type of questions that will be asked in the exam. The same applies to industry or academics, once you understand the entire play-field upside down; it doesn't require any magic potion to trigger the brain to layout the possible loopholes present in the system. Then it lies entirely on the individual's ethics and greed fear balance to execute further actions.

In this article, let's go through three stock market scams in India and how the laws and policies evolved with them.

1. 1992 SCAM

This fraud amounted to around 4000 Cr. and is considered the biggest scam in the history of securities market in India, which lead to complete structural change of banking and financial framework followed by the further insurgence of technology in the system.

Q. WHAT WAS THE FINANCIAL SCENARIO IN 1990'S?

Prior to concepts of dematerialization of physical share certificates, depository participants (DP), demat accounts and direct market access (DMA), everything was paper based i.e. in form of certificates and receipts, with brokerage houses being the sole intermediate between investor and the concerned exchange.

Apart from the differences between the money market and corporate markets in terms of their securities, participants, trading volumes & market capitalization etc., the cost of finance in corporate markets was about twice that of the formal markets. This prompted one to think in the direction of somehow diverting the funds from banking systems to brokers and further to stock market where yields seemed vastly better in comparison. Further, the economic liberalization (June, 1991) brought positive news for private sectors, but had simultaneously put pressure on public sector, financially, to perform well. Also, introduction of portfolio management schemes (Shorn of verbiage-a deposit without interest rate ceiling or reserve requirements) also encouraged competition among banks for PMS funds and to enhance on their own profitability.

Q. WHAT WAS THE SYSTEM FLAW AND MECHANICS OF THE SCAM?

Banks in order to maintain their statutory liquidity ratio (SLR), had to increase or decrease their holdings in liquid assets like Gold and G-secs. Instead of physically buying or transferring holding of these securities through inefficient public debt office (PDO), banks preferred to enter ready forward deals, which are a secured short term loan (~15 days) from one bank to another. A ready forward deal (RFD) can be seen as lending money or borrowing of securities (Illustrated in figure provided below). However, the transactions were done using bank receipts (BR), issued by the borrower. Basically making it unsecured and solely built on trust that seller holds the securities. There was a sudden change Net Demand and Time Liabilities or NDTL.

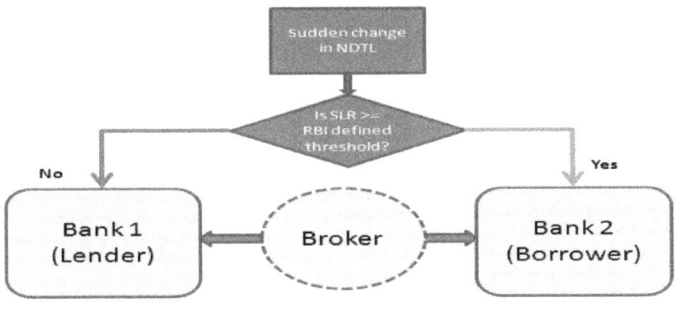

Ready forward deals (RFD)

The figure is a schematic of a ready forward deal between two banks for maintaining statutory liquidity ratio.

Lack of proper control systems in place like credit or counterparty limit further widened the loophole. These flaws were exploited by the broker, who instead of just being an intermediate, also started to engage in their settlement process i.e. the cheques and receipts were now routed through broker. The broker then credited the money to his account even though it was account payee cheque. How?

During that time, when banks made payments to each other, those cheques were cleared on same day. Thus, in order to reduce the clearing time and to save the interest lost for that delay (e.g. 50 Cr. cheques->2 days delay in clearing->Loss of 4 Lakhs @ 15%) certain corporate clients were allowed to clear the account payee cheques in favour of the banks into their own accounts.

Further, the broker persuaded certain small banks to issue counterfeit bank receipts and enter RFD with other banks. Hence with BR with RFD became a pathway for getting unsecured loan from banks to broker to stock market.

Q. HOW DID IT COME UNDER SCANNER?

Eventually, the huge difference in the amount represented by BR's in circulation and the government bonds actually held by the banks led to the discovery of the scam. This lead to a sharp fall in the share prices. Further, one may analyse that technically 4000 Cr impact on a market of size 250,000 Cr. may not too significant. The prices plummeted largely due to the knee jerk response it received afterwards, like declaring all transactions routed through the accused individuals (like brokers) as void leaving several shares worthless as they could not be delivered in the market.

Q. WHAT WERE THE REFORMS THAT FOLLOWED?

The broken financial system of 1990's underwent dramatic structural changes following the scam. To improve transparency, online trading came into light in 1992 which expanded the boundaries of capital market nationally. The satellite communications systems were in place which eliminated the geographical barriers. Regulatory bodies were given more powers. RBI was made the primary agency for banking system regulation in

November 22, 1993. Securities and Exchange Board of India though founded in April 1988, was (through SEBI Act 1992) conferred statutory powers to it. Vigilance towards defaulted paper work was increased with audits and laws in line to deter future offenders................."

The order of sequences of the events that happened given hereinabove are intended to enable the readers to appreciate the tempting facilitation, prompting the securities scam that laid the red carpet in the government circle covering both the politicians and the bureaucrats and in the corridors of the public sector banks, other commercial banks as well as the government owned public financial institutions/PSUs to woo and welcome the leading stock market brokers who had set up their own agencies and concerns under the mentor of the two well-known and acknowledged prudent persons having brilliant brain in the securities and stock markets, the first was former CMD of a reputed government owned bank [Canara Bank] and the other was the CMD of the RBI owned National Housing Bank [NHB].[the former died in 1991 and the latter died in1992 on the break out of the scam]

The brokers did not land into the securities market from sky but were those who landed in the heavenly made securities operational gimmicks. This is not intended to suggest that the brokers were not the fault lines in the securities scam; they were and remained so all through but who created the smooth passage for entry of the secondary market operations into the inner circle of the government system and which was that brain that invented the 'Bank Receipt' method that contained the details of the purchase of specified securities on behalf of the investors, most of whom were those stated before, without the need for taking into possession the securities purchased in physical terms which the commercial banks and their brokers pleaded before RBI for permitting them to deal in securities without possession in physical terms [that involved highly cumbersome process with increasing difficulties in shuffling of the securities within the interbank operation] through the exchange of Bank Receipt [BR} among them for specific maximum period which was consented by the RBI on the condition that such deals in securities would be governed by the Rules on BRs to be issued by the Indian Banks Association [IBA}. The BR system was mainly intended for public sector bonds since they were not government and approved securities but in course of time, this system also got entangled with SLA system.

Six years before the scam came to light, an RBI inspection report of October 1986 found Andhra Bank and Syndicate Bank guilty of misusing BRs. Andhra Bank had issued BRs without having the underlying securities, and Syndicate Bank had issued an SGL transfer form without having adequate balance in its government securities account. Once such a transaction had come to the notice of RBI through its auditors, that was the most appropriate time for the RBI to have gone into depth of the matter and had it taken punitive measures based thereon, the BR operation practice could be been buried under the ground leaving no scope for the scam to come in subsequent years climaxing in April, 1992. I wish to state the following at this stage to enable readers to have a general idea:

Regulations that governed the Banks:

Apart from RBI, other Regulatory authorities include:

- Securities Exchange Board of India (SEBI)

- Banks Bureau of Standard (BBS)
- Insurance Development Regulatory Authority of India (IRDA)
- Pension Fund Regulatory Development Authority of India (PFRDA)
- Indian Banks Association (IBA)
- Banking Codes and Standard Board of India (BCSBI) (since dissolved and a new single Nodal Point is created which is Consumer Education and Protection Department (CPED)
- Banking Ombudsman
- Ministry of Finance (MOF), Government of India.
- Competition Commission of India [CCI]
- Forward Markets Commission

The Banks and Financial Institutions come under the ambit of the following important Acts:

Banking Regulation Act of 1949

Reserve Bank of India Act 1934

Negotiable Instrument Act 1881

State Bank of India Act 1955, (Repeal & Amendment 2018)

The Banking Companies (Acquisition and Transfer of undertakings) Act 1980

Payments & Settlement Systems (Amendment) Act 2015

SARFAESI Act 2002 (Securitization and Reconstruction of Financial Assets and Enforcement of Securities Interest Act 2002)

Foreign Exchange Management Act 1999

Consumer Protection Act 1886

The Limitation Act 1963.

The Bankers' Books of Evidence Act 1891

DICGC (Deposit Insurance & Credit Guarantee Corporation) Act 1961

Excerpts from the Article "The Scam Economy" by Sudeep Chakravarti published in INDIA TODAY - ISSUE DATE: Dec 21, 2015 | UPDATED: Dec 11, 2015 13:34 IST -

"Where does one begin? With ambitious brokers, bankers and bureaucrats brought low? Or a minister diminished-even a Prime Minister? What exactly exploded in April 1992, that year of explosions from which India is yet to recover?

That year the word 'scam' forced its way into India's lexicon. Scam was like an eager house guest, fattened on opportunities provided by increasing liberalisation tripped by faltering oversight and spurred by infinite greed. The story of that time is still so today. Then as now-as several dozen scams emerge each year and, surely, many do not-it's still a world where, to paraphrase a quote by the character Gordon Gecko in the 1987 blockbuster Wall Street, rules are for wimps.

It began with two words: "securities scandal"-which rapidly morphed to "securities scam". Among other things it was about using government bonds, or securities, with borderline and outright illegality, and what was termed "market practice", to make a lot of money in the stock markets………..

The dominoes then began to tumble. In April, an internal State Bank of India (SBI) scrutiny found the bank was caught short by Rs 500 crore that Mehta owed them. He had 'borrowed' it by selling SBI-owned securities, and used bank receipts or BRs that were used to mark sale of government securities between banks, to leverage money elsewhere and fuel his plays in the stock market. Mehta had help in SBI's treasury department. A brokers' strike in Mumbai combined with stock market closure for several days prevented Mehta from cashing in stocks to repay the bank. The discrepancy leaked to media.

In the spirit of full disclosure, credit must go to an uncharacteristically bold article in The Times of India of April 23, 1992. That 'scoop' mentioned that Mehta had been asked by State Bank of India, the country's largest bank, to "square up" Rs 500 crore, a massive sum at the time. The game was up. Mehta soon stood accused by the Central Bureau of Investigation of conspiracy, criminal breach of trust, and cheating under provisions of the Indian Penal Code. The money swirling around this grey space was estimated to be Rs 5,000 crore to Rs 6,000 crore............

As Times and others publications, including Indian Express and INDIA TODAY followed up that newsbreak, there emerged ever newer dimensions that would surely have earned the appreciation of even Wall Street's hardened loophole pirates. Mehta wasn't the only broker in the game, riffling the securities market to make a killing in the share bazaar. SBI wasn't the only bank in the game. Several banks including SBI were fully in the game of using BRs to leverage ever greater amounts and ploughing these into quick loans and 'short-selling' bonds to buy them back at lower rates, looking to maximise revenue any which way in an environment of stifling credit controls. With their portfolio management schemes, several banks acted exactly as Mehta and his ilk: using leveraged funds to play the stock market and reap profits.

Incredibly, even National Housing Bank, a subsidiary of Reserve Bank of India-which, ironically, claimed it was conducting its own investigations into banking capers-was convinced by Mehta to part with BRs. A major INDIA TODAY story from June 1992 pithily highlighted one such transaction: "Promising to deliver a BR later, Mehta persuades NHB to issue a cheque to ANZ Grindlays. ANZ credits this to Mehta. This is not legal, but is said to be common practice." And so Mehta and his broker colleagues-the lines had blurred between securities brokers and share brokers, between banks playing broker and brokers playing banker-had convenient money with which to play. Market bulls like Mehta and their enemies, market bears, alike played the game.

One institution went overboard-some call it overtrading. The Bank of Karad (BoK) was persuaded by a broker, Abhay D. Narottam to issue BRs for which it had no securities to back them, to Standard Chartered Bank. Stanchart, as it was popularly known, paid Mumbai-based BoK, which promptly credited Narottam's account with it. This broker then used the funds to help out bear operators to cover their positions in the stock market. That play bombed, the bears had no money to return, so Narottam had none to return to BoK, and BoK had none to return to Stanchart. Bank of Karad was exposed to Rs 750 crore of scammed money, with its capital and assets unable to cope. The Reserve Bank ordered its liquidation.

Caught in the throes of such churn and near-daily exposures of who scammed whom and how, and clampdown by regulators, the stock market crashed. The Sensex dropped by a third in a month after the scam hit in end-April. Market capitalisation was down by a staggering

Rs 1, 00,000 crore. There were real concerns that the government's privatisation programme would be jeopardised.

Money is like water

The mayhem also took with it reputations. Manohar J. Pherwani, a former Unit Trust of India chairman was at the time chairman of National Housing Bank. The bank had an exposure of over Rs 1,000 crore. Pherwani quit; he died some weeks later. SBI treasury executives were suspended. UCO Bank chairman K. Margabandhu was effectively fired, though he remained defiant, stating his bank played the game of securities-leverage with Mehta as his was a loss-making bank, and the system allowed him no way except that of high-risk returns to turn the bank around. ANZ Grindlays, Stanchart, Bank of America and Citibank N.A., fronted by its high-profile India head Jaithirth "Jerry" Rao and investments chief A.S. Thiyagarajan shuffled executives or fired them. While Citibank scraped through, a couple of quotes of the unrepentant Thiyagarajan, who soon quit Citibank, summed up the attitude: "Trading is a way of life" and, "Money is like water and will flow to where the return is highest."

Stanchart's overseas parent infused 50 million pounds into its Mumbai branch to cover losses. A total of 17 Indian public and private sector banks, and the four foreign banks, came under government scrutiny, along with thirteen major securities and equity brokers. Two committees, including a Joint Parliamentary Committee, tried to make sense of the goings on.

Some like major securities trader Bhupen Dalal, a gentleman of the old school in his mannerisms, and often linked to the bear cartel, steadfastly denied any wrongdoing, in spite of his well-known friendship with the securities broker Narottam, and his directorship in BoK. (Dalal was nevertheless convicted along with two other brokers by a special court in 2014 for their role in the securities scam. Dalal appealed.)

There were other significant casualties. A Bengaluru-based company, Fairgrowth Financial Services floated by a former chairman of Canara Bank, B. Ratnakar, was found to be in the swirl of the scam. So was the fact that India's commerce minister at the time, P. Chidambaram, and his wife Nalini held shares in the firm. Pushed by the expected opposition-led fracas in Parliament, and Prime Minister P.V. Narasimha Rao's need to be seen to do right, Chidambaram held a press conference on the evening of July 9, 1992, to announce the shareholding and plead innocence; he had earlier sent in an offer of resignation to Rao. He accepted with alacrity. High-flying technocrat V. Krishnamurthy, former chief of SAIL Ltd and Maruti Udyog, chair of a committee on public sector divestment, and member of the Planning Commission was probed for his links with Fairgrowth, and for a company controlled by his sons receiving funds from a Mehta-owned firm. Krishnamurthy was over.

Lost in the bloodletting was the trigger. The landmark budget for 1991-92 had sought to drastically reduce the so-called License-Permit Raj that strangled private and state-run industries alike. But banks, especially public sector banks, were choked by a credit policy that forced them to maintain high reserves, buy government bonds, and treat bad loans as matters of political economy. Finance Minister Manmohan Singh acknowledged as much in his speech to Parliament while presenting the budget for

1992-93 on February 29 of the Year of the Scam. He referred to a financial markets review by the government-appointed Narasimhan Committee which flagged "serious problems posed by the deterioration in the financial health of the system because of low profitability, poor portfolio quality and inadequate provisioning for bad debts."

Singh spoke of the need to move toward "a more efficient and competitive banking system", and, in practically the same breath, announced that the government has decided to begin a "phased reduction in the Statutory Liquidity Ratio (SLR) which at present locks up large quantities of bank funds in relatively low yielding Government securities."

As it turned out, banks were a step ahead of the committee and Singh, and those like Mehta and his compatriots in banks and financial services firms were quick to realise that meanwhile, if swashbuckling is what it took to profit, so be it. It took until 1993 for the government to put better financial norms in place. As continuing market scandals and inexplicably rocketing share markets have subsequently shown, oversight is still work-in-progress.

Broken, if not exactly broke

Mehta's, of course, continued to be an amazing story years after the scam broke, even after the entire weight of the system dropped on him, in turn imprisoning him and fining him for causing losses to others and cheating on taxes-let alone several banks raising claims against him. This irrepressible man, who told my colleagues Daksesh Parikh and Lekha Rattanani in September 1992 that he was "living hour to hour" (see accompanying excerpts of the interview), had, incredibly, tried a comeback in 1998. Scraping together a fan club of backers and finding manna in the shares of BPL, Videocon and Sterlite, among others, he again took to the share bazaar. Fortunately, a resurgent Securities and Exchange Board of India-which had over 1991 and 1992 toothlessly watched the capers of Mehta and his spirit brothers of the marketplace-pulled the plug. Mehta again lost money and face. The companies were penalised

That wasn't the apex of Mehta's chutzpah. I met Mehta in his still luxuriously-appointed Worli apartment in November 1992. He was preparing for battle. "I am compiling data on people and bank transactions," he said as his brother Ashwin-many called him the real brain behind Growmore-looked on warily.

The two went on about how their enemies wanted the Mehtas "on the streets", how they had to take permission for every bit of expense, how they were hounded by income tax authorities even as many other protagonists in the scam drama lived easy.

"Enough", said Mehta, settling back comfortably in a deep-set sofa, "is enough." As far as he was concerned it was an eyeball to eyeball situation. Soon, with the ammunition he was stockpiling, his enemies were going to have to blink.

I never thought he would try to take the Prime Minister of India down with him. In June 1993 he held a press conference in Mumbai, his brothers and star lawyers Ram Jethmalani and his son Mahesh in tow, to announce that he had met Prime Minister Rao on November 4, 1991 at the prime ministerial residence, and handed him Rs 1 crore. Then, and later, a large sand-coloured suitcase was shown to the media: the presumably guilty carrier.

Rao's public comeback was as cheesy. He declared: "I will emerge out of this trial by fire in the same manner as Sita did."

The Prime Minister's damage-control team was never able to convincingly prove that he hadn't actually met Mehta; the same as Mehta and his cohorts were never able to conclusively prove that he met Rao. But Mehta's desperate ploy muddied the waters some more. And it tarnished Rao. A comeback Rao loyalists put out was intended as a defence but ended up as a sordid sign of the times: Do you think the Prime Minister of India can be bought with one crore?

Just one crore?

By the time Mehta died of a heart ailment aged 45 in the morning of December 31, 2001, in a hospital in Thane, pressured by a fresh Central Bureau of Investigation case that accused him and his brothers of misappropriating "27 lakh shares of about 90 companies" in 1992, the Big Bull was broken, if not exactly broke. His estate and his family paid much of Mehta's dues a decade after his death; at least the Income Tax Department considers its books with Mehta as closed.

Meanwhile, an enduring Mehta query continues to garnish India's vast, and open, can of worms. "Why blame me alone?" he had asked in 1992 as scam revelations swirled about him. "I'm just part of the system." [Sudeep Chakravarti is an author and independent commentator on socio-political and security issues in South Asia]

"EXCERPT

October 15, 1992

"I'm living hour to hour"

Q. Do you regret the line you chose?

A. There is no regret ... I believe in the theory of karma.

Q. By singling you out (have) other brokers and maybe a few politicians escaped punishment?

A. I am being made a scapegoat. The public cannot be fooled for long.

Q. What is the bear cartel?

A. There are handfuls, about 10 brokers, who have formed a powerful syndicate known as the bear cartel. Some of them also operate in the money market and enjoy a very close nexus with banks and mutual funds. Citibank is one such bank.

Q. Do you see yourself as a Pied Piper?

A. The Indian capital market is under-researched and made up of participants who are largely first timers. They lack conviction and allow themselves to be led rather than lead themselves. I am a product of this vacuum of conviction.]

From Harshad Mehta's interview by Dakshesh Parikh and Lekha Rattanani]"

It is stated at this stage for information of the readers that the words 'Bank Receipt" [popularly known BR] is not defined either in the Reserve Bank of India Act, 1934 or in the Banking Regulations Act, 1949. Then, how did the "Bank Receipt" [BR] came into operation in the securities scam, 1992? This aspect is dealt in more detail in later part of this book.

"……...**Where the RBI Went Wrong [Source: Excerpts from The Securities Scam - A Legal Perspective by Sanjay Bhatia – Citation: Bhatia, Sanjay (1993) "Securities Scam-A legal Perspective," - National Law School of India Review: Vol. 5: Iss. 1, Article 9]**

It is becoming increasingly clear that the securities scam uncovered last April was the culmination of long years of neglect by the RBI.

The story of the scam dates back to 1986 and there is evidence to prove that the Department of Banking Operations of the RBI, had discussed this issue more than once.l! However, nothing concrete was contemplated, let alone taking action against the guilty.

A report authored by none other than the then Deputy Governor of the RBI, Mr. Amitav Ghosh, was tabled on October 8, 1990. The report clearly indicated the facades created by foreign banks to carry out their profit making exercises.

All the documents presented to the DBOD backed their contentions with solid evidence. For example, as early as in 1986, Andhra Bank's involvement in favouring one particular broker had been discovered and pointed out. In fact, the Kurias document+ had also underlined the tendency of the bank to collect securities and SGL on behalf of brokers from the PDO without deduction of tax at source, a facility which is available only to public sector banks. The documents also point out the practice of window dressing of profits by banks as the primary reason for the establishment of the broker-bank nexus.

Similarly, both Kurias and Ranganath had pointed out that a number of banks were trading, not in securities, but in BRs. In other words, transactions were not undertaken for SLR purposes but to accommodate fellow banks or the bank brokers with the full knowledge that the BRs were not backed by security.

The Janakiraman Committee, which was appointed to investigate into the scam, made absolutely no mention of these reports. What the Janakiraman Committee did mention however, was the RBI circular dated July 26, 1991, to most of the banks, alerting them about underhand dealings in securities and the free 'use of BRs. Although the matter caused "great concern" to RBI, it apparently did not consider it necessary, at that stage, to arrest the unfortunate development.

The letter of July 26, instead of being enclosed with a request to forward to the RBI, a copy of the policy framework for undertaking transactions in securities approved by their respective boards, could have been accompanied with a suitable format asking banks to submit to RBI, at regular intervals, till further advice, prescribed details of their holdings in securities and transactions in the securities portfolio during the course of the week or any other such period." This was the obvious course to have been adopted as the RBI, as already mentioned, has enormous powers to call for reports, carry out inspections and give directions. In fact, the RBI has on its rolls, hundreds of officers trained to carry out such scrutiny and there could have been no better occasion than this to press this outfit into service."

Moreover, the RBI guidelines prohibit the issue of BRs in transactions involving government securities. <u>The RBI, being fully aware that BRs were freely used by banks in their trading with government securities, did absolutely nothing to stop this practice. What is more appalling is that the National Housing Bank, A fully owned subsidiary of the RBI, in fact, issued cheques worth over Rs.one thousand crores, without the backing of even a BR.</u> [Emphasis added]

Another major lapse on the part of the RBI was its non-action on banks which did not register their transactions with the PDO. The RBI guidelines are clear on this issue. Every transaction in government securities between banks has to be mandatorily recorded at the PDO. Most of the transactions, as they were on a ready forward basis." did not get reflected in the RBI books at the PDO and therefore escaped the notice of the RBI.

With respect to the State Bank of India (SBI), a management audit team looked into its operations in 1991 and proposed the setting up of an independent back-up section within the bank to oversee securities transactions which would have pre-empted the scam. The audit report, submitted in November 1991, stressed the need to segregate the policy making and monitoring roles from the day to day dealings - roles which are at present, clubbed together. It also pinpointed the lacunae in the supervisory mechanism of the RBI and suggested measures to correct the imbalance. <u>If the RBI had acted and forced to set its functioning in order, the scam could have probably been checked. Mysteriously enough, the RBI itself suppressed the report, which is yet to see the light of the day.</u> [Emphasis added]

It must also be pointed out that the RBI has failed, not just in policing the banks, but the RBI officials, (who are on the board of most banks) could be accused of turning a blind eye to the questionable deals put through by the banks. True, the RBI's nominee directors on the banks' boards would not have been in a position to detect irregularities at the operational level but at least, the RBI nominated directors could have acted as watchdogs and ensured that the guidelines were not violated for several months."

Conclusion

There is very little that can be said in defence of the RBI. It has failed on all counts to play the role of a custodian of the banking sector. The Joint Parliamentary Committee which investigated into the scam has unearthed even more startling information. In the course of the depositions of the officials of the DBOD, it transpired that the Governor of the Reserve Bank had urged, as late as in March 1992, "not to take drastic steps". Although a lot of follow-up action has been taken and banks have been advised to frame their investment policies in strict observance with the existing regulations, the wrongs committed cannot be remedied. The JPC has heavily indicted the RBI for its inaction. However, as the JPC is only a fact finding body, it will be left to the government to punish the guilty." [Emphasis added]

In an ever expanding ambit, the scam has engulfed top executives of large nationalized banks, foreign banks and financial institutions, brokers, bureaucrats and politicians. As is to be expected, everyone is trying to disown the responsibility for the scam. The RBI has blamed the commercial banks, charging them with negligence and extensive violation of banking regulations. The commercial banks are in turn blaming the RBI for inefficient functioning and ineffective supervision. The brokers are being accused by all of downright fraud. The government has chosen the ubiquitous term "systems failure" to describe the reason for the scam. All this has left a lay reader thoroughly confused. The daunting nature of the task of understanding the scam is clear from the arcane terms and acronyms used to describe the scam: ready forward, double ready forward, SGL, PDO, BR, PMS etc. Except the terms SGL and PDO which were in vogue under the RBI Act, 1934, the other terms were born prior to or on eve of the scam period and officialised by the RBI through its directions/notifications. [Emphasis added]

The scam was in essence a diversion of funds from the banking system (in particular the inter-bank market in government securities) to brokers for financing their operations in the stock market. A clear understanding of the government securities market and the stock (corporate securities) markets is a prerequisite for understanding the scam. A brief comparative description of these two markets is as follows:

Characteristic	*Government Securities Market*	*Stock Market*
Securities	Government Securities PSU (Public Sector Undertakings) Bonds Units of the Unit Trust of India	Corporate Securities (shares and debentures)
Trading Volume	Rs. 3000 - 4000 crores (over $ 1 billion) a day	Rs. 50 - 200 crores ($15 - 70 million)
Market Capitalization	Rs. 100,000 crores	Rs. 250,000 crores (at BSE Sensitive Index of 4500)

No of Transactions	250 per day	50,000 per day
Players	Banks Financial Institutions	Individuals Companies Financial Institutions
Inter-mediaries	About a dozen brokers approved by the Reserve Bank of India (RBI)	About 500 brokers in the Bombay Stock Exchange
Finance	Money Market ("Formal" market)	*Badla* Finance Market ("Informal" Money Market)
Cost of Finance	18-20%	35-40%

The crucial part of the comparison however is the last element which indicates that the cost of finance in the informal money market which finance stock market operations is about twice that of the formal market in which banks lend to each other against government securities...............

It is quite clear therefore that there were enormous profits to be had for anybody who could find a way of breaching the artificial wall separating the two markets and arbitrage between them. That in essence was what the scam was all about. To understand the motivation of different players involved in such diversion, it is necessary to examine the changes in the economic environment that preceded the discovery of the scam, and how these changes were affecting the principal players in both markets.

Liberalization of the Economy

After assuming office in June 1991, the new government accelerated the process of economic liberalization under the auspices of the International Monetary Fund (IMF). The opening up of the Indian economy as a result of these measures promised an unprecedented growth and prosperity for the private corporate sector as new sectors of the economy were being allowed private participation and various administrative impediments were being removed. Anticipating the good tidings for the private sector, the stock market started booming - the Bombay Stock Exchange Sensitive Index (Sensex) rose from around 1000 in February 1991 to a peak of 4500 in March 1992 just before the scam came to light. This meant an enormous increase in the scale of finance required by operators in the stock market. Heavy margins imposed by the Bombay Stock Exchange on settlement trading added to the funds requirement.

At the same time, the new free market philosophy confronted the public sector with new challenges. There was immense pressure on the public sector to perform - to perform in financial terms. The nationalized banks too were under the same pressure to improve their bottom line. The proposed increase in capital adequacy requirement (mandated by the Narasimham Committee report) added to the pressure on the banks.

Another innovation in the banking sector in the period preceding the scam was the Portfolio Management Scheme (PMS). Shorn of the verbiage, in operational terms, PMS was simply a deposit which was not subject to interest rate ceilings or to reserve requirements. The scheme was designed to permit deployment of large amounts of surplus cash available with several public sector undertakings

(PSUs) particularly in the oil sector a large part of this surplus cash resulted from borrowings in the international markets (by PSUs, at the instance of the government) to bolster the country's precarious foreign exchange reserves. An intense competition developed among the banks for these funds as they were unfettered by reserve requirements.

To compete for PMS funds from the PSUs as well as to enhance their own profitability, banks were forced to look for higher returns. This was happening at the same time when there was a growing need for funds in the informal money market to finance stock market operations at very high rates of interest. The time was therefore most appropriate for somebody to find innovative ways of diverting funds from the banking system to the stock market. Brokers who were operating in both the markets were ideally placed to do this, and thus the scam was born.

The Ready Forward Deal

The crucial mechanism through which the scam was effected was the ready forward (RF) deal. The RF is in essence a secured short term (typically 15 day) loan from one bank to another bank. The lending is done against government securities, exactly the way a pawnbroker lends against jewellery or other valuables.

In form, however, the RF is not a loan at all. The borrowing bank (Bank 2) actually sells the securities to the lending bank (Bank 1) and buys them back at the end of the period of the loan at (typically) a slightly higher price. The price difference represents the interest on the loan.

The RF is what in other countries is known as repo or repurchase agreement. It is a very safe and secure form of lending and is very common throughout the world. The

US repo market, for example, is about a hundred times larger than the Indian RF market.

The Mechanics of the Scam

As explained above, a ready forward deal is, in substance, a secured loan from one bank to another. To make the scam possible, the RF had to undergo a complete metamorphosis: it had to become an unsecured loan to a broker. How was this transformation brought about?

The three crucial steps to effect the metamorphosis were:

- The settlement process in the government securities market became broker intermediated, that is, delivery and payments started getting routed through a broker instead of being made directly between the transacting banks.
- The broker through whom the payment passed on its way from one bank to another found a way of crediting the money into his account though the account payee cheque was drawn in favour of a bank.
- While the above two steps transformed an RF deal from a loan to a bank into a loan to a broker, it would still be a secured loan. However, the brokers soon found a way of persuading the lending bank to dispense with security for the loan or to accept worthless security.[Vikalpa – IIMA]

Reserve Bank of India (RBI) does not have any information about its chiefs when the securities scam involving Harshad Mehta took place in 1992.

In a surprise reply, the bankers' bank has refused to give the names of its governors when the stock market was rattled and thousands of crores were ripped off in the scam spearheaded by late Harshad Mehta.

Activist SS Ranawat from Bhilwara in Rajasthan, had filed an application under the RTI Act with the RBI seeking to know the details of the scam, names of the RBI governors at that time and their alleged role, if any, in the scam.

Ranawat was left confounded by the reply of Sudarshan Sen, central public information officer of the RBI which said it "does not have any information" about either of the three questions [Source: DNA Website March 17, 2018].

"Swamiji in Scam 1992 is none other than Chandraswami (Tantrik) who was having good hold in politics. Chandraswami was a controversial Indian Tantrik who gained fame when he came in contact with Prime Minister Narasimha Rao. Soon after Rao became Prime Minister in 1991. Swami helped in bringing down the Morarji Desai government and was the most important man of P.V Narsimha Rao's Government.

He took Money from Harshad Mehta for raising the funds in the election but he was a very selfish man and he was also found guilty in many of the scams. Chandra Swamiji used to invest the money of the politicians in the stock market with the help of Harshad Mehta. Chandra Swami was one of the most trusted men of the politicians as he was very close to Prime Minister P.V Narasimha Rao. It was very easy for Chandra swami to manipulate the decision of the police and the other officials in that duration because of his political connections [Emphasis added]

According to a top CBI official, it wasn't long before Mehta's veneer disintegrated. Faced with overwhelming evidence of his role in siphoning money from banks into the stock-market, Mehta is said to have broken down and wept.

The CBI is sure it is only a matter of time before an FIR is filed, detailing charges of misappropriation, cheating and forgery against Mehta and abuse of official position against public sector bank officials.

Said one investigator: "There is prima facie evidence against both Harshad Mehta and State Bank of India (SBI) officials. We can pin them down." But damning evidence - the bank receipts allegedly removed from SBI by Mehta - hasn't yet been traced.

But even as Mehta walked out of the CBI office in Bombay, the visit, <u>say investigators, had served a purpose: of showing up Mehta as being cooperative and strengthening his court defence against a possible arrest and prosecution. There is also speculation that Mehta might turn approver if criminal charges are pressed against him</u>. [Emphasis added]

In exchange for kid-glove treatment, or even full immunity against prosecution, Mehta could provide exceptional information on the rot in the financial system, involving bankers, brokers, bureaucrats and politicians.

Says Mehta: "Why blame me alone? I am just a part of the system." In fact, leaks in the press against some brokers and foreign banks have been ascribed to Mehta's camp.

And last fortnight, Mehta dropped the veil of silence, briefly, in an interview with video magazine Newstrack. In it, the besieged broker opened out, hinting at the wide scope of the securities operations.

Mehta declared that not just Indian and foreign banks, but even the RBI had "full knowledge of what was going on" in the stock-market and were "all party to how best to make money". He added: "Banks were working on how best they could take advantage of the boom on the stock market."

Even as Mehta remained in the eye of the storm, the spotlight appeared to be shifting to others. Reports say that another scandal of Rs 1,000 crore, involving yet another leading public sector bank is likely to surface soon.

A CBI official maintained that after digging into Mehta's nexus with the SBI, over the next eight months, its sleuths will be examining the affairs of 19 banks including State Bank of Patiala, State Bank of Hyderabad, Bank of Karad, Standard Chartered Bank, ANZ Grindlays Bank, Citibank, Bank of America and National

Housing Bank. In any case, the RBI is already going through the records of some of them. Even the income tax authorities have got into the act. And they are sitting on a mine of scam information, <u>but can't use it as they haven't been able to crack the code that will allow them access to computer floppies confiscated from Mehta's premises during the February raid</u>.[Emphasis added]

There was also renewed speculation about the involvement of prominent politicians, including Union ministers, in the securities scam. "Three Union ministers are linked to the scandal, but I will not name them," Janata Dal leader George Fernandes declared.

However, Minister of State for Banking and Insurance, Dalbir Singh, maintained: "So far, I have not heard of the involvement of any politician in the deal. In any case, things will become clear when the interim report is submitted in the first week of June."

The interim report Singh was referring to will come from the RBI, which is focusing on the intricate inter-bank deals. Also, the Securities and Exchange Board of India (SEBI) is conducting parallel investigations into the role of mutual funds in fuelling the artificial stock-market boom.

The CBI probe is the most broad-ranging, but the RBI, SEBI and CBI are not coordinating their investigations or even consulting each other.

Since the CBI probe will naturally be the most extensive, questions are being raised about the agency's ability to unravel the intricacies of Bombay's financial markets. Said a leading foreign banker: "The transactions may prove too complex for the CBI sleuths."

A top Finance Ministry official, however, assured: "The CBI is the prime investigating agency in the country, and I'm sure it will be able to get to the bottom of this."

The scale of the financial mess became evident when the London head office of just one bank, StanChart, made a provision of 50 million (Rs 275 crore) to its Bombay branch in order to meet the possible losses accruing from the securities scam.

Estimates of the total loss incurred by the bank go up to as much as 100 million (Rs 550 crore), a phenomenal figure considering the annual profits of the bank's Indian operations are only Rs 30 crore.

In response to charges that the Bombay branch of the bank had issued bankers' receipts without holding the required government securities, Will Manser, StanChart's group public affairs manager in London, told INDIA

TODAY: "We do not wish to make any further comment while our investigations are in progress."

According to informed banking sources, StanChart lent huge amounts to brokers. The money was given out against a mere promise to deliver securities later. The brokers misjudged the market, and short-sold shares, expecting prices to go down after the budget.

But these bear operators had not contended with Mehta. As share prices zoomed from February-end, brokers who had borrowed heavily from StanChart had to keep buying shares at inflated prices to affect delivery. They incurred enormous losses, and can't repay the bank.

Brokers also raised large amounts of money from foreign banks against bank receipts issued without sufficient back-up government securities by smaller banks. One of the main culprits in such deals is said to be the Bank of Karad which, interestingly, the RBI had investigated a year ago.

A small private bank headquartered in Maharashtra's sugar belt, the bank was allegedly a conduit for channelling money from foreign banks to several brokers.

"It was the brokers' bank of last resort," commented a Dalai Street operator. Bhupen Dalal, a leading broker and Bank of Karad director who is alleged to have accessed large amounts through his company Champaklal Investment and Financial Company Ltd (CIFCO), was served a show cause notice by the RBI last fortnight, CIFCO shares have since tumbled from Rs 250 to Rs 50.

Even the Bombay Stock Exchange is contemplating investigations into Dalal's market operations. And as a sequel to the RBI inquiry, the Bank of Karad chairman was sacked.

On a broader front, the CBI will also be looking into the operations of some of the mutual funds which are believed to have misused the system. Even the SEBI is examining the records of some of the leading mutual funds. Said SEBI Chairman G.V. Ramakrishna: "We'll definitely take penal action if mutual funds are found to have indulged in gross malpractices."

All this is just the beginning of the country's biggest financial whodunit. According to banking experts, many more revelations are yet to come.

But as Umesh Naik, general secretary of the SBI employees' union contends: "In such cases, the big fish go scot free while the small ones are caught and punished. For instance, why were innocent people suspended in SBI while Deputy Managing Director C.L. Khem-ani in charge of treasury operations was only asked to proceed on leave?"

The involvement of so many well-connected senior bank officials raises doubts about how far the investigations into the securities scam will be allowed to proceed. Addressing a news conference at the height of the controversy, RBI Governor S. Venkitaramanan put maximum emphasis on taking action against the irregular activities of foreign banks.

But RBI's initial inaction in the face of inescapable indications that something was seriously amiss in the country's financial world has come in for sharp criticism. In fact, there is considerable bewilderment about the fact that the RBI's Vigilance Cell woke up to the securities scam only in April.

Said a top income tax official: "Things have been especially messed up during the last six months, and Venkitaramanan has not done anything." However, a senior

Finance Ministry official defended the role of the RBI governor, saying: "Remember it was the RBI chief who was responsible for first ordering a probe into the securities deals."

But while allegations are being bandied about, the big question remains: will the authorities succeed in overhauling the country's banking system to safeguard against a replay? Said Hemendra Kothari, a leading broker and chairman of DSP Financial Services: "There is a lesson to be learnt from all this - bring about more transparency in the banking and brokerage businesses."

It is also essential to bring down the artificial barriers erected between different financial sectors. "Money is like water and will flow to where the return is highest. Banks should have the freedom to invest funds where they choose," said Citibank's investments chief A.S. Thiyagarajan.

But before natural laws can prevail, justice will have to be done to bring to book those involved in India's biggest-ever financial scandal." [INDIA TODAY - LEKHA RATTANANI, DAKSESH PARIKH - ISSUE DATE: Jun 15, 1992 | UPDATED: Aug 26, 2013 17:53 IST.

THE BOMBAY SECURITIES SCAM OF 1992: THE SYSTEMIC AND STRUCTURAL ORIGINS Bill Damachis - Policy Organisation and Society Summer 1994 – [Citation: Bill Damachis (1994) The Bombay Securities Scam of 1992: The Systemic and Structural Origins, Policy, Organisation and Society, 7:1, 40-45, DOI: 10.1080/10349952.1994.11876795

"This paper by scrutinising the Bombay securities scam will reveal the structural problems that exist in regard to the government's role in formulating monetary and financial policy and the management of the financial system in India. All types of banking and financial institutions, public, private, cooperative and foreign have been implicated in the scam. This clearly points to a systemic failure. Therefore, the economic policy regime, as well as the broader political and social environment will have to be investigated to assess how such a development as the securities scam occurred. The finance minister, Manmohan Singh, and the governor of the Reserve Bank of India (RBI), S Venkitaramanan, contend that they inherited a legacy of a deficient system, which became a natural breeding ground for fraudulent practices. However, the approach of the media, and the investigative bodies formed by the government, is to concentrate on unravelling individual culpability, which is no doubt important, but fails to produce any new insights into the broader issues that require investigation. While the basic result of the scam was the fall of the stock market indices and the collapse of the bull market, the real issue was the discovery of widespread irregularities in the functioning of the financial sector. Politicians have a lot to answer for in relation to the socio-political environment which has fostered the cutting of corners. Corrupt and short-sighted political leadership have allowed too much leniency to be given to 'flamboyant' operators, and in the process destroyed the vitality of the financial system. After the euphoria over economic liberalisation put together by Rajiv Gandhi and carefully staged news management, it is evident that a lot of work has yet to be done in producing an efficient financial system.

The system has forgotten its basic functions of deposit mobilisation and lending; instead bankers have concentrated on treasury operations, even operations of a completely fictitious nature. Speculation took over from genuine productive activity. The chief irregularities involved Bankers' Receipts2 [Banks trade with each other in securities. Since securities are bulky documents and are cumbersome to transfer, paper is exchanged instead in the form of Bank Receipts, which are non-transferable and can be issued by banks and recognised institutions only between themselves. The Bank Receipt acknowledges a transaction, and promises to deliver securities later. The buyer bank accepts the Bank Receipt and pays the seller bank up front. The Bank Receipt is later exchanged either directly or through the broker for the securities, within 90 days.]For government securities, which are supposed to be traded only between banks, being traded openly with brokers intermediating in these exchanges. Additionally, certain banks were indulging in forward transactions in these receipts so that when the crash occurred, Bankers' Receipts could not be squared with the securities that they were supposed to have been issued against. Although those caught seems to be relatively few, it is now clear that such practices were widespread, involving not just a few banks, but most of the banking sector with foreign and private sector banks involved to a disproportionate extent.3 It is now known that these practices had been going on for quite some time despite RBI regulations to the contrary. Because accounting in securities transactions is manual there is a time lag of a few days between registration of security transfers between banks and movement of funds against Bankers' Receipts. This allowed for profitmaking with the funds in the intervening period, and provided an incentive not only for brokers but also the banks that they acted for.4

In addition, there have been instances of fraud in terms of forged Bankers' Receipts, where some largely public sector banks had advanced money without proper guarantee, and that certain other largely private sector banks had issued guarantees without the required funds. There is clear evidence of insider trading on the exchanges, but since there was no regulation against insider trading in India at the time, such trading could not be deemed as illegal.

At another level, banks were able to obtain large funds for their trading activity, and for boosting deposits from public sector institutions and the corporate sector, under the government run Portfolio Management Schemes (PMS), which enabled short-term deposits to be passed on to banks. State control of the economy ·has made private capital dependent to a degree on political and bureaucratic patronage. It was an open secret in financial markets that there was political involvement, and a system of kick-backs in operation for obtaining most of these deposits. Evidence suggests that politicians, were not just colluding with the bureaucracy but with businessmen in the corporate sector so as to ensure funds reached certain banks. The banks assured PMS clients a fixed return, and earned huge profits by deploying the funds in the capital markets. There was enough left over to pay off the intermediaries whose assistance was required to launder the funds into the stock market.

To highlight how widespread the rush for quick cash was amongst public institutions, in one case under investigation by the Joint Parliamentary Committee, M 0 H Farook, minister of state for civil aviation, presided over a meeting with the top management of the three public sector airlines~ In this meeting it was decided that two of the

Airlines, Air India and Indian Airlines, would loan Rs 10 crore each to Vayudoot, the third Indian carrier, to help it overcome some liquidity problems.6 Vayudoot, in turn, invested the sum with ANZ Grindlays and a number of other banks, and with a number of brokers, instead of using it for operational requirements. This highlights how senior officials in a public institution were in the process of manipulating the system for short-term financial benefits, at the expense of a public institution.

What has been the policy environment encouraging such prolonged treasury operations? This environment was created by the link that was established between the money and capital markets'. Since liberalisation, all five-year plans have relied on the efficiency of the private sector to raise huge funds for capital, much of it through the stock exchange. This had led to a rapid proliferation of financial transactions as funds from the financial sector have moved quickly to the share markets, raising share prices to inflated heights, which is completely unrelated to the actual activity taking place in the economy. Bankers may have recorded huge profits, but they relate more to the fee income generated by underwriting activity in the capital market boom than to any marked improvement in lending portfolios.9 Prior to the scam, the RBI governor had sounded notes of warning on the excessive heating up of the stock markets, and convened a meeting of the heads of major financial institutions to try to curb the speculative trend in equity prices.10 The governor's advice was questioned, and many in his own government advised him not to dampen the revival of the economy as supposedly reflected in the booming share markets. One of the reasons for this was that the government was keen to portray itself as on the right path, so as to keep on side the World Bank, which extends credit to the country. After the scam the governor is now being held accountable for not taking timely action in regard to the share prices boom.

Those implicated or brought down by the scam highlights the extent of deep set structural problems in the financial system. The Commerce Minister, Mr P Chidambaram was forced to resign from the government within a few months of the scam breaking, after it was disclosed that he and his wife held shares in a company that was being investigated.ll Mr V Krishnamurthy, a leading department head in the bureaucracy in charge of a number of public sector concerns had also been forced to resign.l2 The Central Bureau of Investigation is still in the process of a criminal inquiry into the scam, and so far has acted against an ever-increasing number of brokers and bankers Following the latest moves by the RBI, the four foreign banks named in the Janakiraman report (ANZ Grindlays, Bank of America, Citibank and Standard Chartered), will have new chiefs.l4 These four banks handled securities transactions valued at over Rs 9 trillion in the twelve months leading up the scam. lS Managing Director Bob Edgar, of ANZ Grindlays is scheduled to leave and a number of senior executives have lost their positions, and others have been told to sever their links with a number of Bombay brokers.l6 The bank has also agreed to pay, bowing to a RBI request, Rs 5.1 billion to the National Housing Bank to cover transactions involved in the scam.

Standard Chartered has already submitted a list of nineteen names of employees to the Joint Parliamentary Committee. These have been retrenched, reprimanded or asked to resign following the scam, in which the bank has suffered in excess of Rs 900 crore in losses.18 Foreign banks were quick to set up shop in India in the mid-1980s during the start of the liberalisation drive, for they realised the potentialities of the Indian market which contained 20 per cent of the world's potential consumers.19 Standard ·chartered, Citibank and a number of other foreign banks increased their Bombay staff fourfold within four years of Rajiv Gandhi's liberalisation drive, in the anticipation of the profits to be made.2° Free from the burdens of social lending obligations that are imposed on domestic public banks, these banks have been able to attract many corporate customers. Foreign banks quickly interposed themselves in the system by the successful manipulation of government and bureaucratic bodies. The facts are that foreign banks offered lucrative jobs to the kin of important officials, according to the advantages such officials could pass on back to the banks. <u>The Joint Parliamentary Committee has, in fact, demanded and received a list of all children of public servants employed by these banks, which suggests a growing connection between the bureaucracy, the government and the banks.21 [Emphasis added]</u>

After more than a year of investigations by over six agencies, the total amount of money laundered out of the system by the scam still remains untraceable. The Janikiraman Report, set up by the Reserve Bank of India to investigate the scam puts the losses at Rs 4,024 Crores after four reports, with undoubtedly more losses set to be disclosed.22 Most significantly, after over one year of intense interrogation, Harshad Mehta has implicated the Indian Prime Minister P V · Narasimha Rao in the scandal, which will have huge ramifications if substantiated. So far Congress leaders have· stood firmly behind Rao, claiming that the allegations are merely an attempt to destabilise the two year old government. Mehta has claimed he had paid Rs 10 million to the Prime Minister for 'political patronage' in November, 1992.23

Prior to assessing the structural origins of the scam, a number of points have to be addressed concerning its systemic origins. Firstly the loss of money by speculators in the stock market although regrettable is not the issue. Stock markets do fluctuate; therefore investment in stocks and shares involves a degree of risk. However, both the media and the government (wanting to be seen as caring for its constituents), by focusing on this issue, are not addressing the underlining problems in the financial system.

The point is that the fall was inevitable, and simply a matter of timing, as markets does not stay in a bullish24 cycle indefinitely. Furthermore, it has suited the government to portray this bull run solely to the activities of a number of bullish operators led by Harshad Mehta and to a number of directors of certain banks identified as the principal players in the scam, whereas in reality, the main factor behind the speculative run was official encouragement: first, through statements of policy-makers which attributed the boom to the success of their policies (the bull run was interpreted even by the finance ministry as a celebration of the government's liberation and economic reform drive program);25 second, the budget of 1992 abolished the wealth tax on shareholding as well as reducing the capital gains tax upon increases in share values, giving investors the signal to continue with the speculative behaviour. [Emphasis added]

Additionally, the lack of a computerised system, due to trade union resistance, can not in itself be the main reason for the problems attributed to the scam. Computers are simply devices for faster accounting, and whether this is used to keep honest accounts or to 'cook' the books more efficiently depends entirely on the operator. Although lack of computerisation may have broadened the scope for misuse by some unscrupulous operators, it does not explain how some of the most heavily implicated banks are subsidiaries of foreign banks in India, whose operations are fully computerised and whose operation are supposed to be models for Indian banks to follow.

It is also necessary to point out that all types of institutions; both public and private sector banks as well as foreign banks have been implicated in the scam. Thus the government's emphasis on deregulation of the banking industry may not prove to be the panacea it is looking for in the financial economy. The public banks, although some have come out of the scam looking extremely poorly (e.g. the National Housing Bank), have not been the main instigators of the problems. Their main failing was the advance of large sums without proper guarantees, which suggests inexperience at the decision-making level, which gets back to government appointments to senior positions in these institutions, which will be elaborated on below. On the other hand, it has been the private banks, like the Bank of Karad and the Bank of Madura, which have been identified by the RBI as principal sources of dubious Bankers' Receipts. Since the liberalisation push of the 1980s, foreign banks have also been aggressive participants in the blatant disregard of rules and regulations in the financial system.

Several foreign banks, principally Standard Chartered and ANZ Grindlays, have been closely implicated in the scam. Standard Chartered having advanced money without proper security, while ANZ Grindlays allowed itself to be used as a go-between by Harshad Mehta, with what should have been a bank to bank transaction ending up in his personal account.28 Therefore, it is the private sector banks, both private and foreign, who have been the main participants in the market for Bankers' Receipts, obviously as a means of skirting <u>RBI reserve requirements. The RBI seems to have turned a blind eye to such behavior due to the politicisation of public banking</u>, which will be expanded on below.29 [Emphasis added]

To solve such problems, there is a need to devise a rational system of regulation for banks and stock markets. The growth of various kinds of financial intermediaries, which are outside the control of the Reserve Bank of India, poses a serious threat to the efficient supervision of monetary policy in the context of India's rapid economic growth. The regulation of stockbrokers has been ineffectual, which has led to widespread insider trading. If stock markets are to become viable instruments for mobilising savings for productive investment, regulations will require significant tightening. In effect, the scam relates to the 'crooked' use of Bankers' Receipts, so that banks could create money, whereas the whole purpose of compulsory purchase of government securities is to restrict monetary growth. There exists two interrelated aspects. The first is the huge rise in stock market indices, not related to the movements in the real economy, and, second, is the covert practice by the banking sector which allowed the creation through Bankers' Receipts of bogus money. The two fed into each other fostering a self-perpetuating system. The stock market boom made it profitable for banks to create liquidity to allow for more investment in rapidly rising shares, while the inflow of such funds put upward pressure on the stock market which led to a bull run. It is important in both of these aspects to move away from a concentration on the issue of corruption, to a consideration of the processes which allowed them to occur.

Given these features, a number of serious implications emerge for the functioning of the financial system. When the management of public financial institutions is scrutinised a number of flaws arise. The Reserve Bank of India, the head of money management in the country, has become a tool of the government to serve their continued financial needs. According to the Narasimham report, 63.5% of all bank deposits are directed into financing the government's budget deficit or providing cheap funds for the public sector.30 This in turn, has disrupted the RBI's main tasks of designing and implementing an independent monetary policy, managing foreign exchange reserves and policy, backing up fiscal policy with relevant measures, and most importantly supervising and monitoring banks.31 The effect being that such political patronage in India's foremost financial institution has resulted in an inefficiency of operations, poor market intelligence and archaic inspection and supervisory systems becoming the norm, as emphasis shifts from banking to political considerations.

The financial economy needs to be insulated from the consequences of political meddling. Public banks would operate much more efficiently if they were left to their own devices. As the Narasimham Report states, banks can operate effectively without privatisation. In the report's findings' which were released in early 1992, much of the blame for the inefficiency in the banking sector is placed on the pre-emption of their resources by the government.32 Political interference in all operational aspects, investment, credit allocation, branch expansion and even internal management of banks and financial institutions has caused major systemic problems. One of the most ruinous practices is that of the government nominating directors to the boards of the public banks who are affiliated to the ruling political party.33 Since nationalisation; supervisory norms have been violated by this procedure. Selection of persons for the posts of top management has not always been on consideration of their expert knowledge and experience. Their tenure is in accordance with the political considerations faced by the 524 parliamentarians whose obsession with immediate political gain overwhelms all other considerations. This, in turn, affects the morale, discipline and efficiency of the organisation as long-term priorities give way to short-term expediencies. Additionally, recruitment of clerical staff into the banking system takes place through the government run Bank Service Recruitment Boards, minimising autonomy of recruitment by bank management.34

Since Rajiv Gandhi's liberalisation drive a number of ramifications have been felt in the financial economy. Rural lending has been neglected, and the share of priority sector advances has dwindled, as the banking system shifted its focus away from rural and priority sector lending to more 'profitable' ventures. Rural banking in small villages is no longer the norm. As V Mahadevan, managing director of the State Bank of India stated: 'Rural development is acting as a drag on the activities of the commercial banks'.35

Politicians reacted to this development in an expedient manner.

To ensure continued patronage from their rural constituents,36 politicians staged wholesale giveaways of uncollateralised credit, postponed loan repayments or simply wrote-off sizable amounts of bank credit.37 For example, no sooner did Haryana Chief Minister, Devi Lal unseat his predecessor from the ruling Congress Party, than he proceeded to write off Rs 2.3 billion of loans in fulfillment of a campaign promise. Drought, as usual, was used as the excuse.38 Banks are encumbered with unrecoverable loans. Public bank officials who protest at such measures are threatened with transfers to robbery-prone branches in the Punjab or Assam. Banks have been forced to over-extend themselves, and they and the financial institutions have been saddled with portfolios which are infected with dubious assets. The Indian public economy has turned into an elaborate network of patronage and subsidies.39

The government action in setting up the Joint Parliamentary Committee, although essential has failed in setting the exact terms of reference, which has resulted in a plethora of papers and · documents having to be scrutinised. The JPC has been buried under the debris because it failed to plan in advance what ·to look for. It has been common practice in India over the years, that any committee or commission, unable to finds a solution to the problem at hand, sets up a new institution as a solution to not being able to find a solution. So successive solutions, far from resolving the original problems themselves create new problems. It is now clear that between Harshad Mehta and the State Bank of India the fraud would have been swept under the carpet had not a junior employee of the bank naively notified the press, forcing the RBI governor to intervene to stop the roll-over to the broker from the National Housing Bank.

The impact of the scam on the government is that it has slowed down all decision-making. As Swaminanth Anklesaria Aiyar, editor of the Economic Times has stated; 'Nobody wants to take any decisions. It has given people ... a handle to attack the policies of the government'.40 Each political party is using the scam to push their own agenda. Liberalisation has become a big political issue. The Bharatiya Janata Party has condemned economic reforms as a surrender to foreign pressure in terms which are almost identical to those used by the two major Communist Parties in the country, whereas, the Janata Dal, which itself is falling apart due to desertions to Congress, sees the slowing down of liberalisation as the weakness of Congress to pass necessary reform. Up until now divisions within the opposition have enabled the Congress government to weather the fallout of the scandal, however with the new allegations by Mehta implicating the Prime Minister anything is possible. Rao, has based his and his cabinet's legitimacy on their integrity, competence and radicalism on economic management41 If the new allegations prove to be correct that legitimacy is shattered.

In summary, the main issue is that of the proper balance between financial liberalisation and the regulatory aspects required to sustain a credible financial system and an effective monetary policy. The main problem in India is that the Reserve Bank and its regulatory bodies are hostages to government meddling in their affairs. Politicians may want change, but the way the political system is structured, it is not possible for them to distance themselves from the financial sector without harming their own electoral prospects. The Indian state by controlling to a certain extent the industrial, financial, and infrastructural resources allows its politicians the scope for manipulating the economy in directions which are not suited to good management. The Eighth Five Year Plan is now well under way and with its emphasis on employment, especially in the rural sector, it is hardly necessary to stress that financial institutions will have to play a predominant role in the process of economic development.42 To bring about an all-round development of the economy, immense financial resources must be mobilised. One of the primary tasks in the process of development is to mobilise the financial resources of the community and to channel them towards productive investment. Though finance is by no means a substitute for real resources, it has a crucial role in economic development as it places at the command of those who have the technical skill and entrepreneurial talent, the necessary means for expansion. The growth of widely spread networks of financial institutions helps to connect the scattered pockets of saving and investment and in the process the aggregate investment tends to increase.43 But mere sophistication of the financial sector is not likely to push India into higher growth patterns. It is time government and monetary authorities in India examine thoroughly the developments that have taken place in the financial and political structure, and find new methods to make the financial economy more effective and purposeful."

Scam 1992 Explained: How Harshad Mehta, brokers and banks gamed the system – Source: posted

on Storyboard Website - (Edited by: Nazim) - First Published: Nov 6, 2020 5:48 PM IST

Here's a detailed FAQ that takes an in-depth look at the Securities Scam 1992

- Joint Parliamentary Committee Report

The securities scandal of 1992, with Harshad Mehta as its main player, is back in collective consciousness nearly three decades after it was perpetrated, thanks to Sony LIV's popular web series Scam 1992.

While the series has been praised for its largely accurate portrayal of the events that transpired -- down to a fleeting mention of the fiscal deficit in the Budget 1986 speech, as is shown when a character is watching it on TV -- there are only so many details that it can capture given the scope of the medium.

HERE'S A DETAILED FAQ THAT TAKES AN IN-DEPTH LOOK AT THE SECURITIES SCAM 1992.

AT ITS CORE, WHAT WAS THE SECURITIES SCAM 1992 ABOUT?

Stockbrokers wanted to borrow funds to deploy in the market. Stringent RBI regulations restricted them from borrowing from banks, the cheapest source of funds. Brokers found a workaround built on trading in government securities, colluding with banks, circumventing RBI rules, getting their hands on bank funds and diverting it to the stock market.

Brokers and banks got help from public sector undertakings (PSUs), which were looking for avenues to deploy their temporary surpluses. In violation of rules, PSUs started taking positions in the securities market through the portfolio management services (PMS) schemes run by banks.

This wall of money fuelled massive speculation in stocks between April 1991 and May 1992, and caused a near fourfold jump in the BSE Sensex.

HOW DID STOCKBROKERS COME INTO THE PICTURE?

Stockbrokers needed funds to finance their stock market trades. These brokers took up proprietary positions in stocks, or were financiers for *vyaj badla* trades. Many of them were also brokers in the money market, where corporate bonds and government securities were traded.

WHAT IS VYAJ BADLA?

Back in the 80s, stock market trades were settled once in two weeks. But buyers had the option to roll over their position to the next settlement cycle, if they could find somebody to finance it. The financier would charge an interest, which was higher than the rates in the bond markets, as well as the deposit rates offered by banks. Many big brokers were badla financiers as well.

And when they were not financing other traders, the brokers would need funds to roll over their positions, if the market was in an uptrend.

So brokers found it profitable to access funds from the banking system and use it for their stock market operations. They found a loophole in the banking system that was there for everyone to see. They exploited it to the hilt. This was to do with banks' trading in debt securities.

WHY DID BANKS TRADE IN SECURITIES?

For two reasons. One, to meet the RBI regulations of Cash Reserve Ratio (CRR) and Statutory Liquidity Ratio (SLR). CRR, as the term implies, required banks to park a certain portion of their deposits with the RBI at zero interest. For SLR, banks had to park a certain portion of their deposits in government securities and other approved securities.

The second reason was to boost their profits, which were quite low at that time.

WHAT IS THE LINK BETWEEN SECURITIES TRADES AND COMPLIANCE WITH CRR AND SLR REQUIREMENTS?

When the RBI raised CRR, some banks would find themselves short of cash. Similarly, some banks would find themselves short of securities to meet SLR requirements. This meant there both a buyer and a seller, a prerequisite for any market.

BUT BANKS IN NEED OF CASH COULD HAVE DIRECTLY BORROWED FROM THE CALL MONEY MARKET WHERE BANKS LEND TO EACH OTHER?

Till 1988, the interest rate in the money market was capped at 10 percent by the Indian Banks Association. So banks with surplus cash were not keen to lend in the call market. To circumvent the IBA rule, banks devised the 'ready forward' mechanism, and so could lend at a rate higher than the call money rate.

WHAT IS A 'READY FORWARD' DEAL?

Bank A, which temporarily required cash to meet the CRR rule, would sell securities to Bank B. After a few days, Bank A would buy the securities back from Bank B at a slightly higher rate. The difference in the purchase and sale price of securities was the interest paid for borrowing the funds. This would be higher than the call money rate. Note, the coupon rate or yield on the securities had no connection to the trade, which was a pure financing deal.

WHAT WAS THE REASON FOR BANKS' PROFITS BEING LOW?

In the 80s, banks had to park 63.5 percent of their deposits with RBI, in cash or specified securities to comply with the CRR and SLR requirements. This earned either no interest or interest way below market rates. Around 40 percent of the remaining deposits was earmarked for priority sector lending. That left banks—both public sector and private sector--with little funds for commercial lending.

Also, there was a cap on the interest rate that banks could offer its depositors. So bank deposits were not the first choice for corporates with surplus funds.

BANK RECEIPTS ARE SAID TO BE AT THE HEART OF THE SCAM? WHAT EXACTLY WERE THEY?

This was the era of paper trading. Often, there would be a delay in the seller bank handing over the physical securities. Sometimes, the delay was because of the certificates lying at a different centre. In many cases of PSU bonds, the actual issue of certificates was delayed for several years and the holders' evidence of ownership was only an 'allotment letter'. Also, for large ready forward transactions, physical delivery could be cumbersome since the trades were to be reversed shortly.

So the seller bank would issue a 'bank receipt' (BR) to the buyer of the securities, till such time the shares were physically handed over. Once the buyer got delivery of the securities, the BR would no longer be valid.

WHAT WERE THE RULES REGARDING BRS?

Among the main ones, BRs could not be issued for government securities, they could only be issued when PSU bonds or mutual fund units were traded.

The record of government securities held by banks was maintained by the RBI's Public Debt Office in what was known as the Securities General Ledger (SGL). When a bank wanted to sell government securities, it only had to give a SGL transfer form to the buyer.

The buyer would hand the transfer form to the PDO, which would then credit the securities to the buyer's account and debit the seller bank's securities account.

The other key rule was that BRs were valid up to a maximum of 90 days.

HOW WERE BRS MISUSED?

There were multiple violations that eventually led to BRs becoming accepted currency, being traded as securities with the underlying securities rarely changing hands.

- Banks started issuing BRs even for transactions in government securities though RBI rules forbade it.
- Banks buying securities would not insist on delivery within the 90-day limit, and this led to BRs being valid indefinitely.

- A bank holding a BR and yet to receive delivery of the underlying securities would trade in those securities with a third bank, and issue another BR. In effect, BRs were being issued with BRs as the underlying, instead of securities.
- Some banks started issuing BRs, aware that they did not have the underlying securities.

WAS RBI AWARE OF THE MISUSE OF BRS?

Yes. Six years before the scam came to light, an RBI inspection report of October 1986 found Andhra Bank and Syndicate Bank guilty of misusing BRs. Andhra Bank had issued BRs without having the underlying securities, and Syndicate Bank had issued an SGL transfer form without having adequate balance in its government securities account.

DID RBI TAKE ANY STEPS TO PREVENT THE MISUSE OF BRS BY BANKS?

In July 1991, as the misuse of BRs became rampant, RBI issued a circular to banks forbidding sale transactions unless they held the actual securities in their investment account. Also, all transactions put through by the banks either on an outright basis or on ready-forward basis had to reflect on the same day in their investment accounts.

However, the banks ignored the circular and continued to flout the rules on BRs.

HOW DID BROKERS ACCESS FUNDS FROM THE BANKS?

There was a close nexus between some banks and some brokers, which allowed the brokers to have unauthorized access to banks' funds, as well as put through transactions not always authorized by the banks.

Banks lent the funds to the brokers in the guise of ready forward transactions. The rules clearly said that ready forward transactions could be done only between banks and that too for government securities. To circumvent this, transactions were recorded as being entered into with counterparty banks. But the beneficiaries of these transactions were the brokers. In short, certain banks acted as 'routing' banks for brokers.

HOW WERE THE TRADES ROUTED?

The 'routing' banks purchased securities in their own name or sold securities in their own name without indicating that they were acting for the brokers. Where securities were not readily available, they even issued their own BRs.

So when Bank A bought securities from Bank B, the cheque would be made out in the name of Bank B. However, in many instances, the funds would be credited to the individual accounts of brokers. This was possible because every bank dealing in securities had their favoured set of brokers, for whom they were willing to bypass rules.

The brokers would then play the stock market with the funds, earn profits and return the money to the bank.

WHY WERE BANKS WILLING TO ACCOMMODATE BROKERS?

Brokers helped banks meet regulatory requirements and also earn profits on their securities transactions. In addition, brokers also accommodated banks by temporarily taking losses off their books. For instance, when the RBI hiked interest rates, the value of the bonds held by banks would decline, and this would affect their profits. So the banks would temporarily park some of the loss-making bonds with brokers, to minimize the blow to their profits. The brokers would absorb losses on some transaction and would be compensated for those in some other trades. It was a classic 'you-scratch-my-back-I-scratch-yours' arrangement between banks and brokers.

WHAT ABOUT THE ROLE OF FOREIGN BANKS?

The special scrutiny conducted by RBI in 1989 and 1990 revealed gross irregularities in the PMS operations by the foreign banks and non-compliance of RBI circulars. A few of these violations were noticed by the Ministry of Finance as early as 1986, according to an MoF representative's statement to the JPC.

Some foreign banks like Citibank were found to be short-selling government securities, which meant that it sold securities not owned, in violation of RBI rules.

Four foreign banks—Standard Chartered, ANZ Grindlays, Bank of America and Citibank—accounted for 56 percent of all securities transactions by banks between April 1991 and May 1992.

The JPC report said, "ANZ Grindlays, Citibank, American Express Bank, Bank of America and SCB have not only been the major players in the scam but have initiated the entire process of the scam."

WHY THEN DID THE RBI NOT TAKE ACTION AGAINST FOREIGN BANKS?

India's foreign exchange situation was quite fragile in the late 80s and early 90s. "We have to depend on loans and credit from foreign banks in the international market," the then RBI Governor S Venkitaramanan told the JPC, when asked about RBI's inaction against foreign banks

HOW DID PSU FIRMS GET SUCKED INTO SHADY DEALINGS IN THE SECURITIES MARKET?

As the government gradually withdrew budgetary support, PSUs started raising huge sums from the bond markets even when they did not have any capital expenditure plans. Sometimes the large public issues made by the PSUs did not find enough takers. So the PSUs struck deals with banks: the banks subscribed a significant part of the issues and in turn, the PSUs placed the funds in the PMS schemes of the banks who subscribed to the issues. In some cases, the returns from the PMS schemes were lower than the interest that the PSUs had to pay on the bonds.

WERE THERE OTHER REASONS AS WELL FOR PSUS TO MONEY IN PMS SCHEMES?

Yes. Even when PSUs were able to raise money without help from banks, they needed to generate enough returns to be able to pay interest to the bondholders. Many PMS schemes promised handsome returns. Banks offering PMS were not supposed to guarantee returns, but there was an unwritten understanding between the PSUs and the banks, on the expected rate of return.

WHAT WAS THE EXTENT OF PSUS' INVOLVEMENT IN THE SECURITIES MARKET?

Between April 1990 and December 1992, PSUs invested around Rs 36,000 crore in the portfolio management services (PMS) schemes run by foreign banks and NBFC arms of nationalized banks. There were two violations here. Government rules said that PSUs could only invest in government securities, public sector bonds and treasury bills. Having handed over the funds to banks, the PSUs never bothered to check where their money was being invested.

Secondly, PSUs were given permission to transact with foreign banks only in January 1992. But PSUs were dealing with foreign banks even before the formal approval.

HOW DID THE PMS ARRANGEMENT HELP BANKS AND BROKERS?

The funds raised through PMS schemes would be loaned to brokers, and even corporates, in the guise of ready forward transactions. If the banks were to directly lend to brokers and corporates, RBI guidelines would apply. But when done through the PMS route, they were technically investing the funds on behalf of their customers.

Funds for capex being diverted to PMS schemes delayed certain PSU projects because the PMS schemes had a lock-in clause of one year.

WHAT EFFECT DID THE IRREGULARITIES IN THE BANKING SYSTEM HAVE ON THE STOCK MARKET?

Between April 1991 and May 1992, the securities transactions by banks totalled close to Rs 13 lakh crore. Of these, barely 5 percent of the deals by value involved outright purchases or sales of securities. The rest were financing deals.

During the same period, the BSE Sensex rallied from around 1200 to a record high of 4467.

Clearly, the money from the banking system was flooding the stock market and driving stock prices higher.

WAS THERE ANY OTHER DIMENSION AS WELL TO THE SECURITIES SCAM?

A lesser-known aspect is the irregularities in bill discounting by banks. Many banks flouted the RBI guidelines on bill discounting, and advanced funds to corporates and NBFCs even though the bills were not genuine or did not conform to RBI rules. The corporates often use the funds to buy shares of group companies.

WHAT WAS HARSHAD MEHTA'S ROLE IN THE SECURITIES SCAM?

Harshad Mehta was a stock market player as well as a money market broker. He was the favoured broker of State Bank of India and its subsidiaries, National Housing Bank, UCO Bank and ANZ Grindlays. While the banks were supposed to be trading securities with other banks, the funds were mostly credited to Harshad Mehta's individual account. Harshad used the funds for his stock market operations, and peddling the replacement cost theory, sent stock prices soaring to dizzying highs.

WHAT EXACTLY IS THE REPLACEMENT COST THEORY, AND HARSHAD'S VERSION OF IT?

Replacement cost is the cash that a firm needs to replace an old asset at the current market price. In Harshad's view, a manufacturing company's stock market value should be equal to the investment required to set up a similar capacity. For example, if it took Rs 500 crore to build a new cement or steel plant of a certain capacity, then an existing company with that capacity should be valued at Rs 500 crore.

Thanks to this theory gaining acceptance in the market, the share price of cement major ACC rallied from

Rs 300 to Rs 10,000 in less than two years. A similar spike was witnessed in many other stocks as well.

WHAT WAS THE TUSSLE BETWEEN HARSHAD AND THE BEAR CARTEL?

A group of brokers, mainly rivals of Harshad, had short sold many shares, convinced that the exuberance in the stock market was not supported by fundamentals and that the rally would not sustain. Thanks to the banking funds at his disposal, Harshad was able to carry forward his buy positions, and push prices even higher. The continuous rise in prices bled Harshad's rivals financially. To square up their short positions, they had buy shares in the open market, which further fuelled the rally, and cost them more money.

Naturally, they were in a precarious position and faced ruin if share prices rose further.

HOW DID THINGS START UNRAVELLING?

Due to rampant violations in securities trading, 'holes' had developed in the investment portfolio of banks. These holes remained undetected for long because the portfolio was supported by SGL transfer forms or BRs which were either on hand or would be delivered by brokers. Few bothered to check if the SGL transfer forms or BRs were backed by securities. Books were fraudulently balanced by creating a fresh set of transactions with SGL transfer forms BRs not backed by securities.

WHAT WAS THE EVENT THAT FINALLY BLEW THE LID OFF THE SCAM?

In January 1992, RBI began inspecting the books of banks for irregularities in securities transactions. In April, the RBI found a shortfall of Rs 649 crore in SBI's investment portfolio. The bank did not have the securities it had paid its broker Harshad Mehta for. Under pressure from SBI, Harshad paid up around Rs 620 crore between April 13 and April 24. But the RBI dug deeper, and found that Harshad had paid Rs 574 crore from his Grindlay's Bank account. Of this, Rs 489.75 crores was funded by National Housing Bank cheques drawn in favour of Grindlays Bank and credited to Harshad's account. That appeared to be a securities transaction between NHB and Grindlays, but NHB did not have any securities to show for it. The cat was finally out of the bag.

COULD HARSHAD HAVE RESOLVED THE PROBLEM WITH SBI, WITHOUT THE RBI PINNING HIM DOWN?

Unfortunately for Harshad, the BSE stopped trading operations on April 16, as brokers went on strike protesting against the directive from SEBI asking them to re-register and pay a higher registration fee.

That prevented Harshad from being able to sell a part of his holdings and repay SBI. Under pressure from the broking community, SEBI diluted the hike on April 20.

Old-timers say the bear cartel, aware of Harshad's problems, prolonged the strike by making other demands. Harshad is said to have approached a foreign bank with close ties to the bear cartel, offering a part of his holdings at a discount. But that deal did not work out.

Trading finally resumed on April 27, but by then it was too late for Harshad.

WHAT HAPPENED NEXT?

The discovery of the shortfall in SBI and the subsequent disclosure of the payments by NHB created a crisis in the securities market. Other brokers too were unable to hide the 'holes' in the investment portfolios of some banks by replacement deals. One after the other, fictitious deals at various banks started getting exposed. Bank of Karad and Metropolitan Co-operative Bank, which had issued BRs and SGL forms without any underlying securities, suffered massive losses and went under.

By mid-May, the CBI froze Harshad Mehta's bank accounts and seized his assets. Three weeks later, Harshad was arrested by the CBI.

With news of the scam becoming public, and the fund flow into the stock market drying up, share prices nosedived. From a high of 4467 in the last week of April, the BSE Sensex crashed to sub-2600 by August.

WHAT WAS THE SIZE OF THE SCAM?

The Janakiraman Committee estimated the size of the scam at Rs 4024 crore.

A few months before his tenure was to end in 1989, then finance secretary S Venkitaramanan wrote to the finance minister and to the Prime Minister's Office during the Rajiv Gandhi-led Congress government's term. The economy was in a mess, with fiscal deficit well over 8 per cent, and there was plenty of strain on the balance of payments front.

Venkitaramanan's advice essentially was that the economy was vulnerable and therefore, the political leadership ought to consider approaching multi-lateral lenders such as the International Monetary Fund for assistance or a loan. His contention then, according to colleagues of that era, was that India had enough goodwill to ensure multi-lateral assistance without stiff conditionalities.

Any attempt to seek a loan would certainly have created a political uproar those days, given the 'sell-out-of-national-interests' perception attached to such assistance and the conditions which lenders such as the IMF imposed on borrowers. The PMO response to Venkitaramanan's note was that there was no need to make an approach then. A little later, Prime Minister Rajiv Gandhi assigned Venkitaramanan and Vijay Kelkar — then with the Bureau of Industrial Costs and Prices (BICP), the forerunner to today's Tariff Commission — to prepare an agenda for reforms. Even though the Congress government and Rajiv Gandhi had been weighed down by corruption charges on Bofors, they perhaps hoped that the party would retain power and some of the much-needed changes could be carried out later.

By the time the committee completed its interim report, however, the Congress lost power in the 1989 elections. Venkitaramanan, who had finished his civil service career by 1990, moved on to Karnataka as an adviser to the Governor during President's rule there, before taking over as the Governor of the Reserve Bank of India in December 1992 — an appointment that came on the back of Rajiv Gandhi's support whose backing was critical for the survival of the then Chandra Shekhar government.

In the early part of 1991, up to April-May, when the crisis deepened — marked by Indian banks even being denied overnight borrowings from abroad, Non Resident

Indians withdrawing deposits and a downgrade by global credit rating agencies — it wasn't just Finance Minister Yashwant Sinha and his team in Delhi which was on the job. In Mumbai, at the RBI, Venkitaramanan began working on the phone with various central banks. The Bank for International Settlements or BIS — the central bank of central banks — wouldn't help saying India wasn't a member while many other central banks and global lenders weren't willing to risk their money given the then experience of debt-ridden countries such as Mexico. That was when Venkitaramanan, after a mid-week discussion with his officials, got on the phone with his counterpart in the Bank of Japan and quickly fixed an appointment for Saturday. Within a day or two, the visa approval and other clearances were obtained from New Delhi and he managed to convince his fellow governor of the need to provide quick assistance along with another central bank which helped then — the Bank of England.

And when these banks wanted collateral or security in the form of physical gold, which had to be transported to UK, Venkitaramanan managed all of it, including getting the Indian customs not to insist on import clearances or licences for some of the boxes to transport the gold.

Time and decisive action were critical then, given the rapid depletion of India's foreign exchange reserves, which by that time, at a little over $ 1 billion, was enough perhaps to cover just three weeks of imports.

And there was the secrecy of operations: the first tranche of the pledged gold (20 tonnes) helped raise $ 200 million as India went to polls in May 1991 after the tragic assassination of Rajiv Gandhi. Another 47 tonnes of gold raised $ 400 million and subsequent measures by a new government led by Narasimha Rao marked an end to crisis management and fire fighting then.

The new reforms also were welcomed by the private sector as they now were allowed entry into new sectors of businesses that were earlier reserved for government enterprises. The stock market reacted positively to this with the Bombay Stock Exchange touching 4500 points in March 1992.

But liberalization was not the only factor responsible for this. The period also an increase in demand for funds. The Banks were pressured into taking advantage of the situation to improve their bottom line.

The banks are required to maintain a certain threshold of government fixed interest bonds. The governments issue these bonds with the aim of developing the infrastructure of the country. Million-dollar development projects are taken up by the government which are financed through these bonds.

How much is to be invested in these bonds depends on the bank's Demand and Time Liabilities. The minimum threshold that the banks had to maintain as bonds in the 1990s was set at 38.5%. This minimum percentage that banks have to maintain in the form of bonds or other liquid assets is known as the Statutory Liquidity Ratio (SLR).

Along with this, the banks were also pressured to maintain profitability. Banks were, however, barred from participating in the stock market. Hence they were not able to enjoy the benefits of the Stock Market leap during 1991 and 1992. Or at least they were not supposed to.

The banks at times may have temporary surges in the Net Demand and Time Liabilities. In such times banks would be required to increase their bond holdings. Instead of going through the whole process of purchasing bonds the banks were allowed to lend and borrow these liquid securities through a system called Ready Forward Deals (RFD). An RFD is a secured short term loan (15 days) from one bank to another. The collateral here is government bonds.

Instead of actually transferring the bonds the banks would transfer something called Bank Receipts (BR). This is because the bond certificates held by the banks would be of bonds worth 100 crores whereas the requirements by the banks to maintain their SLR would be much lower. Hence BR's were a much more convenient way of short term transfer.

The BR's were a form of short term IOU's (I Owe You). However, when an RF deal was exercised they never looked like a loan transfer but a buy and sale of securities represented by BR's. The borrowing banks would sell some securities represented by BR's to the lending banks in exchange for cash.

Then at the end of the period say 15 days the borrowing bank would buy the BR back (securities) at a higher price from the lending bank. The difference in the buy and sell prices would represent the interest to be paid to the lending banks. Due to the BR's, the actual transfer of securities doesn't take place. BR's could simply be cancelled and returned once the deal was completed.

Was the use of Bank Receipts (BR) Allowed?

The RBI set up a Public Debt Office (PDO) facility to act as the custodian for such transfer of bonds. As per the RBI BR's were not permitted to be used for such purposes. <u>However, the PDO facility was plagued with inefficiencies. Hence the majority of the banks resorted to BR. This</u>

<u>system existed with the knowledge of the RBI which allowed it to flourish as long as the system worked.</u> [Emphasis added]

What Roles did the Brokers Play Here?

Brokers in the markets played the role of intermediaries between two banks in the RFD system. They were supposed to act as middlemen helping borrowing banks meet lending banks. A brokers' role should have ended here where it is done in exchange for a commission.

Where the actual exchange of securities and payments should have taken place only between the bank's brokers soon found a way to play a larger role. Eventually, all transfers of securities and payments were made to the broker. Banks also began welcoming these because of the following reasons

Liquidity: Broker provided a quick and easier alternative to dealing with in comparison to dealing with another bank. Loans and payments would hence be provided on short notice in a quick manner.

Secrecy: When deals were made through a broker it would not be possible for the lending banks to find out where the loans were being moved to. Similarly, the borrowing banks too would not be concerned where the loans would be coming from. The dealings were both done only with the broker.

Credit Worthiness: When banks would deal with each other, the transaction would be placed depending on the creditworthiness of the borrowing bank. However, once brokers took over the settlement process this benefitted the borrowing banks as they would have loans available regardless of their creditworthiness. The lending banks would lend based on the trust and creditworthiness of the broker.

Brokers entering the settlement process made it possible that the two banks would not even know with whom they have dealt until they have already entered into the agreement. The loans were viewed as loans to the brokers and loans from the brokers. Brokers were now indispensable.

The Role played by Harshad Mehta.

Harshad Mehta used to broker the RF deals as mentioned above. He managed to convince the banks to have the cheques drawn in his name. He would then manage to transfer the money deposited in his account into the stock markets. Harshad Mehta then took advantage of the broken system and took the scam to new levels.

In a normal RF deal, there would be only 2 banks involved. Securities would be taken from a bank in exchange for cash. What Harshad Mehta did here was that when a bank would request its securities or cashback he would rope in a third bank. And eventually a fourth bank so on and so forth. Instead of having just two banks involved, there were now multiple banks all connected by a web of RF deals.

Harshad Mehta and the Bear Cartels

Harshad Mehta used the money he got out of the banking system to combat the Bear Cartels in the stock market. The Bear Cartels were operated by Hiten Dalal, A. D. Narottam and others. They too operated with money cheated out from the banks.

The Bear Cartels would aim at driving the prices low in the market which eventually undervalued various securities. The Bear Cartels would then purchase these securities at a cheap price and make huge profits once the prices normalized.

Harshad Mehta countered this by pumping money from the stock market to keep the demand up. He argued that the market has simply corrected the undervalued stock when it revalued the company at a price equivalent to the cost of building a similar enterprise.

He put forward this theory with the name replacement cost theory. This theory was a fallacy on his behalf or an illusion he resented to the public to justify his investments. Such was his influence in the stock market that his words would be blindly followed similar to that of a religious guru.

He would use the money from the banks which were temporarily in his account to hike up the demand for certain shares. He selected well-established companies like ACC, Sterlite Industries, and Videocon. His investments along with the market reaction would result in these shares being exclusively traded. The price of ACC rose from Rs.200 to nearly Rs. 9000 in a span of 2 months.

Harshad Mehta celebrated this victory by feeding peanuts to the bears at the Bombay Zoo as it signified his victory over the bearish trends.

Benefits to Banks

The banks were aware of Harshad Mehta's actions but chose to look away as they too would benefit from the profits Harshad would make from the stock market. He would transfer a percentage to the banks. This would also enable banks to maintain profitability.

THE SCAM WITHIN THE SCAM

Harshad Mehta noticed early on the dependence of the RF deals on BR's. In addition to this, the RF deal system also placed a great deal of reliance on prominent brokers like Harshad Mehta. So he along with two other banks namely Bank of Karad (BOK) and the Metropolitan Co-operative Bank (MCB) decided to further exploit the system. With the help of these two banks, he was able to forge BR's.

The BR's that were forged were not backed by any securities. This meant that they were just pieces of paper with no real value. This is similar to a situation where you can avail of loans with no collateral. Harshad Mehta further would pump this money into the stock market increasing his amount of influence.

The RBI is supposed to conduct on-site inspections and audits of the investment accounts of the banks. A thorough audit would reveal that amount represented by BR's in circulation was significantly higher than the government bonds actually held by the banks.

When the RBI did notice irregularities it did not act decisively against the Bank of Karad (BOK) and the Metropolitan Co-operative Bank (MCB).

Another method through which the collateral was eliminated was by forging government bonds themselves. Here the BR's are skipped and fake government bonds are created. This is because PSU bonds are represented by allotment letters making it easier for them to be forged. However, this forgery amounted to a very small amount of funds misappropriated.

Prelude: The Indian Money Market of the 1980s

The Indian money market was a marketplace where bonds, treasury bills and other fixed income instruments issued by the RBI traded. At its core, the structure was simple: One bank wanting to sell securities to another bank would hire a broker to facilitate the exchange for a small commission.

But the Indian money market was shallow and dominated by five players only - The leader, Citibank and the big brokers, DSP, VBD, C Mackertich and BCD (owned by Bhupen Dalal).

Between 1987-1992, money market brokers underwent a huge transformation. With foreign degrees and technology, they started emulating the foreign banks like Citibank. Brokers like Harshad Mehta, his brother Ashwin Mehta had the expertise, knowledge and understanding that surpassed these banks and soon the non-trading banks started looking like passive brokers.

In a couple of years, money market brokers surpassed the trading volume of the money market mafias. The role of brokers witnessed a massive growth as the Narasimha Rao government moved towards a system driven by markets and not government diktats. This meant that institutions such as IDBI, ICICI etc. who were fed easy money would now be required to raise their own capital from the market with the help of brokers. All of a sudden, brokers like Harshad Mehta had become the key players in the Indian money market.

First Act: Banks forced to invest in high-risk bonds

The 1992 Harshad Mehta Scam was inevitable. The scam was a result of over two decades of over-regulation on paper, lack of regulation in practice, misguided RBI policies and a creaky financial infrastructure.

After the liberalisation of the Indian economy in 1991, the government pressured Indian banks to compete and earn profits as they were close to bankruptcy. But competing with foreign banks and their advanced technology was an uphill struggle, especially since the banks had little freedom and capital for investments.

Till the 1992-93 budget, banks were forced to maintain 38.5% of their deposits as a statutory liquidity ratio (SLR) in low-interest bonds issued by the government and its entities. Another 25% was forced to be maintained as a cash reserve ratio (CRR) in treasury bills. These low-interest bonds financed the government's ever-increasing appetite for cash. Even with the remaining 36.5% 'free' capital, the banks were forced to focus on priority sector and political lending.

This meant that the banks had to dabble in high-risk-high-return bonds issued by other banks to improve their bottom line. Thus, the banks started approaching brokers like Harshad Mehta, to find and execute high return bond deals for them, setting in motion the 1992: Harshad Mehta scam. [Emphasis added]

Second Act: A unique ready forward deal (RFD)

Apart from the SLR and CRR roadblocks, Indian banks were also not allowed to invest in the stock market. So, their entire quest for improving their bottom line was heavily dependent on brokers like Harshad Mehta securing top deals for them.

The Indian banking sector was a jungle with the State Bank of India (SBI) as the dominant player residing with other small sized banks. These small-sized banks often faced temporary SLR and CRR deficits and would borrow from big banks and institutions to avoid being penalised by the RBI.

Before we reveal the second act, it is important to understand the banking system of the 1980s - 1990s. This was an era, where all the records were maintained physically in government offices. There were no digital records. The RBI had a Public Debt Office (PDO), which maintained the records of all the securities issued and transactions between the banks. The records were reconciled by each bank against the PDO records every quarter.

The banks would buy and sell securities through a **Ready Forward Deal (RFD).** A RFD is a secured short-term loan of 15 days against collateral. These RFDs were secured against government bonds.

While on paper the securities were bought and sold, in reality, when banks buy or sell government securities they rarely exchange papers. They exchange **Subsidiary General Ledger (SGL)** notes. SGL was issued as a substitute to exchanging actual securities. But often, **Bank Receipts (BR)** would be used instead of SGL Notes. [[Emphasis added]

A bank receipt was issued by banks who sold the securities but were unable to make immediate deliveries. They specified what had been sold and that funds were received from the lending bank while the securities would be delivered on a later date. Once the delivery was made, the bank receipts stood discharged.

So, a bank receipt would confirm that the borrowing bank will deliver the securities at a later date. This assured the lending bank that the bank receipts were issued against collateral.

Also the settlement cycle was 14 days. So, if SBI loans money to PNB against a BR, then PNB has to deliver the securities within 14 days.

Brokers like Harshad Mehta, were the middlemen of the ready forward deals. <u>Ideally, the lending bank would issue the cheque in the name of the borrowing bank, but Harshad Mehta would promise banks a higher rate of return in exchange for transferring the funds in his personal account. He termed this as making them **'bank-rich'**. So, cheques worth crores of rupees would be made out to Harshad Mehta instead of PNB or other banks.</u> [Emphasis added]

Harshad Mehta would deposit these cheques and since the settlement cycle was 14 days i.e. he had to pay the borrowing bank only after 14 days, so for 14 days Harshad Mehta owned crores of rupees.

He diverted these crores to rupees to the Indian stock market especially rigging the stock prices of his favourite stocks, ACC, Videocon, Sterlite Industries etc and taking the BSE to new heights. He single-handedly tackled all the market bears like Rakesh Jhunjhunwala, Manu Mundra and others, who had short the market, in absence of any fundamental factors driving the market rally.

With an inflow of crores of rupees, the stock prices rose drastically, enticing other investors to invest in the script. As and when investors flocked to these scripts (nearing the end of the 14-day settlement cycle), Harshad would sell his investments, pay the loan amount to the borrowing bank as mentioned in the BR, and deliver the securities to the lending bank.

The game was simple. Everything was squared off after 14 days. The lending bank got the securities, the borrowing bank got the capital, and Harshad made money in the market.

In a normal ready forward deal, only two banks were involved. But the brilliance that is Harshad Mehta, involved multiple banks. He would get the money from Bank A and ask for 14 days to deliver the securities. Consecutively, he would get the securities from Bank B and ask for 14 days to deliver the funds.

For these 14 days he invested the funds in the stock market. After 14 days, he simply had to liquidate his position from the market and pay the funds to Bank B. But what happens when the markets tank and Harshad cannot liquidate his position?

He would then approach Bank C, and get the securities from them and deliver to Bank A and ask for another 14 days to deliver the cash to Bank C. This went on for a while and by the end of it all, Harshad Mehta had 'officially' transferred crores of rupees from the Indian money market to the Indian stock market. Banks were unintentionally a party to the Indian stock market. [Emphasis added]

Third Act: Issuance of fake bank receipts

Remember, brokers were intermediaries in a RFD where lending and borrowing banks remained anonymous. They only knew the broker and an SGL note or a BR was proof enough for them to issue cheques in the name of the broker. And if that broker was the biggest name in the stock market, Mr Harshad Mehta, then no one batted an eyelid while issuing cheques worth crores of rupees.

UCO bank issued 50 crores to Harshad Mehta in clean credit i.e. without any collateral. The biggest bank in

India, the State Bank of India, issued him Rs 500 crores on the basis of unverified bank receipts. This trust and his name was the catalyst in the 1992 Harshad Mehta scam. But Harshad soon realised that he would run short of banks to get the bank receipts from. That is when he decided to print fake bank receipts.

He convinced small sized banks - Bank of Karad (BOK) and Metropolitan Co-operative Bank (MCB) to issue him fake bank receipts, guaranteeing to make them **'bank-rich'**. These bank receipts were just pieces of paper without any collateral. A collateral guaranteed that if the borrowing bank could not repay the lending bank after the agreed period, then the lending bank would take the bank receipts to the PDO and get the securities transferred in their name. Only in this case, there would be no corresponding records with the PDO because the bank receipts were fake.

The climax: The discovery of the Rs 500 Crore SBI 'loot'

In March 1992, CL Khemani, deputy managing director, treasury and investment management at SBI told RL Kamat, the deputy general manager, to start reconciliation work so that SBI's books balanced with the PDO records as on 31st March 1992.

The records were maintained by R. Sitaraman, a junior management grade officer, who later emerged as a key figure in the 1992 Harshad Mehta scam. After the reconciliation, there was a difference of 74 crores between SBI books and PDO records. Khemani became suspicious and asked the assistant manager to get the original records from the PDO.

On 11th April 1992, SBI's balance of the 11.5% central loan of 2010 maturity was 1170.95 crores whereas someone had altered the PDO statement so that Rs 1170.95 crores read as Rs 1,670.95 crores. Someone had looted the biggest bank in the country, the banker to the government worth Rs 500 crores.

After the questioning of R Sitaraman, it was revealed that the mastermind behind the Rs 500 crore loot was none other than the big bull, Harshad Mehta. Harshad Mehta was immediately called in the SBI branch and was asked to pay the bank or deliver the securities.

The market was down and therefore he couldn't sell his shares and pay back the money. Also the bank receipts issued to the SBI were fake, so they had no underlying securities.

Harshad Mehta had made it a habit to stay one step ahead of the others. So when K. Madhavan, joint director of the CBI, arrived in Bombay to head the probe into the Rs 2,500-crore securities scandal, the aggressively ambitious, 38-year-old stockbroker decided not to wait for a summon.

Abandoning his Rs 45-lakh Lexus for a down market Maruti 1000, Mehta drove to the CBI office on Wodehouse Road and offered himself for questioning.

Recently, a web series called "Scam 1992: The Harshad Mehta Story" was launched in India. This series depicted the life of a stockbroker Harshad Mehta who single-handedly took the Indian stock market to great heights in 1992.

The web series revealed the biggest financial exposé that took place in the Indian financial market. This series focused on how such a massive scam could not be pulled off single-handedly by an

individual Harshad Mehta <u>**but involved top executives of nationalized banks, foreign banks, brokers, bureaucrats, and politicians.**</u> **[Emphasis added]**

Thus the scam developed interest in reading and researching the loopholes that were present in the Indian financial system and that led to such an enormous scale of economic irregularities. This article covers how the scam originated, the loopholes in the government system that was uncovered and abused by the stockbrokers, and what reforms were undertaken by the government.

HOW THE SCAM ORIGINATED

In April 1992, <u>Sucheta Dalal</u>, an Indian journalist, wrote a press report stating discrepancies observed in government securities of more than 500 crores INR in the largest government bank of India — <u>State Bank of India</u>. The article did not accuse anyone directly but referenced the 'The Big Bull of Indian Market' laundering bank money and investing in the stock market. And, the Big Bull was none other than Harshad Mehta.

Within a month, it was discovered that this scam was just the tip of an iceberg. in 1992, the governor of Reserve Bank of India (RBI — India's central bank), <u>C.Rangarajan</u> with his subordinates uncovered that the economic irregularities were more than $1.2 billion which is often referred to as the <u>securities scam</u>. While this scam dominated the headlines of Indian newspapers, the immediate repercussion was the fall of the Indian stock market by 2000 points wiping off 100,000 crores INR of money.

THE IMMEDIATE IMPACT OF THE SCAM FOLLOWED BY THE INVESTIGATION FROM CBI

The Bombay stock index dropped steeply from its peak of 4500 points in March 1992 to 2500 points in August 1992 wiping out an exorbitant amount of money from the market. The government set up a special team of Central Bureau of Investigation (CBI just like the FBI from the US) to probe into the matter.

The investigation brought some shocking revelations into the picture. The money swindled from the banks revealed the bribes taken by top officials from the banks to issue fake BRs and uncovered brokers like Harshad Mehta who missed the process. A furore was raised when Mehta made a public announcement of bribing the Prime Minister of India Mr. P.V. Narasimha Rao as a donation to his party in 1992. But all these allegations were subsided and could not be proven.

Harshad Mehta was banned for a lifetime from stock market activities and sentenced to 5 years of imprisonment. He expired in 2001 while serving his sentence.

REFORMS IN THE BANKING SYSTEM OF INDIA AFTER THE 1992 SCAM

This scam forced the government to take some rapid reforms in the Indian stock market. The nationalized market was formed called the National Stock Exchange of India. A regulatory board called the Securities and Exchange Board of India was created to monitor the stock exchange.

The practice of banks giving ready forward deals to other banks was restricted and audited by the central bank (RBI). In 1994, the online trading system was introduced by the NSE that changed the dynamics of stock selling and trading.

This scam clearly indicated that the corrupt government authorities and bank officials were equally responsible as the brokers for the diversion of funds and bringing the GDP of a country to a standstill. This was indeed the worst financial scam that happened in Indian history.

- On April 23, 1992, Journalist Sucheta Dalal in The Times of India reports that the State Bank of India has asked The Big Bull to square up Rs 500 crores of irregularities. This caused mayhem in the country, and the SENSEX crashed. There was chaos in the parliament as well.
- The National Housing Bank, wholly-owned by RBI, was accused of transferring money to Harshad Mehta for him to cover up the displaced amount. The chairman resigned shortly.
- The scam involved officials from SBI, Brokerage Firms, Bureaucrats, Politicians, directors, and small-time employees of banks. There was extensive bribery to run the scheme of affairs. Many were arrested and asked to resign, offices were raided, several assets belonging to businessmen were attached. The country was shaken.
- Standard Chartered, ANZ Grindlays, Bank of America, Andhra Bank, UCO Bank, and many more such banks were involved.
- The CBI, RBI, SEBI, Income Tax Department, State Police. Almost every possible machinery was involved in the investigation.

- P. Chidambaram, who was in the cabinet resigned. His wife owned 25,000 shares in Fairgrowth Financial Services, which was a part of the scandal.
- Finance Minister Manmohan Singh was asked to resign, which was however not accepted by the then Prime Minister PV Narasimha Rao.
- The Jankiraman Committee and a Joint Parliamentary Committee were set up to investigate the claims involved in the scam.
- Mehta claimed that he had bribed the then-PM PV Narsimha Rao almost Rs. 1 crore for clearing him of charges. His claims were refuted by the authorities.

This estimate was based on the exposure of seven financial institutions—National Housing Bank, State Bank of Saurashtra, SBI Capital Markets, Standard Chartered Bank, Canbank Financial Services, Canbank Mutual Fund and Andhra Bank Financial Services. These entities had collectively paid Rs 4024 crore to other institutions for government securities and PSU bonds. But they did not have the securities to show for the money paid, and in some cases, were holding forged securities."

Above submissions suggest how the smooth passage was laid down beginning 1987 until the blow up of the scam in 1992. The laying down of the passage for the entry of the secondary market was contributory covering political, policy [bureaucracy], RBI, the banks and the brokers, to attest which, the material placed before as background for information of the readers could be considered. To believe that the tempting policies that were introduced by the government in 1987 supplemented also by master circulars issued by RBI on those matters to the commercial banks in the same year acted as an open invitation to the scam. I have dealt before about the RBI master circulars. The events introduced, as could be seen, were in serial order, one supporting the other without which, the scam would not have born.

Though the foregoing circumstances impel me to think whether the scam was a deliberate act on the part of the Interested Groups, referred to before; however, I am not an authority to arrive at such thinking conclusively but, at best, I can say they are suggestive of that nature. Activity chart was started in 1987 once it was noticed the outflowing funds at the hands of the PSUs mobilized through issue of tax free public sector bonds at the call of the government in the given circumstances until activities undertaken at various levels among the Interest Groups exploded in 1992 which was expected to happen but believed by the Interest Groups that the system was so fool proof [in negativity] that left little scope for outsiders to think about that in positive sense. All was done in the backyard that also contained explosive materials, one of which was exploded, may be, due to pressure and cracking like what happens when two large dark clouds clash against each other that throws out the lightning and thunder.

Tens of thousands of people officially assigned with functional duties in the PSUs, Banks and Financial Institutions were struck by the lightning unaware even entrapping those who were innocent in the whole process and pushing them into the cage of scam, as also there were and are people who actually made their fortunes out of the scam as stated in the Charge Sheets in hundreds filed before the Hon'ble Special Court in Bombay and also, in some cases, in the Hon'ble CBI Courts in Delhi. Many of them faced convictions based on the Trials and evidence, some of them escaped from the convictions for want of evidence and the last set of people who were innocent having made no pecuniary benefit to themselves or for any of the family members or relatives nor any financial loss to the organization served as admitted in the Charge Sheet itself have been made to hang on. . The Investigating Agency believes its duty is fulfilled once the Charge Sheet is filed while the Hon'ble Courts of Law are waiting for the expeditious action by the Investigating Agencies for completion of the trial. This is the present of state of affairs, a perplex situation beyond the control of the innocents for any remedy. In this process, many of the innocent accused lost their entire professional career built brick by brick maintaining absolute honesty, sincerity and integrity in their performance throughout their services. There is none to listen to their rotten life and advancing age. On account of such inexplicable and inordinate delays, some of the innocent accused passed away while some of them have become octogenarians.. They had incurred substantial expenditure in engaging the lawyers and appearing before the Hon'ble Court on the date of every hearing. They have been financially squeezed, physically beaten and mentally cracked. Their names and existence in the social circles have been blackened. Any film series of such people by anybody? The Search for the Scapegoats:

In Psychology, the scapegoat is the person or group that we want to blame, even though they are innocent, to exonerate the real culprit. Therefore, it is a person on whom fall the accusations or convictions, although he is not the true person responsible for what happened.

History is full of scapegoats since this phenomenon is as old as man himself. Perhaps one of the most tragic and iconic examples of the scapegoat was the process of blame that the Nazis launched against the Jews, just because they seemed to be more successful in their businesses while many other Germans were suffering the devastating consequences of the First World War.

Today, different groups carry the stigma that comes with being considered a scapegoat. Such is the case of immigrants or social minorities on which a part of the society discharges their discomfort. Many political leaders, especially in times of crisis, also unscrupulously exploit the scapegoat mechanism to divert attention from their own shortcomings and attempt to evade their legitimate burden of responsibility by placing it on other actors.

The scapegoat therefore becomes a kind of punching bag, the reservoir where we leave the most painful or complicated problems and conflicts to resolve. Thus we do not have to delve too deeply into its causes. We simplify everything. And we alleviate the psychological pain that would come with accepting certain blames and responsibilities.

The problem is that creating a scapegoat doesn't solve the problems. Closing our eyes to our shadows will not make them disappear. Blaming the other does not resolve our conflicts and creates new problems for the person who is carrying responsibilities that do not correspond to him………..

One may ask why I have brought scapegoat dilemma into the scam that we are presently concerned. There is a popular quote "Search for a scapegoat is the easiest of all the hunting expeditions." – Dwight D. Eisenhower. Once the scam broke out in 1992, the politicians, bureaucrats, bankers' bank, banks started scratching their heads restlessly and came to an unanimous understanding that the search for scapegoats could be most appropriate and be left to the investigation agencies that suggested to keep the names of the persons in the Interest Groups far away from the circumstances of the scam. That worked well. The investigating agency being under realm and control of the political power and bureaucrats joined the musical band and put their best efforts to search for and trace scapegoats as many as they could reach out knowing well, based on the material available in hand, such scapegoats had no role in the scam except having had to discharge their entrusted functions in the organizational set up.

The innocents about whom reference is made before were the most suited class of people whom the agencies in collaboration with the organization apparatus were able to close in, threaten them and forced them to be part of the criminal allegations integrated into the Charge Sheet. Some such people died because of shock and heart attack which hardly mattered to the Interest Groups and the investigating agencies except reporting the fact of death. These people having been interlaced and intertwined with the real offenders named in the Charge Sheet, were also made to merge with them, the function of separating them from the real offenders was considered by the investigating agencies as lying within the discretionary authority of the Hon'ble Trial Courts. One may also say thousands of investors died committing suicides and heart attacks. That is true but the effects were similar if not same in the case of innocents made accused persons also. Those died, died. Those living are livingly dead. The attribution to the existence of scam was one aspect but attributions of the scam to individuals were not at par and pace rather was based from different angles including officialdom influence.

The above narration, based on facts, confirms there was storm in the cup started in 1987 when departures were made by the central government permitting the PSUs to invest the surplus funds in public sector bonds instead of continuing to invest such funds in the Fixed Deposits with the nationalized banks as hitherto. How it was so felt and hurriedly brought into force through the route of confidentiality comes within the political and bureaucratic domain inaccessible to anyone. That opened the doors for dealing in the secondary market which is run and controlled by the brokers for sale and purchase of secondary securities. I have stated before the cumulative circumstances that led to involvement of PSUs in investments in the instruments stated before. The word 'secondary market' used was not defined as stated before. The government instructions on investments to PSUs referred to before did not lay down any specific or general guidelines on how to deal the investments in the secondary market, the PSUs having had no prior experience whatsoever. Example, whether to go through the nationalized commercial banks or any mode suggested by the RBI which ought to have suggested or enter into contracts with the brokers direct and deal in the secondary market. It seems the central government and the RBI left these vital aspects of the instructions on investments to the presumption of the PSUs in order to keep their hands clean so that consequences, if any, could be passed on to the PSUs direct.

Elementary lesson that is taught in the schools to nursery children is from ABC and not from XYZ but instructions so handed out to the PSUs had the effect of starting the learning in reverse order, that is, XYZ to ABC. That was what happened in the central government instructions to PSUs on investment of surplus funds. The master circulars issued by the RBI on operational aspects of the banks are endorsed only to the banks Chiefs whereby the PSUs were made to remain in utter darkness on the operational aspects of investment of surplus funds in the secondary market. Absence of these considerations on the part of the central government and RBI and lack of adequate knowledge and professional expertise at the senior and junior management levels, threw the closed doors open for the rushing entry of the commercial banks through the seasoned brokers in the secondary market. The new system of investment of surplus funds introduced in 1987 referred to before was like rushing water on breach of dam upon the old system neither telling how to deal with nor warning in advance the cautions and precautions to be taken by the PSUs either by the government or the RBI, the commercial banks having been under its domain that were taking up investment of surplus funds of PSUs in the government securities and public sector bonds. There was no training either to the dealing officers and staff in the secondary market securities provided either by the PSU or any other institutions which could have been nominated. It was like keeping the gold in the dark room and asking the dealing officers to search for the gold and tell how best it could be used while the dealing officers were unable to establish whether or not it was real gold. That opportunity was denied to them knowingly all of them were raw hands in handling the new line of investment of surplus funds. It was also like pushing the cats into the places where the pigeons eat grains in groups in thousands and thousands at the roundabouts. Those lucky to fly and escape are saved and those who are not able to fly were caught in between, mauled, injured or died. That is what could be compared to what happened in the secondary market when the crooks operating in that market were also allowed to rush through the surplus funds of the PSUs beginning that period until the scam reached its climax when the authorities woke up to know as to what happened in the stock market. PSUs had no authority to refuse to neither follow such instructions issued by the government /administrative ministries nor even bring to their kind notice of the implications thereof. The administrative ministries were practically not receptive to any kind of voice from the PSUs. They were made to function with their legs and hands tied.

Film series have also been made on the securities scam 1992 where the bones were shown and flesh in the body was guarded, that is the way the thousands of the dealing level officers and staff were made to sacrifice while those big fishes including the politicians, bureaucrats and bankers at the top level who made the richness from rustiness were found enjoying in five star hotels. It is sad that the film made on the subject left them outside their photo frame while shooting the film – it was a great fun for many to enjoy. The water in a vessel does not boil unless there is heat below whether the heat generated is from wood, electricity or gas, end result is that the person watching the boiling water will not put his or her hand in that water, that is what happens when someone goes nearer the big vessels where the degree of heat is much higher than the small vessel. That could be one of the reasons for not making any film on such persons/instances.

That is what is happening in our country in almost all the cases of financial frauds and scams. Let someone in the films industry took pain to detect them and made a film which is worth its cost. Suit, boot, tie and dark glass are good to see in mirror for; the mirror hides the truth but appears to be the only truth. There are greater crooks who are involved in much larger scale scams. This is not to suggest as if I had or have any sympathy towards kingpin of the scam but to point out that that what was shown on the screen was like showing partial eclipse of Sun. Did the central government or the RBI and the investigating agencies make equal efforts to bring them to the surface who have been hiding since several years within and outside the country? The investigating agencies cannot dare to do that because all such crooks are under the shadow of comfort of one or other powerful person. An ant knows it would die once someone puts foot on it but the elephant knows it can kill anyone who comes under its foot. Ant is not afraid of any one and, so silently dies but the elephant is most afraid of ant and feels happy if it is dead. The scientists believe that the elephants are afraid of ants for the same reason they are afraid of bees – They do not like getting swarms of them inside their trunks, which are highly sensitive and full of nerve endings. They may be tiny, but ants can bring giant elephants down to their knees, according to a new study that reveals that elephants in the savannah have good reason to be scared of the tiny insects. The investigating agencies brought the hammer to kill the ants [innocent accused persons] but feared to be near an elephant [the Interest Group that committed crime in reality] thinking the elephant could crush them.

The way the scam was allowed to develop and erupt, as has been submitted before, placed increasing burden on innocent accused persons than those who actually committed crime and made themselves rich. The process of differentiating these two classes of persons is such where the innocent accused persons would have to go through the process as one goes through the fire in one's life. The period is so prolonging stretching over 30 years that wears out such persons and, at times, makes them sick with severe sufferance. He or she who undergoes such journey in life can alone know the terrifying, if not terrorizing life having to remain in a state of mental isolation and whatever kind of consolation one could have built into oneself having done the duties honestly, sincerely and with full integrity torch him or her in a sense of loneliness both at the home and in the social life.

It is easy for the investigating agencies to attempt to prove crime by patching up, stitching the torn out clothes and twisting the circumstances of the case as best suited to them inasmuch as the innocent accused persons have no strength to withstand the illusory or presumable attributions conceived and forced upon such persons at the time they are charged sheeted; though such persons have the opportunity under the law to place before the Hon'ble Court of Law his or her innocence based on the available material and witnesses cross examination but that comes with increasing costs and time consuming process since there is no in between method of periodical review of the procrastinated pendency of the case that does not matter to the prosecuting agency but eats away the existing strength within the body of such persons. The process of law being such that it hardly accords and recognizes the factor of prolongation. Such persons live merely on hopes as long as one is alive not knowing what would happen at the end of the day and whether that day would come at all before his or her last breathing. It is nobody's concern either of the prosecuting agency or of the Hon'ble Trial Court as to how soon justice should be done in such cases. The life of such person remains as that of a caricature. "A caricature is putting the face of a joke on the body of a truth." Joseph Conrad.

There is no law of the land where the investigating agencies and judicial system are bound to go by the rule of law and a drill according to the law that should enable them to consider whether prima-facie there is a case that could be made out to test the innocence or otherwise. More than hundred years laws in vogue are continued to be applied whereas the time as it passes through the years brings with it new techniques and technology intended for the benefit of the humanity, more so, for one who has not done any wrong. **"A machine is a great moral educator. If a horse or a donkey won't go, men lose their tempers and beat**

it; if a machine won't go, there is no use beating it. You have to think and try till you find what is wrong. That is real education." — Gilbert Murray. "I have had a horse. Why would I accept a donkey? — Dr. Hawa Abdi. Time the criminologists and the judicial system presently being practised need to peep into the 'sense' and 'innocence' with open eyes rather than testing them through closed eyes being followed since centuries. Let a bright light be born to make the investigating agencies understand what 'sense' is and what 'innocence' is instead treating an innocent as a criminal and a criminal as an innocent.

Live happily with what comes in life as the only solace that is left to the fate of the innocent accused persons.

This Part 01 sums up combining together the facts and circumstances submitted before that it has become a matter of habit for the politicians, the bureaucrats, the investigating agencies and even for the judicial system to bypass the truth and embrace the false because the truth of the facts and circumstances are more closer to the Interest Groups who have learnt to enjoy the scenes by placing the false as truth for the indictment of the innocent accused persons. They may feel proud to remain to be known as innocents in society but the truth will continue to burn in their Conscience, inescapable for anyone who call a wrong as a right and right as a wrong. Earthly enjoyment is momentary while heavenly enjoyment is permanent that is difference between the false and the truth.

In May 1992, less than a month after the infamous securities scam broke, the former chairperson of the Unit Trust of India and the National Housing Bank (NHB) was found dead in his apartment. Pherwani had been regarded as the mentor of Harshad Mehta. He was also supposed to have lent NHB funds to the scamster and was struggling to recover it from Harshad Mehta and his associates. On May 21 — less than 12 days after resigning as NHB chairperson — Pherwani was found dead by his family members at his Bombay home.

"The journalist (R.C. Murthy, then chief of bureau at *Business Standard*) got a phone call and rushed to the house about 8am," writes Hamish Macdonald in his book *Polyester Prince* which tells the story of Dhirubhai Ambani's rise to power and pelf.

"Pherwani's body looked blue, he (Murthy) remembers. It was cremated at 11.30am the same day with the face covered instead of being kept open in the normal Hindu way. The death was ascribed vaguely to a heart attack. Murthy and many others believe Pherwani committed suicide," adds Macdonald.

Several other bit players involved in the securities scam of 1992 also died during the tortuous investigations and the prolonged court process which continues till this day.

Several mid-sized businessmen who turned bankrupt overnight in the stock market crash after the scam was unearthed also committed suicide in the days that followed [Telegraph Online – 06.03.2011].

The sum total makes it crystal clear that that the series of events that have been brought about as have been submitted in this Part were not accidental but were well thought over by the Interest Groups as justifiable considering the order of the events. Twisting and scrambling by the onlookers are also part of the game of life for; they make something out of anything they have in hand believing what they in have hand is the only truth ignoring the originality of the changing colours that contributed to the birth and death of the scam that called for diving in deep water rather than swimming on the surface.

This Part of the book has made best endeavour to 'Let the cat out of the bag'.

PART 02
JANIKIRAMAN & JOINT PARLIAMENTARY COMMITTEES

RESERVE BANK OF INDIA BULLETIN [JULY, 1992]

Governor's Meeting with Banks and Financial Institutions (June 9, 1992)

The Governor, Reserve Bank of India, Shri S. Venkitaramanan, met the Chairmen and Managing Directors and Chief Executives of banks and financial institutions on June 9, 1992 for a detailed discussion on the findings and recommendations of the Janakiraman Committee's interim report. The meeting noted the public concern at the recent revelations in the securities transactions of banks and financial institutions and emphasised the need to restore public confidence in their functioning as quickly as possible. The Chief Executives informed the Governor that remedial action has already been initiated by them to introduce proper internal control systems, strengthen monitoring, and remove lacunae in existing systems and procedures so as to prevent the recurrence of similar lapses in· future. All the Chief Executives expressed their commitment to implement the further guidelines· being issued by the RBI based on the Janakiraman Committee Report.

The appointment of the Committee headed by the Chairman, IDBI, to look into trading in public sector bonds and units of mutual funds was welcomed.

JANAKIRAMAN COMMITTEE:[Source: RBI Bulletin July, 1992] [Excerpts]

Interim Report of the Committee to Enquire into Securities Transactions of Banks and Financial Institutions (Janakiraman Committee) [June 2, 1992]

"The Committee · headed by Shri R. Janakiraman, Deputy Governor, RBI, which was set up on April 30, 1992 by the Governor, Shri S. Venkitaramanan, · to look into the funds management by commercial banks and financial institutions, in particular in relation to dealings in government securities,· public sector bonds and money market instruments, has submitted an interim report to the Governor. The report was presented to the Government of India and it has, in this connection, issued two press notes today, one highlighting the findings of the interim Report and the other reaffirming the· commitment of the Government and the Reserve Bank · of India to maintain the health of the Indian banking system and to remedy the shortcomings that have come to light. There is no reason for the public to be worried about the safety of their deposits with the banks. A copy of the Report along with a copy each of the press notes is enclosed for necessary action.[Not attached to RBI Bulletin posted on the Website].

GOVERNMENT OF INDIA PRESS NOTE DATED JUNE 2, 1992

Governor, Reserve Bank of India had set up a Committee on 30th April, 1992 to investigate the irregularities in funds management by commercial banks and financial institutions in particular, in relation to their dealings in Govt. securities, public sector bonds, UTI units and similar instruments. The committee has submitted an interim report on 1st June, 1992 which has been made available to the Government today.

The preliminary findings of the Committee indicate serious deficiencies in· the functioning. of the banks and financial institutions involved, lack of necessary internal control in various functions, and massive collusion between the concerned · officials and the brokers involved · in dealings in Govt. securities, public sector bonds and units, etc. The Committee has listed the devices adopted for diversion of funds from the banking system to the individual accounts of certain brokers which prima facie constitute evidence of fraudulent misappropriation. Fund management operations have been conducted in gross violation and with utter disregard of instructions and guidelines issued by RBI from time to time. The breakdown of essential discipline regarding the issue and recording of Bankers Receipts, the receipt and delivery of securities and the receipt and) payment for settlement of the transactions is exposed in many of the transactions detailed in the report. The Committee has also come across instances wherein brokers have been financed by banks through the discounting of bills not supported by genuine transactions.
....

The investigations have revealed that the following banks, subsidiaries of banks and institutions have made payment for purchase of investments for which they do not hold either securities SGL forms or BRs............

The Committee has found that increase in the volume of transactions in securities and capital market instruments since July, 1991 particularly in the form of ready forward deals led to indiscriminate issue of BRs and even SGLs and facilitated diversion of funds to select brokers. Funds have been diverted to Shri Harshad Mehta and his associated concern in a number of transactions put through particularly by NHB, State Bank of Saurashtra, SBI and SBI Cap. In several transactions the counter parties mentioned in the contracts provided by Shri Harshad Mehta are only in name. Further the facility of netting of the contracts afforded by SBI and SBI Cap to Harshad Mehta and collection and credit of banker's cheques issued in favour of SBI in Harshad Mehta's accounts and issue of banker's cheque of SBI as per his instructions have also resulted in irregular operations. The irregularities observed by the Committee in regard to SBI's transactions with Harshad Mehta are extremely disturbing and it appears that the investment account in SBI's books and SBI's accounts with Public Debt Office of RBI have been manipulated to accommodate transactions of the latter.

The Committee has noted the serious implications of the flow of proceeds of the account payee cheques drawn on RBI in favour of SBI and ANZ Grindlays Banks in the account of Shri Harshad Mehta, <u>without any authority of the drawers of the cheques.</u> Serious damage has also resulted from the issue of BRs by Bank of Karad and Metropolitan Cooperative Bank without having the capacity to honour the BRs in. transactions put through Shri Hiten Dalal in the cases of Standard Chartered Bank, CANFINA and Canbank Mutual Fund. The Bank of Karad has issued BRs on brokers' accounts without any backing or against nonexisting securities. A large number of Transactions have been put through in the account of M/s Bhupen Champaklal

Devidas and A; D. Narotam. The BRs. issued by Bank of Karad and presently outstanding of the value of about Rs. 750 crores are those issued in the account of broker. Shri A. D. Narotam who was until recently a director of the Bank. In providing adjustment to the broker Smt. J. HM Mehta (wife of Shri Harshad Mehta), UCO Bank has had to purchase certain shares whose value has depreciated considerably. National Housing Bank deals reveal absence of internal supervision in monitoring, nonpositioning of prudent procedural safeguards and absence of proper records.

The functioning of the Public Debt Office of the Reserve Bank of India evidently requires considerable speeding up and computerisation to effectively handle the large number of transactions and to provide relevant information to the banks for reconciliation at regular intervals to detect fraudulent / irregular transactions.

The committee has made the following recommendations:

(i) The practice of banks entering into ready forward and double ready forward deals with other banks be restricted to Govt. securities only and should be prohibited in other securities including PSU bonds, units and shares.

(ii) Ready forward and double ready forward deals may be prohibited under portfolio management schemes.

(iii) RBI's prohibition regarding banks entering into buy back deals with non-bank clients be strictly' enforced.

(iv) Banks should be required to formulate internal exposure limits' for transactions, including limits in regard to brokers.

(v) Brokers contract notes should indicate counterpart and brokerage charged.

(vi) When banks act as custodians of brokers' or other parties' securities the documentation for all transactions effected for such customers should indicate the banks' status.

(vii) The existing prohibition on banks issuing cheques drawn on their account with RBI for third party transactions should be strictly enforced.

(viii) Banks' transactions on behalf of their merchant banking subsidiaries should be transparent giving full details to the subsidiaries.

(ix) Banks may be required to conduct all their transactions in PSU bonds, units and similar securities through a separate institution like the Stock Holding Corporation, which can be established, to obviate the need to issue BRs.

(x) Speeding up of the work of Public Debt Office through computerisation and furnishing of information to banks.

(xi) Widening of scope of RBI inspections with greater emphasis on the treasury transactions and supplementing of onsite inspection by RBI by reporting of banks' compliance certified by the statutory auditors, with prudential and other guidelines.

(xii) RBI should review the adequacy of the Internal Audit Department of the Banks.

(xiii) Separate audit by' the 'banks'. Statutory auditors for the portfolio management operations of the banks.

(xiv) Strengthening of RBI's organisation responsible for market intelligence.

(xv) Institutional arrangements for inspection of National Housing Bank.

The RBI has accepted these recommendations and necessary follow-up action is being taken. 'Government and RBI have taken serious note of gross violation of RBI guidelines, the failure of internal control systems as also the flouting of banking norms regarding the Account payee cheques. The process for fixing responsibility for lapses and collusion and fraud. is under way. The CBI enquiry is in progress for determining criminal liability

Govt. will take all steps to see that action is taken to recover the dues of the banking system from all those who have abused the system and to punish the guilty.

The Committee expects to produce a second interim report after tracing the flow of funds involving various cheques drawn by banks and the brokers."

SUMMARY OF INSTRUCTIONS ISSUED BY RESERVE BANK OF INDIA ON REPOS - ANNEXURE VI POSTED ON ITS WEBSITE:

"1. Ready Forward (buy-back) deals in4Government and other approved Securities:

1.1 In April 1987, banks were advised to follow the guidelines given hereunder in respect of their buy-back arrangements with banks and others.

[Author's view: It is to be noted here that 'while the Summary of Instructions stated above mentions to follow the guidelines of April, 1987 given hereunder, after going through the guidelines, one finds that the guidelines go beyond April, 1987, even covering the guidelines issued up to 1995. All such guidelines/instructions issued beyond 1991 are to be ignored. These guidelines/instructions did not exist during the scam period, issued subsequent to the scam period and were therefore, did not exist during the scam period.]. Mixing them up with RBI guidelines of April, 1987 was inappropriate

A. Prohibition against buy-back arrangements in respect of Corporate Securities and Bonds issued by Public Sector Undertakings:

Banks should not enter into buy-back arrangements in respect of their holdings of public sector bonds or corporate shares and debentures.

B. Buy-back arrangements in Government and Other Approved Securities with (non-bank) clients:

(i) The buy-back deals should be exclusively confined to Government and Other Approved Securities and the re-purchase dates should be fixed after a minimum period of 30 days from the date of sale of the securities in question.

(ii) The purchase/sale prices under the arrangement should be in alignment with the proximate market rates prevalent on the date of the original transaction for the relevant Government and Other Approved Securities.

(iii) No sales of Government and Other Approved Securities under the arrangement should be effected by banks unless the same were actually held by them on their own investment portfolio either in the form of actual scrips or in Subsidiary General Ledger (SGL) account maintained with Reserve Bank.

(iv) Immediately on sale, the corresponding amount should invariably be deducted from the investment account of the bank and its SLR assets for the entire period.

(v) (Minimum 30 days) of holding by the purchasers/counterparty.

(vi) Interest on the securities at coupon rates would be paid by the banks after deduction of tax on the lines indicated in the communication dated 14th August 1986.

C. Inter-Bank Buy-back Arrangement in Government and Other Approved Securities

(i) While inter-bank buy-back transactions in Government and Other Approved Securities may be undertaken for short periods without the stipulation of any minimum period, the net differential in sale and repurchase prices of the securities in question (spread over the transaction period), together with the coupon rate of interest on the securities, should not in aggregate exceed the prevailing ceiling on call-money rate in the interbank market. In other words, the transactions should be done to yield a net return at the lower of the following:

(a) difference in sale and repurchase price of the securities (spread over the transaction period) together with interest at the coupon rate on the securities in question; or

(b) the prevailing ceiling on call-money rate in the inter-bank market.

(ii) The other stipulation mentioned at B (ii) to (v) above would be equally applicable to transactions with banks

1.2 Banks were also advised that a report on the buy-back arrangements indicating, interalia, profitability of transactions, should be submitted to their Board of Directors on a quarterly basis. Further, they should place before the Board of Directors a copy of this communication for their information, under advice to the Reserve Bank.

1.3 Thereafter, in December 1987, following inquiries from banks whether they could enter into buy-back arrangements in units of Unit Trust of India (UTI) under 1964 Scheme, it was advised that the units were not approved security for buy-back arrangements in terms of the instructions of April 1987.

1.4 As there was a sharp increase in the commitments of banks under buy-back Arrangements, they were cautioned in October 1987 to moderate their commitments as a sudden unwinding of these arrangements by investors could result in a serious liquidity bind. However, these commitments remained large and had a depressing effect on the growth of deposits, apart from having an adverse impact on the profitability of banks. The banks were, therefore, prohibited from entering into buy-back arrangements in Government and Other Approved Securities with non-bank clients with effect from 4th April 1988 and were advised that all such existing arrangements must be terminated on the date they expire or 1st July 1988, whichever was earlier.

1.5 Banks were further advised in April 1988 that while they were permitted to undertake outright purchases/sales, such transactions must be effected at market prices. Besides, while existing procedures for outright purchase/sale transactions could be continued, the spirit of the instruction prohibiting buy-back arrangements with non-bank investor was required to be scrupulously observed. It was to be noted that outright sale and purchase transactions with the same party and for identical or similar amounts would be construed by the Reserve Bank as tacit arrangements violating the instructions prohibiting buy-back arrangements with nonbank clients. Accordingly, the instructions conveyed in April 1987, stood modified.

1.6 It was added that banks may continue to enter into buy-back arrangements with other banks (inter-bank) in Government and Other Approved Securities subject to strict adherence to guidelines of April 1987. It was emphasised that the top executives in banks should bestow their special attention to inter-bank buy-back arrangements to ensure that the guidelines on the subject were strictly complied with in both letter and spirit, any deviation/s was/were viewed seriously and accountability fixed at all levels.

1.7 In conclusion, it was advised that a report should be submitted to the Board of Directors setting out compliance with the instructions prohibiting buy-back arrangements with nonbank investors. The position regarding the phased unwinding of buy-back commitments was to be advised to the Reserve Bank at the end of each month and a full compliance report was also to be submitted to it immediately after 1st July 1988.

1.8 In January 1991, banks were informed that it had come to Reserve Bank's notice that some banks had entered into buy-back deals with certain financial institutions like National Bank for Agricultural and Rural Development.

Industrial Development Bank of India and Unit Trust of India. It was clarified that buy-back arrangements in Government and Other Approved Securities were permitted between scheduled commercial banks only and for the purpose of the instructions issued in April 1988, financial institutions set up under Acts of Parliament or otherwise, both at the all-India and State levels and not undertaking banking business within the provisions of the Banking Regulations Act, 1949, were deemed as nonbank clients, and banks should not enter into any buy-back arrangements with them.

1.9 In this connection, banks were advised in January 1992 that the issue whether the prevailing 'repos' facilities in 182 days Treasury Bills (Government Securities) by Discount & Finance House of India Ltd. (DFHI) to banks would amount to violation of the instructions of April 1988 and January 1991, was examined by the Reserve Bank. It was clarified that as the basic objective of setting up of DFHI was to facilitate the development of active money market by smoothening short-term liquidity imbalances, DFHI was expected to actively trade in money market instruments, particularly in 182 days Treasury Bills. It was, accordingly, decided to exclude DFHI from the term ''non-bank clients'' for the purpose of buy-back arrangements in Government and Other Approved Securities by commercial banks...................

1.10 In June 1992, following the initial recommendations of the Janakiraman Committee, the following instructions were issued regarding 'Ready-Forward' (buy-back) deals:

(i) Banks were prohibited with effect from 22nd June 1992, and until further instructions, from undertaking inter-bank Ready Forward deals in dated Government and Approved/Trustee Securities. Existing deals in dated securities should be completed on due dates without resorting to any extension or roll overs. As such, inter-bank Ready Forward transactions might thereafter be undertaken only in Treasury Bills (of all maturities)

(ii) All double Ready Forward deals in Government securities, including Treasury Bills, were strictly prohibited.

(iii) No Ready Forward and double Ready Forward deals should be put through even among banks, and even on their own Investment Accounts in any other securities, such as Public Sector Undertakings' bonds and units of UTI.

(iv) Similarly, no Ready Forward and double Ready Forward deals should be put through in any security, including Government securities, on behalf of other constituents, including brokers.

1.11 In August 1994, banks were informed that the Notification No.S.O.2561 dated 27th June 1969, issued by the Central Government in exercise of the powers conferred by subsection (I) of Section 16 of the Securities Contracts (Regulation) Act, 1956, with respect to restriction on sale or purchase of securities, had been further amended, vide Notification No.S.O. (E) dated 1st June 1994 and a copy each of the two Notifications was forwarded to them.

(These are furnished in Annexure I.) [Annexure 1 not produced]. It was added that in terms of the amended Notification Ready Forward contracts may be entered into by

(I) a banking company
(II) a co-operative bank and
(III) the Discount and Finance House of India Ltd. in Treasury Bills of all maturities issued by the Government of India and in such dated securities of the Government of India, as were approved by the Reserve Bank of India, in consultation with the Central Government, provided all such Ready Forward transactions were put through SGL Account with the Reserve Bank of India.

1.12 Banks were further informed that in pursuance of the aforementioned Notification dated 1st June 1994, the Reserve Bank of India, in consultation with the Government of India, had approved the following four dated securities of the Government of India for the purpose of Ready Forward contracts :

Sl. No. Nomenclature of Security

1) 12.00 percent Government Stock 1995

2) 12.75 percent Government Stock 1996

3) 12.00 percent Government Stock 1999

4) 12.50 percent Government Stock 2004

1.13 In February 1995, banks were advised that the Reserve Bank of India in consultation with the Government of India, had approved the Zero Coupon Bonds, 2000 of the Government of India for the purpose of Ready Forward contracts, in addition to the four dated securities listed in the communication dated 16th August 1994.

1.14 Soon thereafter, the banks were advised that the Government of India vide their Notification F.No. 1/9/SE/94 dated October 18, 1994, (copy furnished in Annexure II),[Not reproduced] had notified Securities

Trading Corporation of India Ltd. as an eligible institution, in addition to the institutions indicated in the communication dated 16th August 1994, to undertake Ready Forward transactions in Treasury Bills and in such dated securities of the Government of India as were approved by the Reserve Bank in consultation with the Government. It would, therefore be in order for banks to enter into Ready Forward transactions in the securities specified above with Securities Trading Corporation of India Ltd.

1.15 Banks were further advised in March 1995 that it had been decided that Ready Forward deals in all the five approved securities (advised in the communications of August 1994 and February 1995) would be permitted only if the transactions were effected at Bombay and the deals were put through SGL Accounts.

1.16 Subsequently, banks were advised through different communications, that they may undertake Ready Froward transactions in the following securities subject to the condition that

(a) the transactions were effected at Bombay and
(b) the deals were put through SGL Accounts :
- (i) 13.25 percent Government Stock, 1997.(in conversion of 12 percent Government Stock 1995)
- (ii) Government of India Zero Coupon Bonds, 2000. (Second Series).
- (iii) 13.65 percent Government Stock, 1998.
- (iv) 13.50 percent Government Stock, 1997.
- (v) 14.00 percent Government Stock, 2005.
- (vi) Government of India Floating Rate Bonds, 1999.

(vii) 13.50 percent Government Stock, 1997. (Second Issue)
(viii) 14.00 percent Government Stock, 2005. (Second Issue)
(ix) 14.00 percent Government Stock, 2005. (Third Issue)
(x) Government of India Floating Rate Bonds, 1999.(Second Issue).
(xi) 13.85 percent Government Stock, 2000.

1.17 It was observed by the Reserve Bank that Ready Forward transactions were being used for as short a period as one day merely as a change in nomenclature from call money. With a view to ensuring that banks resort to Ready Forward transactions in accordance with the spirit of this facility, banks were advised on 29th September 1995, that effective from 30th September 1995, the minimum period for Ready Forward (repos) transactions will be three days.

2. Need to hold the security before sale

2.1 <u>In July 1991,</u> banks were advised inter alia, that it was observed that certain banks were resorting to buy-back deals in Government Securities amongst themselves without actually holding sufficient securities either in physical form or in their Subsidiary General Ledger (SGL) account (<u>resulting in substitution of Bank Receipts (BRs)/ return of SGL forms for want of sufficient balance</u>), at rates which had no relevance to market, with a view to window-dressing their profitability/ maintenance of SLR requirement, with the tacit understanding with the counter party banks. Some of the banks appeared to be taking outright oversold position in securities and in their desperate bid to cover the oversold position in a particular security/ies they had entered into double Ready Forward deals and other banks had obliged them in the matter. [Emphasis added]

In this regard, banks were instructed as under:

(i) Under no circumstances, a bank should hold a oversold position in any security; that is to say that no sale transactions should be put through without actually holding the security in its investment account.

(ii) All the transactions put through by a bank, either on outright basis or Ready Forward basis and whether through the mechanism of SGL Account <u>or BR, should be reflected on the same day in its investment account and accordingly for SLR purpose, wherever applicable.</u> [Emphasis added]

(iii) Any instance of return of SGL form from the Public Debt Office (PDO) of the Reserve Bank for want of sufficient balance in the account should be immediately brought to Reserve Bank's notice with the details of the transactions.

2.2 Notwithstanding the issue of the above instructions, irregularities on the part of banks persisted and following the initial recommendations of the Janakiraman Committee, the following comprehensive instructions on the above subject were issued in June 1992 (along with those on other issues relating to investment transactions) :

(i) All transactions in Government securities for which SGL facility was available should be put through SGL Accounts only,

(ii) Before issue of SGL transfer forms covering their sale transactions, banks should ensure that they had sufficient balance in their respective SGL Accounts.

Accordingly, under no circumstances, a SGL transfer form issued by a bank in favour of another bank should bounce for want of sufficient balance in the SGL Account.

The purchasing banks should issue the cheques only after receipt of the SGL transfer forms from the selling banks.

(iii) The SGL transfer form received by purchasing banks should be deposited in their SGL Accounts immediately. No sale should be effected by way of return of SGL form held by the bank.

(iv) SGL transfer forms should be signed by two authorised officials of the bank whose signatures should be recorded with the respective PDOs of the Reserve Bank and other banks.

(v) The SGL transfer forms should be in the standard format prescribed by the Reserve Bank and printed on semi-security paper of uniform size. They should be serially numbered and there should be a control system in place to account for each SGL form.

(vi) If a SGL transfer form bounces for want of sufficient balance in the SGL Account, the (selling) bank which had issued the form would be liable to the following penal action against it ;-

(a) The amount of the SGL form (cost of purchase paid by the purchaser of the security) would be debited immediately to the current account of the selling bank with the Reserve Bank.

(b) In the event of an overdraft arising in the current account following such a debit, penal interest would be charged by the Reserve Bank on the amount of the overdraft at a rate of 3 percentage points above the Discount and Finance House of India's (DFHI) call money lending rate on the day in question, and

c) If the bouncing of the SGL form occurs thrice, the bank would be debarred from trading with the use of the SGL facility for a period of six months from the occurrence of the third bouncing. If, after restoration of the facility, any SGL form of the concerned bank bounces again, the bank will be permanently debarred from the use of the SGL facility in all the PDOs of the Reserve Bank.

[2.3 not stated in the copy posted on Google Website]

2.4 Thereafter in December 1993, banks were advised [with reference to item (iii) of para. 4.3.3 above] that it was observed that the SGL transfer forms received by the purchasing banks were not being deposited in their SGL Accounts immediately and delays (of as much as 10 days in certain cases) had been observed. It should, therefore be ensured that SGL transfer forms were lodged in the SGL Accounts with the PDO immediately, i.e. within a maximum period of two working days from the date of transaction. It was added that any delay beyond the above mentioned period would be viewed seriously.

2.5 Subsequently, in respect of item (vi) (b) of para. 4.3.3 above, banks were advised in January 1994 that if the DFHI's closing call money rate was lower than the minimum lending rate of banks, as stipulated in the Reserve Bank's interest rate directive in force, the applicable penal rate to be charged would be 3 percentage point above the minimum lending rate.

3. Internal Control System in respect of investment transactions

3.1 The comprehensive instructions on Investment portfolio issued to banks in June 1992 following the initial Report of the Janakirman Committee included the following on Internal Control System of banks (which have been included in the Chapters on Frauds, Annual Accounts, etc.)

    (i)   There should be a clear functional separation of (a) trading, (b) settlement, monitoring and control and (c) accounting. Similarly, there should be a functional separation of trading and back office functions relating to banks' own Investment Accounts, Portfolio Management Scheme (PMS) Clients' Accounts and other Constituents' (including brokers') Accounts. While providing portfolio management service to their clients, the banks should strictly follow the guidelines in regard thereto issued by the Reserve Bank on 18th January 1991. (These have been covered separately). Further, PMS Clients' Accounts should be subjected to a separate audit by external auditors.

(ii) For every transaction entered into, the trading desk should prepare a deal slip which should contain data relating to nature of the deal, name of the counterparty, whether it was a direct deal or through a broker, and if through a broker, name of the broker, details of security, amount, price, contract date and time. The deal slips should be serially numbered and controlled separately to ensure that each deal slip had been properly accounted for. Once the deal was concluded, the dealer should immediately pass on the deal slip to the back office for recording and processing. For each deal there must be a system of issue of confirmation to the counterparty. The timely receipt of requisite written confirmation from the counterparty, which must include all essential details of the contract, should be monitored by the back office.

(iii) Once a deal had been concluded, there should not be any substitution of the counterparty bank by another bank by the broker, through whom the deal had been entered into; likewise, the security sold/purchased in the deal should not be substituted by another security.

(iv) On the basis of vouchers passed by the back office (which should be done after verification of actual contract notes received from the broker/counterparty and confirmation of the deal by the counterparty), the Accounts

Section should independently write the books of accounts.

(v) In the case of transaction relating to PMS Clients' Accounts (including brokers), all the relative records should give a clear indication that the transaction belonged to PMS Clients/Other Constituents and did not belong to banks' own Investment Account and the bank was acting only in its fiduciary/agency capacity.

(vi) Records of Subsidiary General Ledger (SGL) transfer forms issued/received should be maintained. Balances as per bank's books should be reconciled at quarterly intervals with the balances in the books of PDOs. If the number of transactions so warrant, the reconciliation should be undertaken more frequently, say on a monthly basis. This reconciliation should also be periodically checked by the internal audit department. Any bouncing of SGL transfer forms issued by selling banks in favour of the buying bank should immediately be brought to the notice of the Central Office of the Department of Banking Operations and Development of the Reserve Bank by the buying bank. <u>Similarly, a record of Bank Receipts (BRs) issued/received should be maintained. A system for verification of the authenticity of the BRs and SGL transfer forms received from the other banks and confirmation of authorised</u>

<u>signatories should be put in place.</u> [Emphasis added]

(vii) Banks should put in place a reporting system to report the top management, on a weekly basis, the details of transactions in securities, details of bouncing of SGL transfer forms issued by other banks and BRs outstanding for more than one month and a review of investment transactions undertaken during the period.

(viii) Banks should not draw cheques on their account with the Reserve Bank for third party transactions, including inter-bank transactions. For such transactions, bankers' cheques/pay orders should be issued. (Detailed instructions in this regard have been covered separately.)

(ix) The Internal Audit Department should audit the transactions in securities on an on-going basis, monitor the compliance with the laid down management policies and prescribed procedures and report the deficiencies directly to the management of the Bank.

3.2 In this regard, banks were advised in August 1992 that it was the primary responsibility of the bank managements to ensure that there were adequate internal control and audit procedures for ensuring proper compliance of the instructions in regard to the conduct of the investment portfolio. Banks were instructed to undertake an immediate review of the adequacy of their internal audit departments and indicate details of their existing organisational set up and the scope of their operations to the Reserve Bank to enable it to review the adequacy of the internal machinery to oversee the implementation of the instructions given to banks. It was added that banks should also institute a regular system of monitoring compliance with the prudential and other guidelines issued by the Reserve Bank of India. Further, banks were advised to get compliance in key areas certified by their statutory auditors and to furnish such audit certificate to the Reserve Bank.

4. Engagement of brokers for Investment transactions

4.1 In July 1991, banks were advised to frame suitable investment policy. The various guidelines then furnished to them in this regard have been covered separately.) As regards engagement of brokers, they were advised as under:

Transactions between one bank and another bank should not be put through the brokers' accounts. The brokerage on the deal payable to the broker, if any (if the deal was put through with the help of a broker), should be clearly indicated on the notes/memorandum put up to the top management seeking approval for putting through the transaction and separate account of brokerage paid, broker-wise, should be maintained.

4.2 Thereafter, following the initial recommendations made by the Janakiraman Committee, Reserve Bank issued, in June 1992, comprehensive instructions to banks on the various aspects of conduct of their Investments Portfolio. As regards dealings through brokers, the following instructions were issued:

(i) If a deal was put through with the help of a broker, the role of the broker should be restricted to that of bringing the two parties to the deal together.

(ii) While negotiating the deal, the broker was not obliged to disclose the identity of the counterparty to the deal. However, on conclusion of the deal, he should disclose the counterparty and his contract note should clearly indicate the name of the counterparty.

(iii) On the basis of the contract note disclosing the name of the counterparty, settlement of deals between banks, viz., both fund settlement and delivery of security, should be directly between the banks and the borker should have no role to play in the process.

(iv) With the approval of their top managements, banks should prepare a panel of approved brokers which should be reviewed annually, or more often if so warranted. Clear-cut criteria should be laid down for empanelment of brokers, including verification of their creditworthiness, market reputation, etc. A record of broker-wise details of deals put through and brokerage paid, should be maintained.

(v) A disproportionate part of the business should not be transacted through only one or a few brokers. Banks should consider fixing aggregate contract limits for each of the approved brokers and ensure that these limits were not exceeded.

4.3 Thereafter, in December 1992 banks were informed that on a scrutiny of the investment policies evolved by the banks, it was observed that a number of them had not fixed aggregate contract limits for each of the approved brokers (vide item (v) above). The matter was, therefore reviewed by the Reserve Bank and it was decided that a limit of 5% of total transactions (both purchase and sales) entered into by a bank during a year should be treated as the aggregate upper contract limit for each of the approved brokers. This limit should cover both the business initiated by a bank and the business offered/brought to the bank by a broker. Banks should ensure that the transactions entered into through individual brokers during a year normally did not exceed this limit. However, if for any reason it became necessary to exceed the aggregate limit for any broker, the specific reasons therefor should be recorded, in writing, by the authority empowered to put through the deals. Further, the Board should be informed of this, post facto.

4.4 In this regard attention of banks was drawn to the instructions on 'Audit', Review and Reporting' contained in the communication dated 20th June 1992 and it was reiterated that the concurrent auditors who audit the treasury operations should scrutinise this aspect also and include it in their monthly report to the Chief Executive Officer of the bank. Besides, the business put through any individual broker or brokers in excess of the limit, with the reasons therefor, should be covered in the half-yearly review to the Board of Directors/Local Advisory Board. It was added that these instructions shall also apply to subsidiaries and mutual funds of the banks.

4.5 Subsequently, some of the banks sought certain clarifications on the instructions of December 1992 and these were examined by the Reserve Bank. The clarifications sought and the replies thereto, issued in July 1993, are furnished in the Annexure.

4.6 On further review of the matter, banks were advised in November 1994 that it had been decided that inter-bank securities transactions should be undertaken directly between banks and no bank should engage the services of any broker in such transactions. Banks may, however, undertake securities transactions among themselves or with non-bank clients through members of the National Stock Exchange (NSE), wherein the transactions were transparent. Transactions with non-bank clients, if such transactions were not undertaken on the NSE, should be undertaken by banks directly, without engaging brokers.

4.7 Banks were also cautioned that any violation or circumvention of Reserve Bank's instructions would invite penal action against banks, which could include raising of reserve requirements, withdrawal of refinance from the Reserve Bank and denial of access to money market, as also such other penalty under the provisions of the Banking Regulation Act, 1949, as the Reserve Bank may deem fit.

4.8 After the issue of instructions of November 1994, some of the banks sought clarification on the coverage of the term 'securities' appearing therein. Banks were advised in December 1994 that although the Securities Contracts (Regulation) Act, 1956 defines the term 'securities' to mean corporate shares, debentures, Government Securities and rights or interest in securities, for the purpose of the communication dated 16th November 1994, the term 'securities' would exclude corporate shares. Further, as regards the coverage of term 'non-bank clients' appearing in the aforementioned communication, it was clarified that Provident/Pension Funds and Trusts registered under the Indian Trusts Act, 1882, would be outside the preview of the expression 'non-bank clients' for the purpose of that communication......... {Clarifications by RBI to Banks' Queries – Not reproduced]

5. Accounting standards for Investments

5.1 The comprehensive instructions issued by the Reserve Bank in April 1992 on Income Recognition, Asset Classification, Provisioning and Other Related Matters included the following on Accounting standards for Investments :

The investment portfolio of a bank would normally consist of both "approved securities" (predominantly Government securities) and "others" (shares, debentures and bonds). It has been decided that the investments in approved securities should be bifurcated into "permanent" and "current" investments. Permanent investments were those which banks intended to hold till maturity and current investments were those which banks intended to deal in, i.e. buy and sell on a day-to-day basis. On this basis, banks should classify the existing investments in approved securities into the aforesaid two categories. To begin with, banks should keep not more than 70 percent of their investments in the permanent category from the accounting year 1992-93. This ratio would have to be brought down to 50 percent in due course. All subsequent purchases would also be required to be classified suitably. Reserve Bank would have no objection to banks inter-changing the investments from one category to another with the prior authorisation of the Board of Directors, in which case depreciation, if any would have to be fully provided for.

5.2 While the depreciation in respect of permanent investments was not likely to affect their realisable value and, therefore, need not be provided for, depreciation in the current investments should be fully provided for. Permanent investments could be valued at cost unless it was more than the face value, in which case the premium has to be amortised over the period remaining for maturity of the security. Banks were not expected to sell securities in the permanent category freely, but if they do so, any loss on such transactions in securities in this category has to be written off. Besides, any gain should be taken to capital reserve account. (It was subsequently advised in December 1992 that banks which experienced difficulties in adopting the above standards could discuss the matter separately with the Reserve Bank.)

5.3 The detailed instructions relating to Investment transactions issued in June 1992 following the initial Report of the Janakiraman Committee, included the following additional instructions/ modifications relating to Accounting Standards:

(i) All investments in securities, other than approved securities, should be classified under ''current'' category and should be valued at market price or cost whichever was less and depreciation should be provided for the shortfall, if any.

(ii) In the instructions of April 1992, the manner in which banks' investments in approved securities should be bifurcated into ''permanent'' and ''current'' categories had been indicated. Dealing securities were marketable securities that were acquired and held with the intention of reselling them in the short term. The financial results arising from such transactions must be seen as volatile, generating trading profit or loss from deliberate position taking. Investment securities, on the other hand, were acquired and held for yield or capital growth purposes (apart from for compliance of SLR requirement) and were usually intended to be held till maturity, except when liquidity needs arise. Unless governed by the special rule described below, gains and losses on sale of securities should be recorded at the time of sale as capital gains/losses. As stated earlier, approved debt securities classified under "current" category should be carried in the Balance Sheet at market price or cost whichever was lower, whereas approved debt securities classified under "permanent" category should be carried in the Balance Sheet either at book value (cost) or at market value, at the discretion of the banks, subject to their following a consistent accounting policy. Accounting of securities under various categories should be as under :

Approved debt securities under "permanent" category

   (a) If the investments were carried at book value, the difference between the acquisition price (acquisition cost) and the redemption price should be accrued over the period from the acquisition to the redemption date and should be recognised as income or expense.

   (b) Alternatively, the banks may choose to value such investments, on a consistent basis, at market value.

   (c) Should the banks elect to adopt the practice described in (a) above, when the securities were redeemed or sold before the original redemption date, the unaccrued portion of the amount referred to at (a) above should immediately be charged to the profit and loss account as capital gain or loss, as the case may be.

(d) Should banks elect to follow the practice described in (b) above, the resulting revaluation gains/losses should be recognised as capital gain/loss. Investments under ''current'' category

(e) The investment under ''current'' category should be carried at lower of cost or market value, on a consistent basis.

(f) Costs, such as, brokerage fees, commission or taxes, incurred at the time of acquisition of trading securities, should immediately be recognised as expenses, without any accrual.

(g) The carrying value of securities under current category should be revalued at market prices on a quarterly basis. The gains/losses arising out of this revaluation should not be taken to interest income/expenses accounts. Instead, revaluation gains/losses should be segregated by entering them in specific "realised/unrealised gains/losses on trading of debt securities" account. The net amount of gains/losses from trading of debt securities shall be taken to the income statement.

(iii) Each time a security was acquired, the bank should immediately record whether it was for investment account or for trading account and accordingly account for them in the respective accounts on the basis of laid down accounting policies. Transfer of securities from one account to another (i.e. Investment Account to Trading Account or vice versa) should be done only with the prior approval of the Board of Directors of the bank and should be properly documented.

(iv) Potential losses should be recognised prior to the transfer of securities from ''current'' category to ''permanent'' category where market value as on the date of transfer was less than the carrying value in the books.

(v) Banks may treat equity investments in subsidiaries as permanent investment.

5.4 It was clarified in January 1994 that, in respect of Zero Coupon Bonds (issued by Government of India, vide its Notification No. F. 4(5) W & M/93 dated 7th January 1994), the value of these Zero Coupon Bonds for the purpose of determining "cost" may be reckoned after taking into account the accrued discount pro rata. After this adjustment of the "cost", banks could use the standard valuation procedures.

5.5 The clarifications/fresh guidelines issued to banks on 'Income Recognition, etc.' in February 1994, included those relating to 'Valuation of Securities'. Thus, banks were informed that it was observed by the Reserve Bank that the practices followed by banks and auditors differed in respect of valuation of investments in ''current'' category. It was, therefore, decided that the Indian Banks' Association (IBA), in consultation with the Institute of Chartered Accountants of India (ICAI), would evolve a method for valuation of Government and other securities and banks and auditors should adopt the method so evolved while finalising the balance sheet as on 31st March 1994.

5.6 In the context of bifurcation of investments in Government securities into "permanent" and "current" category, banks were not required to make provisions for depreciation in respect of investments held under "permanent" category. Hence, it was not necessary to show the difference between the book value and the market value of the investments under this category as a footnote to the balance sheet and the instructions contained at "Notes and instructions for compilation of balance sheet and profit and loss account", advised in February 1992, were withdrawn. However, the difference between the book value and market value could be mentioned by Statutory Auditors in the Long Form Audit Report for the information of the bank's management.

5.7 In this connection, a reference was also invited to the instructions on accounting Standards advised in June 1992. It was clarified that while banks may, at their option, value the approved debt securities under the "permanent" category on a consistent basis at market value, they should refrain from doing so in respect of securities whose market price was higher than the book value (cost) on the balance sheet date. In other words, in these cases it was not permissible to carry these securities at a value higher than cost, as this would result in recognising unrealised gains in respect of such investments.

5.8 At a meeting of the Bank Audit Committee, comprising representatives of the Institute of Chartered Accountants of India (ICAI) and Chairmen of some major banks, held in March 1995, the guidelines on valuation of investments were reviewed and, in the light of the discussions held in the meeting, banks were advised as under in April 1995. :

(i) Valuation of "permanent" investments

Banks' attention was drawn to the instructions of June 1992, in terms of which if the "permanent" investments were carried at book value, the difference between the acquisition price (acquisition cost) and the redemption price should be accrued over the period from the acquisition to the redemption date and should be recognised as Income or expense. Further, in February 1994, it was clarified that while banks may, at their option value the approved debt securities under the "permanent" category on a consistent basis at market value, they should refrain from doing so in respect of securities whose market price was higher than the book value (cost) on the balance sheet date. In other words, in these cases, it would not be permissible to carry these securities at a value higher than face/redemption value as this would result in recognising unrealised gain in respect of such investments. It had since been decided that the "permanent" investments should be valued at cost and in case the cost price was higher than the face value, the premium should be amortized over the remaining period of maturity of the security. On the other hand, where the cost price was less than the face value, the difference should be ignored and should not be amortized or taken to income account since the amount represents unrealised gain.

(ii) Investments to be carried at gross or net of depreciation

It was decided that "investments" should be shown in the balance sheet net of depreciation. It would, however, be open to the banks, for disclosure purposes, to show in the balance sheet the book value of investments, the depreciation there against and net amount of investments separately.

(iii) Valuation of investments on a quarterly basis

In the instructions of June 1992, it was mentioned that the carrying value of securities under "current" category should be revalued at market prices on a quarterly basis. It had since been decided that the investments under "current" category should be carried at lower of cost or market value, on a consistent basis and that the valuation should be done on a quarterly basis. In other words, the basis of valuation on quarterly basis would be the same as that followed for annual accounts. It was also decided that the rates of Yield To Maturity (YTM) of different kinds of securities circulated by the Reserve Bank for the final accounts of each year should be used for the subsequent quarters also for the purpose of quarterly valuation of investments. The banks may arrive at on notional basis gains or losses on the basis of such quarterly valuation and it may not be necessary to pass entries booking such gains or losses.

(iv) Treatment of excess depreciation, if any

It was decided that depreciation on "current" investments should be shown in the profit and loss account as a debit item under Schedule 14. It was also decided that where depreciation was provided on "current" investments but, in a subsequent year, the market price of the relevant securities had improved, the excess provision towards depreciation could be taken to the profit and loss account and, thereafter, it could be appropriated to the "capital reserve" account.

(v) Treatment of recapitalisation bonds

The recapitalisation bonds would not form part of "permanent" or "current' 'investments. It would not be necessary to provide for depreciation on the recapitalisation bonds received by the nationalised banks from Government. In case, however, banks acquired recapitalisation bonds of other bank for investment purposes, the depreciation, if any, would have to be provided for.

(vi) Modification of percentages in respect of classification of investments under "permanent" and "current" category

It was advised in June 1992 that, to begin with, banks should keep not more than 70% of their investments in "permanent" category for the accounting year 1992-93, which would be brought down to 50% in due course? It was suggested in the meeting that there was a need for bringing down the ratio to 60:40. It was however, decided to maintain the ratio of approved securities into "permanent" and "current" investments at 70:30 for the year ended 31st March 1995 also.

(vii) Routing of gain from sale of securities

While in April 1992 banks were advised that any gain on sale of securities in the "permanent" category should be taken to "capital reserve" account, it had since been decided that such gain should be first taken to the profit and loss account and thereafter it could be appropriated to the "capital reserve" account.

6. Audit, review and reporting of Investment transactions

For implementing the recommendation contained in the initial Report of the Janakiraman Committee, the following instructions on the captioned subject were issued (alongwith other instructions on conduct of the investment portfolio) :

(i) Banks should undertake a half-yearly review (as of 30th September and 31st March) of their investment portfolio, which should, apart from other operational aspects of investment portfolio, clearly indicate and certify adherence to laid down internal investment policy and procedures and Reserve Bank guidelines, and put up the same before their respective Boards within a month, i.e., by end-April and end-October.

(ii) A copy of the review report put up to the bank's Board, should be forwarded to the Reserve Bank by 15th November and 15th May respectively.

(iii) In view of the possibility of abuse, treasury transactions should be separately subjected to a concurrent audit by internal auditors and the results of their audit should be placed before the Chairman and Managing Director of the Bank once every month. These audit reports should be sent to the Regional Office of Department of Banking Operations and Development (now to Department of Supervision) of the Reserve Bank under whose jurisdiction the Head Office of the bank fell.

7. Reconciliation of holdings of Government Securities, etc.

7.1 Following the initial report of the Janakiraman Committee, comprehensive guidelines/ instructions regarding the conduct of the Investments Portfolio were issued by the Reserve Bank in June 1992. In regard to the

Subsidiary General Ledger (SGL) facility provided at the Public Debt Offices (PDOs) of the Reserve Bank, apart from detailed instructions (which have been covered separately), it was advised that records of SGL transfer forms issued/received, should be maintained by banks. Further, balances as per bank's book should be reconciled at quarterly intervals with the balances in the book of PDOs. If the number of transactions so warrant, the reconciliation should be undertaken more frequently, say on a monthly basis. This reconciliation should also be periodically checked by the internal audit department. It was also advised that any bouncing of SGL transfer forms issued by selling banks in favour of the buying bank, should immediately be brought to the notice of the Central Office of the Department of Banking Operations and Development (now Department of Supervision) of the Reserve Bank by the buying bank. Similarly, a record of Bank Receipts (BRs) issued/received should be maintained. A system for verification of the authenticity of the BRs and SGL transfer forms received from other banks and confirmation of authorised signatories should be put in place.

7.2 In this connection, banks were further advised in December 1992 that during the course of scrutiny of security transactions of banks/Financial Institutions, instances of shortages in holdings of securities had come to Reserve Bank's notice. Therefore, banks and their subsidiaries/Mutual Funds should reconcile the securities held by them, both on their own Investment Account, as well as Portfolio Management Scheme (PMS), as on 31st December 1992. Further, a reconciliation statement, in the prescribed proforma, should be furnished to the Reserve Bank, duly certified by the bank's auditors. (The format for the Statement is at Annexure I, while the instructions for compiling it are in Annexure II.)

7.3 In this connection, it was clarified in February 1993 that there was no objection to the aforementioned verification/certification being done either by the bank's own internal auditors or by external auditors.

8. Transactions in Securities — Custodial Functions

8.1 In continuation of the detailed instructions in regard to management of investment portfolio of banks, particularly relating to transactions in securities, issued in June 1992, banks were advised in August 1992 that when they exercised custodial functions on behalf of their merchant banking subsidiaries, these functions should be subject to the same procedures and safeguards as would be applicable to other constituents. Accordingly, full particulars should be available with the subsidiaries of banks of the manner in which the transactions had been executed. Banks were instructed to issue suitable instructions in this regard to the department/office undertaking the custodial functions on behalf of their subsidiaries.

8.2 Banks were advised in January 1963 that under Section 6 of the Public Debt Act, 1944, no notice of any trust was receivable by Government in respect of Government securities. Consequently, the Public Debt Office of the Reserve Bank treats, and has to treat, every person, in whose name a Government security stands, as the full owner thereof, even though the said per Son may be having no personal interest in the security but may be holding it merely as a trustee of a particular trust or as an office-holder of a society or a fund, i.e., in a fiduciary or representative capacity. Holding of securities in the personal names of officials or trusts was liable to lead to considerable difficulties under certain circumstances. Since the Public Debt Office was bound to treat the "holder" as the "owner", it followed that if a trustee or office-holders, in whose personal name a security (belonging to a trust or society) was held, dies, the Public Debt Office would refuse to make any payment on the security to the trust or society unless the said trust or society obtained legal representation (i.e. Probate, Letters of Administration or Succession Certificate) in the estate of the deceased trustee/office-holder. As the obtaining of such a grant entailed considerable inconvenience and expenses, the societies or trusts concerned were, as a rule, unwilling to adopt this course and approach the Reserve Bank for relaxations, which the Public Debt Office was understandably reluctant to make, except on the condition that the claimant body executed a bond of indemnity in the Reserve Bank's favour jointly with one or two sureties. Very often, it was difficult for the claimants to arrange for sureties of the requisite financial standing. It also sometimes happened that the office-holder/trustee, in whose favour a security was held, resigned and omitted or refused to transfer the security to his successor-in-office. In such cases, the Public Debt Office was unable to help the real beneficiary whose only course was to bring a suit against the ex-trustee or the ex-official in a civil court for obtaining a proper decree to enable the Public Debt Office to recognise the claimant's title.

It was further mentioned that a body which had a corporate status could, of course, hold Government securities in its corporate name, but this recourse was not available in the case of unincorporated bodies — to which category most trusts, provident funds, etc., usually belonged. The most convenient course for such bodies was to hold securities in the form of Stock Certificates (and not in the form of Government Promissory Notes). Under Rule 8 (2)(b) of Public Debt Rules, 1946, Stock Certificates could be issued in favour of officials/trustees ex-officio without mentioning their personal names, so that in the event of death or resignation, the security could be dealt with immediately by the successor-in-office, without any formality. No question of legal representation or indemnity bond would arise if securities were so held. Besides the above advantage, holding in stock was very convenient from the point of view of a long-term investor. For example, the periodical interest on Stock Certificates was remitted by the Public Debt Office to the holder or to the holder's bankers on the due date, without any cost to the holder, whereas a Government promissory note had to be physically presented for drawal of interest every time such interest was drawn. Again, if a Government Promissory note was lost, the procedure for obtaining a duplicate was a long and expensive one, whereas a lost/destroyed Stock Certificate could be replaced by the Public Debt Office on the holder merely reporting the loss and executing an affidavit. It was added that like Stock Certificates, Treasury Savings Deposit Certificates and Defence Deposit Certificates could also be issued in favour of office holders and trustees, ex-officio.

Usually, all organisations like provident funds and trusts, made investments through, or on the advice of their bankers and, therefore, the expense and inconvenience caused to the beneficiaries in such cases would be obviated, if banks were to advise the above position to their customers. Banks were advised that they might, therefore, take note of these instructions and also communicate them to such of their customers as belonged to the above categories with the advice that if any securities were held by their officials/trustees in their personal names, they would be well advised to contact the nearest Public Debt Office for getting the matter regularised.

In conclusion, it was indicated that in case any clarification or further information on any point was required, reference may be made to the Public Debt Office. The stipulation of minimum period of three days for ready forward transactions has been withdrawn from October 31, 1998."

Chapter 4: Planning for the Development of Repo Market

4.1. This Chapter deals with areas which are of immediate concern to the Group in the context of development of the repo market in India. As mentioned in the earlier Chapter, over the course of its discussions the Group made observations on the need for expansion of the repo market in terms of enhanced participation and eligible instruments. It also pondered over the need for uniform accounting standards and documentation. The other areas of its concern are dealing and settlement systems which required to be put in place and the need for evolving a code of conduct for the market participants. Also, need for removal of certain procedural irritants has been suggested by the Group as an integral part of the plan for development of the repo market.

LEGAL POSITION

4.2. At the outset, the current legal position is that the forward or second leg of a repo transaction will be legal and valid only if it is not hit by the Government Notification prohibiting repos. Accordingly, in order to legally facilitate the repos transactions RBI had to take up the issue with the Government to exempt banks, etc. from this prohibition. As long as the June 1969 notification is operative, RBI would have to continue to take up with the Government to issue necessary notification exempting, such of those entities as deemed necessary by the Bank, from the prohibition contained in the notification. It will not be possible for most intending parties (other than the few permitted) to legally participate in repos unless the Notification is withdrawn by the Government. Hence, the first basic legal requirement for developing repos is to withdraw the Government Notification dated June 27, 1969.

4.3 Repos undertaken by RBI, however is exempted in terms of Section 28 of the Securities Contract (Regulations) Act as the provisions of the Act do not apply to the Government, RBI and any local authority or any corporation set up by a special law or any person who has effected any transaction with or through the agency of any of these authorities. Till such time, the above mentioned notification is not repealed there would, however be need to notify institutions by names to make them eligible for undertaking repos. Mere withdrawal without regulatory framework is not advisable and it is necessary for RBI to have legal authority to regulate the repos market.

4.4 Repo being short term money market instrument, is being used for smoothening volatility in money market rates by central banks through injection of short term liquidity into the market as well as absorbing excess liquidity from the system. Regulation of repo market, thus becomes a direct responsibility of RBI. As expansion of the repo market with wider participation and variety of

> instruments would require RBI to have enhanced regulatory powers over the debt market there is need to amend Section 29A of SCR Act. to enable the Government to delegate regulatory powers in respect of trading in Government Securities and other debt instruments to the Reserve Bank. While the "Internal Working Group to Study Legal and Regulatory Aspects of Financial Markets" has already made recommendations to this effect, there is need to pursue the amendments vigorously as they would provide the required legal base for regulating the repo market.

4.5 In view of the developments which are envisaged to take place in the financial market in general, and the repo market in particular, there is need for a computerised system linking the participants and PDO for trading and settlement. The system should ideally provide facility both for trading, confirmation and settlement. The Group recognises the legal impediments in the way to electronic transfer of gilt securities which is not possible under the Public Debt Act, 1944 and the need to effect early replacement of the Public Debt Act by the proposed Government Securities Act has assumed great expediency. The Group urges that immediate steps should be taken to resolve the legal and procedural difficulties in the way to achieve a modern market infrastructure It may be worthwhile to take due cognizance of the changing face of securities settlement systems, the world over with the use of information technology.

WIDENING AND DEEPENING OF THE MARKET

4.6. The position regarding participation and eligible instruments for undertaking repo transactions at present is as under:

    (I) All banks, cooperative banks, Primary Dealers (by name) and Satellite Dealers (by name) are permitted to undertake ready forward transactions in all Central Government securities including Treasury Bills provided the transactions are settled through SGL Accounts maintained at Public Debt Office, Mumbai;

    (II) Nonbank entities as notified by the Central Government are permitted to undertake reverse repos subject to restrictions on counterparties and instruments as mentioned above.

4.7 Further, keeping the usefulness of repos in view as an instrument for the development of the money market it was decided in the Monetary Policy for the first half of 1997-98 to allow repos in such PSU bonds and private corporate debt securities which are held in dematerialised form in a depository and the transactions done in recognised stock exchanges. Till recently, pending a resolution on stamp duty these instruments could not be used for undertaking repos. However, with the announcement in the current budget on removal of stamp duty on transactions in debt instruments in demat form these instruments are expected to be used in repo transactions subject to Government's notifying their eligibility for the purpose.

WIDER PARTICIPATION

4.8 The repo market in India operates under a controlled environment and the Group examined the need for expansion of repo market in terms of participation and eligibility of instruments. The Group is of the view that in terms of the participants there is need to expand the market to include all entities including corporates while in terms of eligible instruments it could be possible to make all government securities including those issued by State Governments and debt securities issued by PSUs, corporate entities and All India Financial Institutions eligible for undertaking repo transactions.

4.9. The Group observed that repos have been restricted to interbank market in India and it has thus kept away a large number of potential users such as financial institutions, corporates and pension funds from its purview. It is well recognised that extension of repos to these institutions would provide them with access to financing at competitive rates in case of need. These institutions, otherwise need to resort to distress sale of securities when there is a need for funds.

4.10. A case for widening participation is also justified from the point of view of the recommendations of the Narasimham Committee II which has observed that the participation of nonbanks in the call money market resulted in volatility in the market. It has advocated that call/notice/term money market should be a pure interbank market including Primary Dealers. The exit of nonbanks from call money market would reduce the funds available in the call money market considerably as the lendings by non-bank institutions constitute about 40 per cent of the total lending in the call money market. Consequently these funds are expected to seek avenues for deployment. It has already been announced in the Monetary Policy Measures for the second half of 1998-99 that the move towards pure interbank call money will be implemented in a manner that the existing lenders in the market will have operational flexibility to adjust their asset-liability structure.

4.11 The decision to exit the nonbank participants from the call money market raises the issue about the instruments in which the nonbank institutions may be allowed to invest their surplus funds which are presently deployed in call money market. (of the order of Rs.5,000 crore). While at present the non-bank entities can undertake reverse repos they are not allowed to repos – thus they do not have two-way access in the repos market. If provided two way access the need to keep large 'cash balances' will be reduced and these institutions could invest across the yield curve without anxiety thus facilitating their cash management as also development of a yield curve. The Group is, therefore of the view that permission to nonbank entities to enter the repo market two ways would be beneficial both from the point of view of the non-bank entities as also the market.

4.12 Further, keeping the usefulness of repos in view as an instrument for the development of the money market RBI has already been advocating the need to widen participation in the repo market in a phased manner. The facility has already been extended to Primary Dealers and Satellite Dealers in the recent past.

4.13 Inclusion of non-banks as participants in the repo market would have the following advantages.

4.13.1 It will enhance liquidity in respect of Government securities held encouraging them to enlarge their holdings voluntarily which would be very much welcomed in the context of the Government's market borrowing programme of higher amounts, in future;

4.13.2 Nonbanks, when are allowed to operate two way instead of the existing one way by taking part in reverse repos only, would help the market to narrow the spreads between repo and reverse repo rates making efficient allocation of liquidity possible; and

4.13.3 It would give rise to varying maturities as far as repo transactions are concerned as the market participants would go in for periods of their choice thus giving rise to the development of a term money market through price discovery.

4.14. There are however, arguments against any further expansion of the participants in the repo market. They are as under:

4.14.1 RBI has a promotional role to play in developing and activating market in money market instruments and government securities which have direct bearing on Monetary Policy. Repo is a money market instrument and money market is not open to all players. In this context, the Group is aware that there is an existing view on the implications of the signals the repo market could have for policies pursued and it would be desirable that only participants in the money market should be made eligible to participate in the repo market.

4.14.2 Repos are money market instruments which are treated variously as borrowing/lending and selling/buying by different market participants. The impact of this on accounting and the asset-liability patterns could be significant. The regulatory concern about non-bank participation related to the fact that borrowing from non-bank results in increase in the liabilities and consequently the levels of CRR/SLR to be maintained thus impacting the maintenance of statutory reserves by banks. Also, a bank could meet its cash requirements by doing a repo with the non-bank, treating the repo instrument as a transaction of sell/buy and it could be viewed as being aimed at avoiding the booking of liability.

4.15 To the extent non-banks switch their investment from money market to the repos market, the reserve base would be diminished but this is possible even under the present regulation allowing non-banks to participate in reverse repo transactions. Further, as long as banks have surplus SLR, borrowing against repos is 'reserve free' as compared to borrowing in money market and the banks are then on level playing field with non-banks in this sense. Provided there is uniformity in accounting treatment of repos by the different participants in the repos market, efficient DVP systems for all repos transactions undertaken, prudent ALM guidelines laid down and followed by bank and non-bank financial entities, 'haircuts' or 'margins' levied and maintained on an ongoing basis repos could bring about enhanced flexibility and liquidity to the financial markets.

ADDITIONAL INSTRUMENTS

4.16 The Group observes that currently, the repo transactions are driven by two considerations and they comprise compliance with SLR requirements and use of SLR securities to raise short term finance. In fact, there is enough evidence to show that neither of these types of transactions actually contribute to the depth and liquidity of the Government securities market, in the real sense. There is a need to make eligible a variety of other instruments such as bonds of all India financial institutions, public sector units and corporate entities to make a vibrant and active repo market.

4.17 As in the case of widening participation, deepening of the repo market through introduction of eligible instruments as well, needs to be thought of. The Group is, therefore, of the view that PSU bonds and corporate bonds as also bonds of All India Financial Institutions held in demat form which enjoy high level of safety and liquidity can be considered for repo transactions and the time is opportune enough to add more to the existing instruments.

4.18 Since some of the State Government securities have also acquired liquidity over a period of time as an addition to the existing stock of securities eligible for repo transactions if the outstanding amount of all State Government securities are also made eligible it would further add Rs.60,000 crore or so, in value to the existing stock of instruments thus enhancing the quantum of eligible instruments to around Rs.3,85,000 crore. Since State Government stocks are risk free and therefore, on par with Central Government dated securities with a comfortable margin by way of higher coupon for comparable maturities to compensate for their illiquidity, once they become eligible as an instrument for repo transactions, there is reason to believe that their liquidity as well, would improve. The Group's recommendations would be justified on grounds that although all Central Government marketable securities are now eligible for repos only bench mark securities are liquid enough for the purpose. While repo transactions in respect of State Government securities may be restricted to SGL Accounts at Mumbai, in due course with the introduction of computerisation of PDOs it should be possible to extend repo transaction settlement to all PDOs.

"OVER THE COUNTER" AND EXCHANGE TRADED "REPOS"

4.19 Since PSU bonds and Corporate Debt Securities in dematerialised form in a depository are already eligible (subject to issue of notification by Government) for undertaking repos transactions through a Stock Exchange, it was felt that this arrangement could be extended to Government securities as well, thus making "exchange traded" repos in Government securities a reality. However, since the memories of the irregularities committed in the Government securities market through ready forward transactions are still very fresh such an expansion needs to be undertaken with caution. The Group is of the view that keeping the needs of the market participants a system of "over the counter" and "exchange traded" repos with adequate checks and controls could be introduced, as under:

(i) All entities who have SGL Account and Current Account with RBI may be allowed to undertake 'over the counter' repos and reverse repos in all Government securities (including those issued by the State Governments). For the present, such repos may be restricted to SGL Accounts at Mumbai and in due course with successful linking of all RBI offices; it could be extended to other RBI centres.

(ii) All entities including corporates may be allowed to undertake repos and reverse repos in all Government securities, PSU bonds, Private Corporate Debt Securities and bonds issued by All India Financial Institutions provided firstly, the debt instruments are held in dematerialised form in a depository and the transactions are undertaken through approved stock exchange with a well-capitalised clearing corporation functioning as legal counter party.

Transactions under (ii) above, involving triparty could be permitted provided the triparty agent is a well-capitalised Clearing Corporation[2] licensed to function as a legal counterparty in all such transactions and where such an agency would define acceptable securities from within the specified broad categories as mentioned above, execute required haircuts, do daily marking to market, ensure that all participants maintain adequate collateral at all times, the quantity traded is in standardised lots and the settlement is done under "novation", maintaining anonymity of counterparties all the time.

Under "novation" , an entity A does a repo against a Clearing Corporation and the Clearing Corporation does a repo against an entity B. The Clearing Corporation would view both A and B as sources of crdit risk and insist on collateral from both sides. There could be a defined number of Clearing Corporations, licensed for the purpose. The regulating authority would vet the policies and audit the operations of the Clearing corporations. The clearing corporation would define acceptable securities and haircuts, do daily marking to market and ensure that all participants maintain adequate collateral at all times. The Clearing Corporation being the legal counterparty in all transactions, the proposal when implemented would help remove credit risk from the repo market. The concept of "novation" , in fact, helps alignment of the enforcement objectives of the

Clearing Corporation with the enforcement objectives of the regulator.

ACCOUNTING TREATMENT

4.21. The complication in accounting of repos arises from the fact that the transaction involves an outright sale of securities with an irrevocable commitment to repurchase at an agreed price after a certain period while the transaction could also be considered as a borrowing of money against the collateral of securities. In consonance with the International Accounting Standards (IAS -1) and the Accounting Standards (AS-1) set out by the Institute of Chartered Accountants of India, the "substance" has to take a precedence over the "legal form" while incorporating any accounting transaction in the financial statements. This would mean that the underlying nature and spirit than the form of the transaction should reflect the financial statements, since, these statements are used for making evaluations of the financial strength of the entity concerned and thus facilitate most appropriate financial decisions. On the other hand, it also helps management to take appropriate and timely action.

4.22. In India, the accounting treatment given to repos in majority of the cases does not follow the "substance" approach. There are two broad type of accounting treatment observed as under:

(i) Some entities treat repos as money market borrowing/lending operations against the collateral of securities, thus reporting the cost of repo as interest expense;

(ii) A majority of the entities strictly go by the definition of repos and treat them as an outright sale in the first leg and a repurchase in the second leg.

4.23 The second approach leads to booking the capital gains/losses in the first leg itself, though in fact, the securities are to be repurchased in the second leg. Further, during the repo period there is a presumption that the coupon would accrue to the lender of money.

4.24. There is need for uniformity in treatment of similar transactions by all market participants and accounting treatment has to be standardised. There is a view that the confusion over accounting of repos in India is on account of treating them as "buy/sell back repos". The Group, therefore examined the advantages and disadvantages of a shift to "classic repo" and whether a classic repo could address most of the accounting problems encountered in the case of a buy/sell back repo. In a classic repo:

4.24.1 The starting and end prices of the securities are same and the payment of "interest" is made separately, thus establishing clearly the spirit or substance of the underlying transaction. i.e. a borrowing/lending transaction.

4.24.2 If the buyer of the bond receives a coupon payment while holding the bonds, the same is paid to the seller immediately, whereas in the case of a buy/sell back repo, it is incorporated in the repurchase price. This is one reason why in India during "shut period" repos in Government securities are not preferred;

4.24.3 Since the interest component is not embedded in the repurchase price, it allows the repo cost as an item of expenditure/income in the financial statements of counterparties, treating the repo transactions as borrowing activity against the collateral of securities;

4.24.4 Unlike in the case of buy/sell repo where low coupon securities are not considered for repo transactions for fear of booking of losses, classic repo would release a huge portfolio of low coupon government securities for the purpose of repos;

4.24.5 Marking to market to take care of the market risk on a daily basis is possible;

4.24.6 Open trades i.e. repos terminable at any time at the instance of either of the contracting parties are feasible.

4.25 Although there are major advantages in going in for classic repos it would be difficult to get the transactions legally accepted in India as the two legs of the repo are still being not considered generally as a part of a composite instrument. . Also, under classic repo it may not be desirable to allow the cash taker to include securities sold, for calculation of SLR as the country is still under minimum SLR requirements. Further, classic repo does not allow the purchaser of securities recon the securities for SLR purposes, during the repo period.

4.26 Thus, while a total shift to "classic repo" could address most of the accounting problems encountered, it may not be possible to implement the proposal in view of the legal treatment of repos as buy sell back transactions. In the circumstances, the Group is of the view that it would be better to continue with "buy sell back" repo.

4.27 In this context, it may also be recalled that following the Janakiraman Committee, RBI advised banks that all repos should be done at market rates to ensure transparency. While the Group is totally in agreement with the view that off market rate repos can hide a variety of payments it is necessary that the system allows for haircuts or margins to be maintained for market and liquidity risk. This is essentially a risk management function and management of banks would in addition to laying down haircuts could also specify the extent of "haircuts" or margins to be applied for different types of instruments. The money market dealer would then only be responsible for fixing interest rate. In order that there is uniform accounting treatment and sufficient transparency, the Group has accepted continuance of the "buy-sell back repo concept" and has suggested standardised accounting norms for repos so that there is uniformity in approach towards accounting in general and applying haircuts/margins, booking of capital gains/loss and separation of the interest paid/received in the transaction, in particular. The uniform accounting treatment of repos is accordingly placed at Annexure II.

DEALING AND SETTLEMENT

4.28 The existing mode of trading is 'over-the-counter' with a system of confirmation of the deals. If the deal is through a broker, broker's note also forms part of the deal documentation. Settlement is done at PDO in the SGL system which provide for DVP settlement providing for end-of-day settlement. Consequently no transaction can be treated as final till the end of the day, exposing the participants to a systemic risk of one deal being dishonoured leading to a sequential transaction failure. As long as the SGL/Current Account system is open to creditworthy parties who come under RBI's system of monitoring, the above risk may not crystallise. But the position will be significantly different when the participation to Repo market is enlarged. The above position underlines the need for introducing sophistication in trading and settlement systems in tune with the increasing level of participation in the Repo Market.

4.29 As regards settlement, the existing system of end-of the day DVP cannot be considered risk free due to bottlenecks in movements of securities and cash. as explained above. A system of provision of Day-Light overdraft to the current account holders by RBI may be thought of to avoid such eventuality.

4.30 While the proposed entry of all non-bank institutions maintaining Current and SGL Account with RBI may not exert much pressure on the existing system, entry of corporates would be critical from the point of view of the preparedness of the physical settlement systems and legal and regulatory environment. Firstly, the corporate entities generally hold their gilt securities indirectly in the Constituents' SGL Accounts maintained with RBI by banks and PDs/SDs (hereinafter called Gilt Dealer (GD), for the sake of convenience).

4.31 Banks, Primary Dealers and Satellite Dealers are provided the facility to maintain a second SGL Account in the books of Public Debt Offices. The eligible entities can hold Government securities in these Constituents' SGL Accounts, where the beneficial ownership belongs to their constituents. The system is meant to facilitate a simple and indirect form of investment in Government securities by investors. However, such beneficial ownership of the constituents is not recognised in the Public Debt Act, 1944. The relationship between the entities holding Constituents' SGL Accounts and their constituents are contractual where as the formers' relationship with RBI and Government is governed by the Public Debt Act and the rules made, thereunder.

4.32 As the transfer of securities would be made in the books of the GD a framework of DVP has to be designed to rule out settlement failures. In addition, it would also be necessary that clear guidelines are issued by RBI to regulate the maintenance of Constituents' SGL Accounts by GDs particularly emphasising the fiduciary role of the GD. While the guidelines could provide for GDs obligations and a code of conduct in dealing with the constituents' securities, in the area of repos deals between the corporate and a bank/PD, it is necessary that the settlement is done by DVP in the books of RBI using the GD's funds subject to the GD ensuring that the DVP at RBI is invariably preceded by the recovery of funds from the constituent.

4.33 In the context of gradual deepening of the Government securities market and the policy to promote the retail segment of the market, it is felt expedient to frame a set of guidelines governing the maintenance of the Constituents' SGL Accounts by these entities. The Guidelines should lay down eligibility conditions to hold Government securities in the indirect form, responsibilities of Constituent Account holders, Custody, transfer and mechanics followed for settlement of transactions. This would go a long way in elimination of undesirable practices which could crop up in the wake of an active Government securities market in general and a repo market, in particular.

4.34 The Working Group, in its draft guidelines for maintenance of Constituents' SGL Account placed at Annexure III, has provided for obligations and code of conduct including transparency and safety in dealing with the Constituents' securities. These Guidelines could be finalised after discussion with representative self regulatory organisations of the market participants.

4.35 To avoid differences in practices followed it would be desirable to stipulate deal date and settlement date. At present deals undertaken take, often more than stipulated number of days for execution and settlement. In order that there is no confusion deals can either be settled on the same day or the next day of the deal and this should be clearly indicated in the contract/terms of deal to ensure that there is no confusion/variance in settlement date of repos.

DOCUMENTATION

4.36 The two main risks are default risk and the issuer risk. The credit risk involved in repo transaction is offset to a great extent by the fact that on default by counterparty the lender can liquidate the securities received . Similarly, the seller of securities holds cash against no return of securities by the purchaser. However, when the realisable value of securities does not match the exposure, such offsetting is not adequate. Also, illiquid issues, defect in title and enforceability of contractual terms pose problems. Under the issuer risk, the market volatility of the security (market risk) and the risk of default by the issuer are the main risks. If proper legal documents are available, on default by issuer, the counterparty would remain bound to make good the fall in market value of security. A suitable legal agreement also needs to be signed with the counterparties.

4.37 Accordingly, the Group felt that it is essential to settle and standardise the matters to be covered under a legal agreement governing a repo transaction. The agreements could have provisions for:

4.37.1 Transferring of title to securities (including any securities transferred through substitution or mark-to-market adjustment of collateral);

4.37.2 Marking to market of transactions daily bais;

4.37.3 Specifying clearly the events of default and the consequential right and obligations of the counterparties;

4.37.4 Clarifying the rights of the parties regarding substitution of collateral and the treatment of coupon and interest payments in respect of securities subject to it, including, for example, the timing of any payments.

4.38. Working Group has attempted a draft document which could be modified suitably to meet actual requirements in repo transactions. The Draft Master Repurchase Agreement on the lines of the global master repurchase agreement of the Public Securities Association, New York, placed at Annexure IV has provisions for absolute transfer of title of securities (including any securities transferred through substitution or mark to market adjustment of collateral), daily marking to market of transactions, specifying clearly the events of default and the consequential right and obligations of the counterparties, clarifying the rights of the parties regarding substitution of collateral and the treatment of coupon and interest payments in respect of securities subject to it, including , for example the timing of any repayments. In the event of default, repo counterparty should have to stand in queue along with other creditors and this aspect has especially been taken care of. A final master repurchase agreement based on the draft could be prepared in consultation with the representatives of the market participants.

CODE OF CONDUCT

4.39 The Group is of the view that as the market for repos is being expanded there is the immediate need for evolving a code of best practice and this could be done by a working group of market practitioners and regulators to ensure that the repo market is adequately controlled and understood. Such a code of conduct would include issues participants should address before undertaking repo transactions, legal agreements in prevalence, margins, marking to market, exposure limits on counterparties, custody of collaterals, right to declare a counterparty in default, confirmation of deals, matters to be covered before trading with a new counterparty, information to be exchanged at point of trade etc. The Group has included a draft code of conduct which has been included as a part of this report and placed at Annexure V for the benefit of the market practitioners.

SUPERVISION

4.40 The memories of the irregularities committed in the Government Securities Market is still very fresh in the minds of the market participants and the regulators. As more participants and instruments are made eligible for undertaking repo transactions RBI may like to monitor the size, growth and orderliness of the repo market . RBI could also seek reports institution wise, on the value of repo contracts entered into, broken down by original maturity for specific periods, total number of deals undertaken during the period, the value of repo transactions outstanding at the end of the period, broken down by residual maturity As money market on line dealing system is installed and made operative it should become possible for RBI to monitor the market online focusing on participants, market rates, trading patterns etc.

OPERATIONAL IRRITANTS

4.41 There are a few operational irritants which have been plaguing smooth undertaking of securities transactions in general and repo transactions in particular. These include inability to roll over repos, and confusion over maximum period for repos contract which needed to be addressed by the Group.

Roll Over of Repos

4.42 As a part of its policy on repos, RBI does not permit roll over of Repos. The rationale for this is when one repos is replaced with another especially with another especially since the requirement of funds could be a constraint. As long as the securities are valued at the prevailing market prices at time of roll over haircuts freshly applied cash payables/receivables settled rollover is at rates of interest in alignment with prevailing market rates, the Group is of the view that rollover of repos (which is somewhat akin to rollover of forex swaps) could be permitted. The rollovers could be for any period as agreed to by the parties and need not have any relationship with the original contract period.

Duration

4.43. There are at present no restrictions on the duration of repos. Effective October 31, 1998, RBI has already withdrawn the restriction of a minimum of 3 days for a repo transaction which has been operative. However, the convention of 14 days for forward leg came perhaps due to the concept of reporting by banks on fortnightly basis and reserve requirement on inter-bank liabilities. A clarification stating that such restrictions do not exist would help the market.

(2) The arrangement for Tripartite repos will involve the concept of Clearing Corporation which would act as a counterparty and perform novation. It will guarantee all trades done on an exchange as per the terms and conditions of its guarantee framework. In this context, all participants who will use this facility will be governed by the Rules and Regulations framed by the Clearing Corporation. The rules and regulations will focus on various factors as under:

1. Applicability comprising entities and eligibility criteria, eligible securities, eligible trades/contracts
2. Procedures for trade execution, confirmation etc.
3. Methods of settlements, settlement periods etc.
4. Settlement procedure viz. Obligation generation etc. under broad categories comprising securities settlement and cash settlement
5. Guarantee Framework with details on settlement fund, contributions etc.
6. Risk containment framework including, top ups, withdrawals, initial margins, exposures, margins, re-pricing, modifications of a transaction. Substitutions depending upon the volatility and risk issues arising in the market etc. Clearing Corporation may introduce other

appropriate measures for containment of risk from time to time.

7. Events of defaults and closing out which would include auctions, shortages/exception handling, auto assign, fines and penalties, inflation adjustment to the principal etc. The rules and regulations will act as a binding agreement between Clearing Corporation and participants.

(Ref : Paragraph No. 4.7.5)

Investment port-folio of banks-Transactions in securities-Aggregate contract limit for individual brokers-clarifications

Sr. No.	Issue Raised	Response
1.	The year should be calendar year or financial year?	Since banks close their accounts at the end of March, it may be more convenient to follow the financial year. However, the banks may follow calendar year or any other period of 12 months provided, it is consistently followed in future.
2.	Whether the limit is to be observed with reference to total transactions of the previous year as the total transactions of the current year would be	The limit has to be observed with reference to the year under review. While operating the limit the bank should keep in

known only at the end of the year?	view the expected turnover of the current year which may be based on turnover of the previous year and anticipated rise or fall in the volume of business in the current year.
3. Whether to arrive at the total transactions of the year, transactions entered into directly with counter-parties i.e. where no brokers are involved would also be taken into account?	Not necessary. However, if there are any direct deals with the brokers as purchasers or sellers the same would have to be included in the total transactions to arrive at the limit of transactions to be done through an individual broker.
4. Whether in case of ready forward deals both the legs of the deals i.e. purchase as well as sale will be included to arrive at the volume of total transactions?	Yes. This is, however, only theoretical as R/F transactions in Govt. securities are now prohibited except in Treasury Bills and the 3 year dated securities issued by conversion of Treasury Bills recently
5. Whether central loan/state loan/treasury bills etc.	No as brokers are not involved as

purchased through direct subscriptions/auction will be included in the volume of total transaction?	intermediaries.
6. It is possible that even though bank considers that a particular broker has touched the prescribed limit of 5% he may come with an offer during the remaining period of the year which the bank may find it to be to its advantage as compared to offers received from the other brokers who have not yet done business upto the prescribed limit.	If the offer received is more advantageous the limit for the broker may be exceeded, the reasons therefor recorded and approval of the competent authority/Board obtained post facto.
7. Whether the transaction conducted on behalf of the clients would also be included in the total transactions of the year?	Yes. If they are conducted through the brokers.
8. For a bank which rarely deals through brokers and consequently the volume of business is small maintaining the broker wise limit of 5% may mean splitting the orders in small values amongst different brokers and there may	There may be no need to split an order. If any deal causes the particular broker's share to exceed 5% limit, our circular provides the necessary flexibility in as much as Board's post facto

also arise price differential.	approval can be obtained.
9. During the course of the year it may not be possible to reasonably predict what will be the total quantum of transactions through brokers as a result of which there could be deviation in complying with the norm of 5%.	The bank may get post facto approval from the Board after explaining to it the circumstances in which the limit was exceeded.
10. Some of the small private sector banks have mentioned that where the volume of business particularly the transactions done through brokers are small the observance of 5% limit may be difficult. A suggestion has therefore been made that the limit may be required to be observed if the business done through a broker, exceeds a cut-off point of, say Rs. 10 crores	As already observed, the limit of 5% can be exceeded subject to reporting the transactions to the competent authority post-facto. Hence, no change in our instructions is considered necessary.

5. Accounting standards for Investments

5.1 The comprehensive instructions issued by the Reserve Bank in April 1992 on Income Recognition, Asset Classification, Provisioning and Other Related Matters included the following on Accounting standards for Investments :

The investment portfolio of a bank would normally consist of both "approved securities" (predominantly Government securities) and "others" (shares, debentures and bonds). It has been decided that the investments in approved securities should be bifurcated into "permanent" and "current" investments. Permanent investments were those which banks intended to hold till maturity and current investments were those which banks intended to deal in, i.e. buy and sell on a day-to-day basis. On this basis, banks should classify the existing investments in approved securities into the aforesaid two categories. To begin with, banks should keep not more than 70 percent of their investments in the permanent category from the accounting year 1992-93. This ratio would have to be brought down to 50 percent in due course. All subsequent purchases would also be required to be classified suitably. Reserve Bank would have no objection to banks inter-changing the investments from one category to another with the prior authorisation of the Board of Directors, in which case depreciation, if any would have to be fully provided for.

5.2 While the depreciation in respect of permanent investments was not likely to affect their realisable value and, therefore, need not be provided for, depreciation in the current investments should be fully provided for. Permanent investments could be valued at cost unless it was more than the face value, in which case the premium has to be amortised over the period remaining for maturity of the security. Banks were not expected to sell securities in the permanent category freely, but if they do so, any loss on such transactions in securities in this category has to be written off. Besides, any gain should be taken to capital reserve account. (It was subsequently advised in December 1992 that banks which experienced difficulties in adopting the above standards could discuss the matter separately with the Reserve Bank.)

5.3 The detailed instructions relating to Investment transactions issued in June 1992 following the initial Report of the Janakiraman Committee, included the following additional instructions/modifications relating to Accounting Standards :

(i) All investments in securities, other than approved securities, should be classified under "current" category and should be valued at market price or cost whichever was less and depreciation should be provided for the shortfall, if any.

(ii) In the instructions of April 1992, the manner in which banks' investments in approved securities should be bifurcated into "permanent" and "current" categories had been indicated. Dealing securities were marketable securities that were acquired and held with the intention of reselling them in the short term. The financial results arising from such transactions must be seen as volatile, generating trading profit or loss from deliberate position taking. Investment securities, on the other hand, were acquired and held for yield or capital growth purposes (apart from for compliance of SLR requirement) and were usually intended to be held till maturity, except when liquidity needs arise. Unless governed by the special rule described below, gains and losses on sale of securities should be recorded at the time of sale as capital gains/losses. As stated earlier, approved debt securities classified under "current" category should be carried in the Balance Sheet at market price or cost whichever was lower, whereas approved debt securities classified under "permanent" category should be carried in the Balance Sheet either at book value (cost) or at market value, at the discretion of the banks, subject to their following a consistent accounting policy. Accounting of securities under various categories should be as under :

Approved debt securities under 'permanent' category

(a) If the investments were carried at book value, the difference between the acquisition price (acquisition cost) and the redemption price should be accrued over the period from the acquisition to the redemption date and should be recognised as income or expense.

(b) Alternatively, the banks may choose to value such investments, on a consistent basis, at market value.

(c) Should the banks elect to adopt the practice described in (a) above, when the securities were redeemed or sold before the original redemption date, the unaccrued portion of the amount reffered to at (a) above should immediately be charged to the profit and loss account as capital gain or loss, as the case may be.

(d) Should banks elect to follow the practice described in (b) above, the resulting revaluation gains/losses should be recognised as capital gain/loss.

Investments under "current" category

(e) The investment under "current" category should be carried at lower of cost or market value, on a consistent basis.

(f) Costs, such as, brokerage fees, commission or taxes, incurred at the time of acquisition of trading securities, should immediately be recognised as expenses, without any accrual.

(g) The carrying value of securities under current category should be revalued at market prices on a quarterly basis. The gains/losses arising out of this revaluation should not be taken to interest income/expenses accounts. Instead, revaluation gains/losses should be segregated by entering them in specific "realised/unrealised gains/losses on trading of debt securities" account. The net amount of gains/losses from trading of debt securities shall be taken to the income statement.

(iii) Each time a security was acquired, the bank should immediately record whether it was for investment account or for trading account and accordingly account for them in the respective accounts on the basis of laid down accounting policies. Transfer of securities from one account to another (i.e. Investment Account to Trading Account or vice versa) should be done only with the prior approval of the Board of Directors of the bank and should be properly documented.

(iv) Potential losses should be recognised prior to the transfer of securities from "current" category to "permanent" category where market value as on the date of transfer was less than the carrying value in the books.

(v) Banks may treat equity investments in subsidiaries as permanent investment.

5.4 It was clarified in January 1994 that, in respect of Zero Coupon Bonds (issued by Government of India, vide its Notification No. F. 4(5) W & M/93 dated 7th January 1994), the value of these Zero Coupon Bonds for the purpose of determining 'cost' may be reckoned after taking into account the accrued discount pro rata. After this adjustment of the 'cost', banks could use the standard valuation procedures.

5.5 The clarifications/fresh guidelines issued to banks on 'Income Recognition, etc.' in February 1994, included those relating to 'Valuation of Securities'. Thus, banks were informed that it was observed by the Reserve Bank that the practices followed by banks and auditors differed in respect of valuation of investments in "current" category. It was, therefore, decided that the Indian Banks' Association (IBA), in consultation with the Institute of Chartered Accountants of India (ICAI), would evolve a method for valuation of Government and other securities and banks and auditors should adopt the method so evolved while finalising the balance sheet as on 31st March 1994.

5.6 In the context of bifurcation of investments in Government securities into ''permanent'' and ''current'' category, banks were not required to make provisions for depreciation in respect of investments held under ''permanent'' category. Hence, it was not necessary to show the difference between the book value and the market value of the investments under this category as a footnote to the balance sheet and the instructions contained at ''Notes and instructions for compilation of balance sheet and profit and loss account'', advised in February 1992, were withdrawn. However, the difference between the book value and market value could be mentioned by Statutory Auditors in the Long Form Audit Report for the information of the bank's management.

5.7 In this connection, a reference was also invited to the instructions on accounting standards advised in June1992. It was clarified that while banks may, at their option, value the approved debt securities under the ''permanent'' category on a consistent basis at market value, they should refrain from doing so in respect of securities whose market price was higher than the book value (cost) on the balance sheet date. In other words, in these cases it was not permissible to carry these securities at a value higher than cost, as this would result in recognising unrealised gains in respect of such investments.

5.8 At a meeting of the Bank Audit Committee, comprising representatives of the Institute of Chartered Accountants of India (ICAI) and Chairmen of some major banks, held in March 1995, the guidelines on valuation of investments were reviewed and, in the light of the discussions held in the meeting, banks were advised as under in April 1995. :

    (i) Valuation of "permanent" investments Banks' attention was drawn to the instructions of June 1992, in terms of which if the "permanent" investments were carried at book value, the difference between the acquisition price (acquisition cost) and the redemption price should be accrued over the period from the acquisition to the redemption date and should be recognised as income or expense. Further, in February 1994, it was clarified that while banks may, at their option value the approved debt securities under the "permanent" category on a consistent basis at market value, they should refrain from doing so in respect of securities whose market price was higher than the book value (cost) on the balance sheet date. In other words, in these cases, it would not be permissible to carry these securities at a value higher than face/redemption value as this would result in recognising unrealised gain in respect of such investments. It had since been decided that the "permanent" investments should be valued at cost and in case the cost price was higher than the face value, the premium should be amortized over the remaining period of maturity of the security. On the other hand, where the cost price was less than the face value, the difference should be ignored and should not be amortized or taken to income account since the amount represents unrealised gain.

(ii) Investments to be carried at gross or net of depreciation

It was decided that "investments" should be shown in the balance sheet net of depreciation. It would, however, be open to the banks, for disclosure purposes, to show in the balance sheet the book value of investments, the depreciation there against and net amount of investments separately.

(iii) Valuation of investments on a quarterly basis

In the instructions of June 1992, it was mentioned that the carrying value of securities under "current" category should be revalued at market prices on a quarterly basis. It had since been decided that the investments under "current" category should be carried at lower of cost or market value, on a consistent basis and that the valuation should be done on a quarterly basis. In other words, the basis of valuation on quarterly basis would be the same as that followed for annual accounts. It was also decided that the rates of Yield To Maturity (YTM) of different kinds of securities circulated by the Reserve Bank for the final accounts of each year should be used for the subsequent quarters also for the purpose of quarterly valuation of investments. The banks may arrive at on notional basis gains or losses on the basis of such quarterly valuation and it may not be necessary to pass entries booking such gains or losses.

(iv) Treatment of excess depreciation, if any

It was decided that depreciation on "current" investments should be shown in the profit and loss account as a debit item under Schedule 14. It was also decided that where depreciation was provided on "current" investments but, in a subsequent year, the market price of the relevant securities had improved, the excess provision towards depreciation could be taken to the profit and loss account and, thereafter, it could be appropriated to the "capital reserve" account.

(v) Treatment of recapitalisation bonds

The recapitalisation bonds would not form part of "permanent" or "current" investments. It would not be necessary to provide for depreciation on the recapitalisation bonds received by the nationalised banks from Government. In case, however, banks acquired recapitalisation bonds of other bank for investment purposes, the depreciation, if any, would have to be provided for.

(vi) Modification of percentages in respect of classification of investments under "permanent" and "current" category

It was advised in June 1992 that, to begin with, banks should keep not more than 70% of their investments in "permanent" category for the accounting year 1992-93, which would be brought down to 50% in due course. It was suggested in the meeting that there was a need for bringing down the ratio to 60:40. It was however, decided to maintain the ratio of approved securities into "permanent" and "current" investments at 70:30 for the year ended 31st March 1995 also.

(vii) Routing of gain from sale of securities

While in April 1992 banks were advised that any gain on sale of securities in the "permanent" category should be taken to "capital reserve" account, it had since been decided that such gain should be first taken to the profit and loss account and thereafter it could be appropriated to the "capital reserve" account.

6 Audit, review and reporting of Investment transactions

For implementing the recommendation contained in the initial Report of the Janakiraman Committee, the following instructions on the captioned subject were issued (alongwith other instructions on conduct of the investment portfolio) :

(i) Banks should undertake a half-yearly review (as of 30th September and 31st March) of their investment portfolio, which should, apart from other operational aspects of investment portfolio, clearly indicate and certify adherence to laid down internal investment policy and procedures and Reserve Bank guidelines, and put up the same before their respective Boards within a month, i.e., by end-April and end-October.

(ii) A copy of the review report put up to the bank's Board, should be forwarded to the Reserve Bank by 15th November and 15th May respectively.

(iii) In view of the possibility of abuse, treasury transactions should be separately subjected to a concurrent audit by internal auditors and the results of their audit should be placed before the Chairman and Managing Director of the Bank once every month. These audit reports should be sent to the Regional Office of Department of Banking Operations and Development (now to Department of Supervision) of the Reserve Bank under whose jurisdiction the Head Office of the bank fell.

7. Reconciliation of holdings of Government Securities, etc.

7.1 Following the initial report of the Janakiraman Committee, comprehensive guidelines/ instructions regarding the conduct of the Investments Portfolio were issued by the Reserve Bank in June 1992. In regard to the Subsidiary General Ledger (SGL) facility provided at the Public Debt Offices (PDOs) of the Reserve Bank, apart from detailed instructions (which have been covered separately), it was advised that records of SGL transfer forms issued/received, should be maintained by banks.

Further, balances as per bank's book should be reconciled at quarterly intervals with the balances in the book of PDOs. If the number of transactions so warrant, the reconciliation should be undertaken more frequently, say on a monthly basis. This reconciliation should also be periodically checked by the internal audit department. It was also advised that any bouncing of SGL transfer forms issued by selling banks in favour of the buying bank, should immediately be brought to the notice of the Central Office of the Department of Banking Operations and Development (now Department of Supervision) of the Reserve Bank by the buying bank. Similarly, a record of Bank Receipts (BRs) issued/received should be maintained. A system for verification of the authenticity of the BRs and SGL transfer forms received from other banks and confirmation of authorised signatories should be put in place.

7.2 In this connection, banks were further advised in December 1992 that during the course of scrutiny of security transactions of banks/Financial Institutions, instances of shortages in holdings of securities had come to Reserve Bank's notice. Therefore, banks and their subsidiaries/Mutual Funds should reconcile the securities held by them, both on their own Investment Account, as well as Portfolio Management Scheme (PMS), as on 31st December 1992. Further, a reconciliation statement, in the prescribed proforma, should be furnished to the Reserve Bank, duly certified by the bank's auditors. (The format for the Statement is at Annexure I, while the instructions for compiling it are in Annexure II.)

7.3 In this connection, it was clarified in February 1993 that there was no objection to the aforementioned verification/certification being done either by the bank's own internal auditors or by external auditors.

8. Transactions in Securities — Custodial Functions

8.1 In continuation of the detailed instructions in regard to management of investment portfolio of banks, particularly relating to transactions in securities, issued in June 1992, banks were advised in August 1992 that when they exercised custodial functions on behalf of their merchant banking subsidiaries, these functions should be subject to the same procedures and safeguards as would be applicable to other constituents. Accordingly, full particulars should be available with the subsidiaries of banks of the manner in which the transactions had been executed. Banks were instructed to issue suitable instructions in this regard to the department/office undertaking the custodial functions on behalf of their subsidiaries.

8.2 Investment in Government securities by Trusts etc.

Banks were advised in January 1963 that under Section 6 of the Public Debt Act, 1944, no notice of any trust was receivable by Government in respect of Government securities. Consequently, the Public Debt Office of the Reserve Bank treats, and has to treat, every person, in whose name a Government security stands, as the full owner thereof, even though the said person may be having no personal interest in the security but may be holding it merely as a trustee of a particular trust or as an office-holder of a society or a fund, i.e., in a fiduciary or representative capacity. Holding of securities in the personal names of officials or trusts was liable to lead to considerable difficulties under certain circumstances. Since the Public Debt Office was bound to treat the 'holder' as the 'owner', it followed that if a trustee or office-holders, in whose personal name a security (belonging to a trust or society) was held, dies, the Public Debt Office would refuse to make any payment on the security to the trust or society unless the said trust or society obtained legal representation (i.e. Probate, Letters of Administration or Succession Certificate) in the estate of the deceased trustee/office-holder. As the obtaining of such a grant entailed considerable inconvenience and expenses, the societies or trusts concerned were, as a rule, unwilling to adopt this course and approach the Reserve Bank for relaxations, which the Public Debt Office was understandably reluctant to make, except on the condition that the claimant body executed a bond of indemnity in the Reserve Bank's favour jointly with one or two sureties. Very often, it was difficult for the claimants to arrange for sureties of the requisite financial standing. It also sometimes happened that the office-holder/trustee, in whose favour a security was held, resigned and omitted or refused to transfer the security to his successor-in-office. In such cases, the Public Debt Office was unable to help the real beneficiary whose only course was to bring a suit against the ex-trustee or the ex-official in a civil court for obtaining a proper decree to enable the Public Debt Office to recognise the claimant's title.

It was further mentioned that a body which had a corporate status could, of course, hold Government securities in its corporate name, but this recourse was not available in the case of unincorporated bodies — to which category most trusts, provident funds, etc., usually belonged. The most convenient course for such bodies was to hold securities in the form of Stock Certificates (and not in the form of Government Promissory Notes). Under Rule 8 (2)(b) of Public Debt Rules, 1946, Stock Certificates could be issued in favour of officials/trustees ex-officio without mentioning their personal names, so that in the event of death or resignation, the security could be dealt with immediately by the successor-in-office, without any formality. No question of legal representation or indemnity bond would arise if securities were so held.

Besides the above advantage, holding in stock was very convenient from the point of view of a long-term investor. For example, the periodical interest on Stock Certificates was remitted by the Public Debt Office to the holder or to the holder's bankers on the due date, without any cost to the holder, whereas a Government promissory note had to be physically presented for drawal of interest every time such interest was drawn. Again, if a Government Promissory note was lost, the procedure for obtaining a duplicate was a long and expensive one, whereas a lost/destroyed Stock Certificate could be replaced by the Public Debt Office on the holder merely reporting the loss and executing an affidavit.

It was added that like Stock Certificates, Treasury Savings Deposit Certificates and Defence Deposit Certificates could also be issued in favour of office holders and trustees, ex-officio. Usually, all organisations like provident funds and trusts, made investments through, or on the advice of their bankers and, therefore, the expense and inconvenience caused to the beneficiaries in such cases would be obviated, if banks were to advise the above position to their customers.

Banks were advised that they might, therefore, take note of these instructions and also communicate them to such of their customers as belonged to the above categories with the advice that if any securities were held by their officials/trustees in their personal names, they would be well advised to contact the nearest Public Debt Office for getting the matter regularised.

In conclusion, it was indicated that in case any clarification or further information on any point was required, reference may be made to the Public Debt Office.

The stipulation of minimum period of three days for ready forward transactions has been withdrawn from October 31, 1998.

Above status report of the action taken by the RBI on the recommendations of the Janakiraman Committee is placed here as could be found from the RBI Website. Fact remains that almost all the guidelines/instructions/master circulars notified by the RBI relate to the later part of the scam period as a measure to make up the deficiencies existed on the eve of the scam period though, as noted above, part of the instructions/guidelines/master circulars related to status in December, 1987 that pertained to the same period when the central government issued fresh instructions to PSUs on investment of their surplus funds public sector bonds, government securities, as deposit with the government. For the first time, the government instructions stated before permitted PSUs entering into the Secondary Market, an unknown secondary securities operational area or field exclusively mastered by the commercial banks and the brokers. That was precisely the reason why the PSUs did not enter into direct contracts with the brokers and preferred, as a safeguard, to route their surplus funds in public sector bonds through the government owned commercial banks. Fact also was that these commercial banks were already dealing in the secondary market through the brokers. The object was to earn higher return in order to show higher profit in the accounts which had the implicit understating with or approval of the top management of those commercial banks. The investigations done by the investigating agencies later on support this view.

Though the Janakiraman Committee Reports in six volumes do not attribute any kind of deficiency or lapse on the part of the officers and staff of the RBI but what was not noted as a serious lapse was about the very working of the PDO especially in dealing with SGL transactions with the commercial banks. RBI admits, as noted before, in place of SGL operational system, the Bank Receipts were substituted. This substantiates the fact that the RBI was well aware of the prractice of BR since 1986 but except cautioning the concerned banks, the RBI did not act upon for enforcing the penal provisions. So, the onus of mischief of Bank Receipt [BR] cannot be solely placed upon the commercial banks nor the brokers when the PDO of the RBI itself accepted them for SGL transactions. . This can, at best, be termed as escapism. It is like blaming a blindman that he doesn't know how to walk on the road. That is what could be attributed to the BR. Thus, RBI based on the irregularities committed by the Syndicate Bank and the Andhra Bank, also noted before, found during the audit of their account by RBI Auditors coupled with the fact that PDO which is integral part of RBI allowed substitution of the SGL practice by the Bank Receipt practice, had complete knowledge of the what was going on in the stock market/secondary market which was the right time for the RBI to have had taken severest possible action against commercial banks on use of BRs in lieu of securing physical possession of the securities purchased that was otherwise mandatory. That didn't happen. Why? Best known to the RBI.

PSUs were not aware of the guidelines issued by RBI stated before regarding interbank transfer of securities against physical possession of the securities sold and purchased since the RBI guidelines issued to the banks are not endorsed to the PSUs, may be as a matter of policy of the RBI, the PSUs not being under its jurisdiction. PSUs were also unaware of the reality that was happening using the Bank Receipts behind the scene between the commercial banks and the brokers, they having satisfied having received the BRs that contained the relevant particulars of the investments made by the commercial banks and having received back the invested amount along with the interest due and payable on the due dates whereupon they discharged the Bank Receipts and returned to the commercial banks. This was not the case with all the PSUs in some of whose case the commercial banks defaulted in return of invested money along the interest on the due date which resulted in serious concern due to the absence of the securities in hand that triggered scam into open, more so, starting with deals done by the SBI with the brokers including in particular Harshad Mehta's firm. That was too late to have acknowledged the reality of the scam. It cannot be conceivably ruled out that the concerned ministries in the central government, the politicians and the bureaucrats were not aware of what was happening in the stock market before the scam broke out. It is unthinkable because the relaxations in the government policies on investment of surplus funds with PSUs and the RBI's guidelines issued in December, 1987 which coincided with the change in the government policies that paved the way for build-up of the scam and its explosion in the second quarter of 1992. I am of the firm belief that the commercial banks and the brokers would not have dared to do what they had done without susceptible support of the politicians, the bureaucrats and the management of the commercial banks. That is what emerges if one could take pains to trace the consensual circumstances that were allowed to develop towards the conceivability of the scam by those who were nearer to corridors of power.

What I have submitted above is not intended either to offend or to defend anybody but the analysis of the available material herein contained suggests one would not have happened without the other.

I have dealt more about the Bank Receipts which was epicentre of the scam in the later part of this book.

JOINT PARLIAMENTARY COMMITTEE [JPC]

The second JPC was formed in August 1992. It was headed by former Union minister and senior Congress leader Ram Niwas Mirdha. It was set up to probe Irregularities in Securities and Banking Transactions in the aftermath of the Harshad Mehta scandal. The motion was moved by the then minister for parliamentary affairs Ghulam Nabi Azad in the Lok Sabha on August 6, 1992. The Rajya Sabha concurred with it the next day. The recommendations of the JPC were neither accepted in full nor implemented.

JPC is the collective body of the Members of both the Houses of Parliament comprising of highly learned, knowledgeable and gifted with great wisdom. Any reference of a matter of national importance involving injurious implications to the interests of the nation in the nature of scam is normally referred to the JPC that called for closest scrutiny and in-depth study and examination of multifarious issues associated with such matters. JPC completed the process it was mandated to and made several observations/recommendations for taking action by the central government, some of which were of serious nature. The Terms of Reference of JPC and its Report containing its detailed recommendations could not be found on the Google Website. Some of the Action Taken Reports {ATRs] numbering more than thirty submitted by the central government to the Parliament are posted on the Website as listed below but these are not reproducible. Other ATRs could not be found on the Website.

1. THIRD PROGRESS REPORT ON THE ACTION TAKEN PURSUANT TO THE RECOMMENDATIONS OF THE JOINT PARLIAMENTARY COMMITTEE ON STOCK MARKET SCAM AND MATTERS RELATING THERETO – DECEMBER, 2004
2. FOURTH PROGRESS REPORT ON THE ACTION TAKEN PURSUANT TO THE RECOMMENDATIONS OF THE JOINT PARLIAMENTARY COMMITTEE ON STOCK MARKET SCAM AND MATTERS RELATING THERETO – JULY, 2005
3. SIXTH PROGRESS REPORT ON THE ACTION TAKEN PURSUANT TO THE RECOMMENDATIONS OF THE JOINT PARLIAMENTARY COMMITTEE ON

STOCK MARKET SCAM AND MATTERS RELATING THERETO – MAY, 2006
4. SEVENTH PROGRESS REPORT ON THE ACTION TAKEN PURSUANT TO THE RECOMMENDATIONS OF THE JOINT PARLIAMENTARY COMMITTEE ON STOCK MARKET SCAM AND MATTERS RELATING THERETO – DECEMBER, 2006
5. 8TH PROGRESS REPORT ON THE ACTION TAKEN PURSUANT TO THE RECOMMENDATIONS OF THE JOINT PARLIAMENTARY COMMITTEE ON STOCK MARKET SCAM AND MATTERS RELATING THERETO – MAY, 2007
6. 9TH PROGRESS REPORT ON THE ACTION TAKEN PURSUANT TO THE RECOMMENDATIONS OF THE JOINT PARLIAMENTARY COMMITTEE ON STOCK MARKET SCAM AND MATTERS RELATING THERETO – DECEMBER, 2007
7. 11TH PROGRESS REPORT ON THE ACTION TAKEN PURSUANT TO THE RECOMMENDATIONS OF THE JOINT PARLIAMENTARY COMMITTEE ON STOCK MARKET SCAM AND MATTERS RELATING THERETO – DECEMBER, 2008
8. 12TH PROGRESS REPORT ON THE ACTION TAKEN PURSUANT TO THE RECOMMENDATIONS OF THE JOINT PARLIAMENTARY COMMITTEE ON STOCK MARKET SCAM AND MATTERS RELATING THERET – JUNE, 2009
9. 27th PROGRESS REPORT (December, 2016) OF THE ACTION TAKEN PURSUANT TO THE

RECOMMENDATIONS OF JOINT PARLIAMENTARY COMMITTEE ON STOCK MARKET SCAM AND MATTERS RELATING THERETO – DECEMBER, 2016
10. 30th PROGRESS REPORT ON THE ACTION TAKEN PURSUANT TO THE RECOMMENDATIONS OF THE JOINT PARLIAMENTARY COMMITTEE ON STOCK MARKET SCAM AND MATTERS RELATING THERETO – JULY 2018
11. PROGRESS OF OGRESS OF THE ACTION TAKEN PURSUANT TO THE RECOMMENDATIONS OF JOINT PARLIAMENTARY COMMITTEE ON STOCK MARKET SCAM OCK MARKET SCAM AND MATTERS RELATING THERETO - 2002

What could, however, be found are the proceedings of the JPC subjecting high profiles to close questions and examination as accused, the JPC acting in its capacity as a court, as reported in the leading newspapers/magazines, that throw light on the implicit or explicit connection of such profiles in the process of the development of the scam and in the scam itself which was rather the main intent of their questioning and examination by the JPC. Such proceedings of the JPC as could be found on the Google Website have been considered relevant and useful and are, therefore, reproduced below:

"It can either be the greatest whitewash in recent memory. Or the greatest investigation. It's up to Ram Niwas Mirdha to figure out which way it goes.

As chairman of the Joint Parliamentary Committee (JPC) that took up the securities and stock-market scam investigation on August 20, Mirdha is laying his, and his government's credibility on the line. The soft-spoken politician from Rajasthan and the 30-member JPC wield enormous power.

The committee can summon whoever it wishes for questioning - businessmen, brokers, bureaucrats and politicians. Technically, it does not have to ask for permission or clearance to interrogate and indict anybody, which places it way above the clout of investigating agencies such as the CBI and the Income Tax Department. These agencies now have to keep the JPC posted.

Currently, the JPC is schooling itself - it has yet to start questioning any of the accused. It had met four times by the end of August. In these sessions, members were briefed by experts from the RBI, nationalised banks, the stock exchanges and the Planning Commission.

The subjects: the intricacies of banks' functioning, stock-market operations, and the explanation of terms such as securities, bank receipts,' ready-forward deals and so on, covering the institutions and their instruments which played a role in the scam. Says Congress (I) MP, Mani Shankar Aiyar, a JPC member: "It was basically a tutorial session for all of us."

The crucial part will begin in September, when the CBI presents its findings-it is presently putting together a document for the JPC-about the scam to the members. It is only after this stage that summons will go out to suspects and witnesses. And a political drama is likely to unfold.

The Congress (I) dominates the JPC, but opposition member George Fernandes claims he has inside information on ministers' involvement in the scam. The BJP'S Jaswant Singh is more restrained, but his party is demanding that the finance minister and RBI governor resign.

But Prime Minister P.V. Narasimha Rao seems well prepared to duck the opposition attack. Unlike Rajiv Gandhi over the Bofors JPC, Rao's strategy is to engage the Opposition in the JPC and let the political parties themselves examine what went wrong with the system. Consequently, speculation about the Government's whitewashing efforts is deflected, at least for some time.

The other element of Rao's game plan, say insiders, is to divert the focus of the bank scam issue-from a government scandal to pegging blame on individuals. Basically, a bad apple approach. The ease with which Rao accepted P. Chidambaram's resignation and allowed the CBI to arrest high flying bureaucrat V. Krishnamurthy indicates - publicly - that Rao is willing to dump anyone involved in the scam".[Source: INDIA TODAY - ZAFAR AGHA - ISSUE DATE: Sep 15,. - 1992 | UPDATED: Aug 1, 2013 13:38 IST].

Plagued by procedural wrangles and controversies, the Joint Parliamentary Committee struggles to establish its autonomous identity.

Jaswant Singh feels the JPC is responsible **"to clear India's fair name internationally and to restore confidence in the country's fiscal systems"**.

For a seasoned politician like P.V. Narasimha Rao, pushed into a corner by constant opposition heckling on the multi-crore securities scam, the Joint Parliamentary Committee (JPC) provided the ideal instrument with which to buy time.

Rao, who had witnessed even the brute majority of Rajiv Gandhi's regime crumble before the might of the Bofors juggernaut, did not want to expose his minority government to a similar fate. With the setting up of the JPC,

Rao also hopes to establish the sincerity of his intentions in getting to the bottom of the scandal, even if he sacrifices some of his own party men in the process.

Unlike the Bofors JPC, which comprised only the Congress (I) and its allies and essentially carried out a whitewash job, Rao has made a concerted effort to make this JPC truly representative. The 16 Congress (I) members, including Chairman R.N. Mirdha, are well matched by the 14 members of the Opposition.

In fact, so high is the credibility of the committee so far that even such ardent critics of Rao as Janata Dal leader George Fernandes have admitted: "I believe the Congressmen are also keen to unearth the truth."

This impression was further strengthened by the fact that it was a Congress(I) MP, S.S. Ahluwalia, who blew the whistle on the document which had been surreptitiously circulated by Minster of State for Finance Rameshwar Thakur, to Congress(I) members of the JPC on September 3.

Honest intentions apart, the JPC has still to establish its separate identity, despite clearly laid down terms of reference. According to these, the JPC is to fix responsibility; identify the misuse and failure of the system; make recommendations for the elimination of such failures; and suggest changes in policies and regulations to be followed in future.

But with the CBI investigating the criminal aspect, the Janakiraman Committee looking at the flaws in the banking system and the Nadkarni Committee suggesting reforms, many observers feel the role of the JPC may overlap with other agencies.

In fact, the last chapter of the third Janakiraman report states categorically: "The committee feels that its continuing with further investigations would not only involve duplication of efforts but is also likely to hamper the work of the JPC" Indeed, given the constitutional supremacy of the JPC, it is likely to force all other agencies investigating the scam to re-examine their role in much the same way that the Janakiraman Committee had to.

The head of the JPC, **Ram Niwas Mirdha**, has greater credibility than B. Shankaranand, of the Bofors JPC. **"At the committee level, party differences get completely obliterated."**

But BJP leader Jaswant Singh is unperturbed. "The JPC is not a committee of detectives, nor is it to review the working of the CBI or the Janakiraman Committee. Our terms of reference are far more comprehensive."

Some JPC members feel there are many areas that have still escaped scrutiny. These include the role of the RBI and the Finance Ministry. Says Fernandes: "Janakiraman's intention was to see how best the RBI could be covered up." He also points out the limitations of the CBI in arresting suspect ministers.

A self-proclaimed crusader against corruption, George Fernandes is doing his own digging and has his own list of scam suspects. Says he: "The JPC must uncover the truth."

Realising the magnitude of the task before them and the deadline of the last week of December, the JPC was divided into three groups for an intensive study of a limited number of subjects.

One group, with Jaswant Singh as the convenor, examined the role of the Government, the Finance Ministry and the RBI. Another group under former speaker and Janata Dal MP Rabi Ray looked at banks, financial institutions and financial companies.

The third group, led by Congress (I) member Jagesh Desai studied the stock exchange, SEBI and the public sector units. On the basis of their research, the groups presented a list of documents they wanted from the Government, its various agencies and companies. They also listed the witnesses they wanted to cross-examine and prepared a questionnaire.

T.N. Chaturvedi, the former CAG whose report on the Bofors deal indicted the Rajiv government, is cautious about success this time because **"the JPC is in an uncharted sea"**.

The list of witnesses reads like a Who's Who. Topping it is former Prime Minister Chandra Shekhar, Finance Minister Manmohan Singh, Defence Minister Sharad Pawar, Minister for Parliamentary Affairs Ghulam Nabi Azad and Petroleum Minister B. Shankaranand.

CBI Joint Director K. Madhavan, RBI Governor S. Venkitaramanan, V. Krishnamurthy and Harshad Mehta, will also be summoned before the JPC beginning September 15.

The lack of a precedent and the absence of a definite law governing the functioning of the JPC could, however, be the single biggest hurdle. As BJP leader and former comptroller and auditor general of India T.N. Chaturvedi, says: "We are sailing in uncharted waters. There is nothing to go by."

And this is why even the issue of whether the JPC meetings should be witnessed by the media or held in-camera became a subject of debate. Such investigations, especially by the US Senate, are televised 'live'. For now, the JPC meetings will be held in-camera with Mirdha giving regular briefings.

MANI SHANKAR AIYAR

I am, an ardent defender of the Gandhi family, may use the JPC to protect V Krishnamurthy. Krishnamurthy is my friend and I will not conceal it."

Another ramification is that while the JPC insists that it has the right and privilege to have access to all information, agencies such as the CBI are reluctant to part with all their leads and argue that this could hamper the future course of investigations.

Even such adept parliamentarians such as CPI (M)'S Saifuddin Chowdhary are not clear how the JPC would deal with a situation in which information or assistance was not forthcoming. All he can visualise is "a serious problem".

There is another potential tangle: the JPC verdict has to be arrived at through consensus, and not by vote. No norm has been established to tide over a split decision-the only recourse for the Opposition will be a note of dissent. Fernandes, however, feels that such a note could become a political issue outside the JPC.

Also, unlike the US Senate committees, which have a dedicated secretariat staffed with specialists, the JPC is still working with the Parliament's secretariat. This means that technical and financial matters will have to be referred to outside experts and could lead to uncomfortable situations.

For instance, to explain some banking transactions, the JPC may have to refer it to employees of the bank itself. Says Chaturvedi: "The JPC should have a strong, informed secretariat."

Unlike the past, S.S. Ahluwalia attacked his own government on the plea, "If I have to choose between my party and motherland, I will stand by my motherland."

Yet another vexed issue is the clash of interests in the event of the JPC and other agencies diverging in their views. For instance, in the Bofors case, Win Chadha was able to use the JPC report to get the CBI FIR quashed in the Delhi High Court recently.

And in the present scandal, the central figure, Harshad Mehta, has already started appealing to the JPC chairman, pronouncing his innocence and arguing that he was being used as a scapegoat.

Observers fear that if the JPC is convinced of Harshad's innocence, the CBI's handiwork could come to naught. JPC members, themselves, however, are optimistic that such situations will not arise if the CBI shares information with them.

They are far more concerned with any attempt that the Government might make to scuttle the investigation by either withholding information or conducting a bureaucratic filibustering exercise.

While these fears may be unfounded, given the Government's pronounced intentions to provide all the necessary support, there is an undoubted possibility that the JPC's probe may get diverted into procedural and other minor wrangles, while the primary questions remain unresolved.[Source: INDIA TODAY - W.P.S Sidhu ISSUE DATE: Sep 30, 1992 | UPDATED: Aug 21, 2013 12:38 IST.]

Perhaps it is the spirit of the season. The hearings of the Joint Parliamentary Committee (JPC) on the stocks scam have become a resounding series of fireworks, lighting up dark secrets and blasting at the citadels of foreign banks, the RBI and even the office of the attorney-general. But pyrotechnics can be dangerous. At least one charge is threatening to singe the hand that ignited it.

The JPC charged Attorney-General G. Ramaswamy with taking an unsecured loan of Rs 15 lakh from the Standard Chartered Bank (Stanchart) in return for legal advice. But Ramaswamy is fighting back and is accusing the JPC of being "unfair" by reading between the lines..... . Stanchart has issued a clarification, backing Ramaswamy and denying the JPC's reading of the situation.

The JPC, however, is sticking to its guns that boom louder each day. In fact, the dramatic revelations made by the JPC last fortnight have silenced its most vocal critics. Right from September 15, when it began by examining two RBI departments, there has not been a dull moment within the committee room or outside.

It concentrated on trying to unravel the connections between the public sector units (PSUs) and the banks and through them to the brokers; the politicians and bureaucrats behind the PSUs; and the senior officers of the accused banks who are hoping to go scot-free. The JPC, according to Janata Dal leader S. Jaipal Reddy, used the Janakiraman report as "a compass to sail through uncharted waters",

The focus so far has been on exposing the irregularities committed by multinational banks. Chiefs of Stanchart, Citibank and Bank of America (BankAm) have testified before the JPC and each has admitted to flouting the RBI's guidelines. But the banks have turned the tables by putting the RBI in the dock. Its directives, they say, were flouted with such monotony that the violations were taken to be "normal banking practices".

Stanchart's testimony was sensational. It began by telling the JPC that it had lost around Rs 890 crore in the scam but ended up confessing that it had been hoodwinking the RBI with the full knowledge and implicit consent of its head office. The admission did not come about by chance. The JPC was already armed with damning evidence which the bank could not refute.

The JPC had the note written by Prakash Yardi, former assistant director in charge of risk management for Stanchart, to his bosses in London on September 10, 1990. The note, which mentioned that the bank was indulging in transactions that were neither safe nor above board, found its way into the hands of some JPC members.

It demolished what JPC chief Ram Niwas Mirdha called "the constant refrain that Stanchart's corporate office did not know what was happening". For Yardi had spelt out the irregularities in specific terms. He was sacked on December 14, 1990, three months after writing the note.

The bank had been accepting funds for short-term investment from PSUS-even after the RBI banned transactions between PSUS and foreign banks-and had gone about loaning them to private parties without security. Yardi listed a number of such transactions in which dubious loans amounting to over Rs 83 crore had been made. Confronted with this note, the bank's officials saw their defence crumble.

Mirdha said it was evident that Stanchart had been receiving money from PSUS for portfolio management well before the RBI sanctioned the scheme in 1992. Indian Railway Finance Corporation, Indian Oil and HUDCO, among others, had deployed huge sums in Stan-chart's Customer Cash Deposit Scheme in 1990 and 1991.

This scheme, he said, was nothing but "a thinly disguised version" of the portfolio management scheme. Rattled by the barrage of questions from JPC members, Stanchart apparently went on to admit that it had given an unsecured loan to G. Ramaswamy.

Interestingly, the JPC was tipped off about the Ramaswamy connection by some journalists who had information about his overdraft, but did not have access to documents. Stanchart was hardly unique in its aberrations. BankAm admitted that in 1990, three PSUS-ONGC, HUDCO and Oil India-had placed huge sums with the bank as term-deposits. Instead, the bank used these sums to play the securities market. The bank also credited massive amounts in the accounts of Harshad Mehta.

More revealing was the bank's excuse for trading in subsidiary general ledger (SGL) forms that had bounced. This was happening on such a large scale, said BankAm, that it assumed that such trade was "normal practice", RBI's public debt office functioned only in fits and everyone re-traded rejected SGLS, they said.

The bank's Indian manager, Vikram Talwar, maintained that while the RBI's Deputy Governor, R. Janakiraman, had specifically told him that there was nothing against the bank, he went on to castigate it in his report.

Even as JPC members were totting up technical points against the RBI, the name of its former deputy governor, Amitav Ghosh, cropped up. BankAm revealed it had intended hiring Ghosh, the very man who had been issuing a list of do's and don'ts to the bank. And it might well have, had the RBI not vetoed the idea.

Citibank tried to pull a fast one on the JPC by dumping documents running into thousands of pages on it, just a few hours before the sitting was scheduled. Smart thinking saved the day for the JPC. Instead of putting off the questioning, the members divided the documents among themselves-each of them reading a section-and proceeded to grill Jerry Rao, the bank's chief executive in India.

Rao's lecture on banking was cut short by members who got him to admit that PSUS had placed funds with it for portfolio management, even while it was prohibited. Rao and company, however, remained quite unfazed by the JPC assault. Citibank tried to shift the blame on to others. If the boards of various PSUS approved placing funds with the bank for portfolio management, it was their fault, said Rao.

And in any case, he said, the third Janakiraman report, which contained allegations against Citibank, was full of holes. The bank was in the process of exposing it, he said. Equally suspect, he claimed, was Stanchart's claim that Citibank owed it Rs 115.69 crore worth of securities in connection with bogus Bank Receipts (BRS). Stanchart has now initiated proceedings in the US against Citibank NA for the recovery of the securities.

So sustained was each bank's attack on the RBI and the Janakiraman report that JPC member George Fernandes commented: "The report has lost all its charm." In fact, it has also paved the way for a closer scrutiny of the central bank's role by the JPC.

The top RBI officials, including Janakiraman and its governor, are slated to be examined in November. In the JPC's next session which will be held in mid-October, PSUs such as the national airlines, oil companies, along with finance institutions will be put under its microscopic examination.

On October 16, more fireworks are expected when Andhra Bank officials will be cross-examined. A member of the JPC has learnt that the nationalised bank gave 'accommodation' of Rs 140 crore to Hiten Dalal for one day through Stanchart, and will confront the witnesses with this information.

The JPC certainly isn't making any friends. Its list of enemies has burgeoned after it instructed all bureaucrats above the rank of joint secretary to declare their complete shareholdings, including those in the companies of Harshad Mehta, Krishnamurthy and B. Ratnakar. The banks, the bureaucrats and the attorney-general are all livid. The JPC could not have asked for a better testimonial. [Source: INDIA TODAY - RAHUL PATHAK - ISSUE DATE: Oct 31, 1992 | UPDATED: Aug 16, 2013 18:51 IST.

RAJYA SABHA (1992): Point of privilege Attempt to influence some members of a Joint Parliamentary Committee by a Minister and a Government official.

Facts of the case and reference to the Committee of Privileges on 4 September, 1992,

Shri George Fernandes, a member, gave notice of a question of privilege against Shri Rameshwar Thakur, the then Minister of State for Finance, and Shri P. G. Lele, Additional Secretary in the Ministry of Finance, for allegedly attempting to influence some members of the Joint Parliamentary Committee probing into the securities scam with a view to obstructing the work of the Committee.

2. Shri George Fernandes stated inter alia in his notice that the Finance Ministry resorted to a patently

clandestine operation by circulating to some selected members of the Joint Parliamentary Committee, a 22 page document in an unofficial envelope without any covering note and contended that if the Government's intentions were honourable, there would have been no question of suppressing the authorship of the note and it should have been sent to all members of the JPC through the JPC Secretariat. Shri Fernandes in his notice charged the Minister of State for Finance and the Additional Secretary (Finance) with committing gross breach of privilege by making attempts by improper means to influence members and of obstructing members in the discharge of their duties. The member further stated that a breach of privilege of a Committee of Parliament is tantamount to breach of privilege of the House. He requested the Speaker to refer the matter to Committee of Privileges.

On 11 September, 1992, the Speaker, in terms of the procedure laid down in the Report of the Joint Sitting of the Committees of Privileges of Lok Sabha and Rajya Sabha and adopted by both Houses of Parliament, forwarded the notice given by Shri Fernandes to the Chairman, Rajya Sabha, for "appropriate action" as Shri Rameshwar Thakur, the then Minister of State for Finance, was a member of Rajya Sabha.

On 16 November, 1992, the Chairman, Rajya Sabha, referred the matter to the Committee of Privileges for examination, investigation and report. Findings and recommendation of the Committee.

The Committee of Privileges after considering the notice of question of privilege given by Shri George Fernandes, MP, and other relevant documents in their Thirty-second Report presented on 19 March, 1993, reported inter alia that the matter did not involve any breach of privilege.

Action taken by the House No further action was taken by the House in the matter.

[Source: Microsoft Word - PRIV-158.htm (rajyasabha.nic.in]

SECURITIES SCAM: MANMOHAN SINGH PLEADS 'NOT GUILTY' TO ALL CHARGES MADE BY JPC

The securities scam was the result of failures to check irregularities in the banking system and stock markets and also "liberalisation without adequate safeguards".

Charge: The securities scam was the result of failures to check irregularities in the banking system and stock markets and also "liberalisation without adequate safeguards".

Despite being aware of the unhealthy trend in the country's bourses since mid-1991, the ministry acted indecisively and did not discuss the matter during the meeting with the presidents of stock exchanges in March 1992. In fact, Singh took credit for the rising share prices as being an indicator of the success of reforms.

Foreign banks were allowed to "play havoc with the economy" and there was a "deliberate lack of action" to bring them in line with the Government's policies during 1990-92. The delay in the reconstitution of the RBI's central board for nine years showed the "lack of urgency" in the ministry. [Emphasis added]

The ministry failed to take corrective steps after the scam became public and delayed punishing the guilty. The JPC concluded that any deregulation without effective checks would be "an unmitigated disaster".

Verdict: Under the Parliamentary system, the accountability of the Finance Minister cannot be denied and ministers cannot make a distinction between direct and indirect responsibilities.

Defence: Singh says he directed the RBI to ensure bank credit was not used for speculation in shares in September 1991 and repeated it three months later. He kept quiet at the presidents' meeting as he felt it would have been "foolish and unethical" for him to say what level the stock exchange index should be.

The scam was due to the collusion between bankers and brokers and the "systemic" failure in the banking sector. Requisite steps have been taken to stop such failures in the future. He pleads "not guilty" to all charges made by the JPC. [INDIA TODAY - ALAM SRINIVAS - ISSUE DATE: Jan 15, 1994 | UPDATED: Jul 2, 2013 14:46 IST].

Officials of Air India, Power Finance Corporation of India and Indian Railway Finance Corporation reveal a series of suspect investment deals.

Torquemada, the dreaded grand inquisitor of 15th century Spain would have envied the alacrity with which the Joint Parliamentary Committee (JPC) is extracting confessions from its victims. In fact, every time a set of witnesses appeared before the high powered committee last fortnight, new skeletons came tumbling out of the closet.

So many that for a while it seemed to complicate the financial scam instead of unravelling it. Consider this:

- Air India officials readily admitted that they had followed verbal instructions and had fudged accounts to show that they had put the money in State Bank of India when, in fact, it had been deposited with Citibank.
- Power Finance Corporation officials revealed that they had raised Rs 150 crore from both Citibank and UCO Bank at 17 per cent interest and then deposited the funds back with these banks for earning 14.25 per cent interest on the same day.
- Officers of the Indian Railway Finance Corporation confessed that they had parked Rs 515 crore with Canbank Financial Services Limited (Canfina) to fulfil the condition laid down for Canfina to buy railway bonds. Result: the amount is now locked up with Canfina.

But the most dramatic revelation was, undoubtedly, the linking of Petroleum Minister B. Shankaranand name to the unorthodox investment deal made by the Oil Industry Development Board (OIDB)

According to documents presented to the JPC, Shankaranand - ironically, the chairman of the last JPC on Bofors - as chief of the OIDB ordered that Rs 114.72" crore be placed with the Syndicate Bank at an interest rate of 19.51 per cent.

The transaction was suspect because the Syndicate Bank letter offering the highest interest rate of 19.51 per cent had been entered in the diary only a day *after* - on April 28, 1992 - the letter was acted upon. Worse, according to some JPC members who examined the file, the figure 19.51 appears to have been tampered with.

Shankaranand is also implicated in another OIDB investment worth Rs 63.89 crore. Initially, the board had decided to invest Rs 48.89 crore with the Corporation Bank at 20 per cent and another Rs 15 crore with the Bank of India Finance Limited at 19.75 per cent. But a letter, again from Syndicate Bank, addressed to the chairman's office offering 20.05 per cent, which was not entered and directly put into the file, changed the decision.

Shankaranand wrote: "Since Syndicate Bank is the highest at an interest rate of 20.05 per cent, the entire amount of Rs 63.89 crore may be invested with them for one year."

While OIDB officials argue that both the investments were legitimate and made commercial sense, the JPC members were not convinced. Says one: "Culpability has been established in the case of Shankaranand." Some members have also demanded that the minister be called before the JPC for further questioning.

Another minister who may be hauled up before the JPC is M.O.H. Farook, minister of state for civil aviation. The minister presided over a meeting with the top management of the three public sector airlines - Air India (AI), Indian Airlines (IA) and Vayudoot - on February 6, in which it was decided that AI and IA would loan Rs 10 crore each to Vayudoot to help it tide over its present financial crisis.

Vayudoot, in turn, invested the sum with ANZ Grindlays, Stanchart and Canara Bank, instead of using it for operational requirements.

Similar charges have also been made against AI. Going by what the current airline management says, the blame lies with former acting chairman and managing director S.R. Gupte. But Gupte has denied his role and has asked to be examined by the committee.

In a letter to JPC Chairman R.N. Mirdha, he says that the present AI management has presented a "totally wrong and one-sided picture".

The present AI Chairman Y.C. Deveshwar, while deposing before the JPC, had disclosed that Gupte verbally ordered the investments to be made after receiving instructions from the Civil Aviation Ministry.

Gupte, now working with the private airline, UB Air in Bangalore, however, denies the charges: "How can anyone prove I gave verbal instructions? Besides, in the public sector no one will take verbal instructions for one year."

Interestingly, JPC members quote a note written by Gupte in which he had argued in favour of AI participating in forward deals. Meanwhile, in a second letter to Mirdha, the former AI chief has asked to see the minutes of the committee's meeting with the AI officials, before he appears. So far the JPC has not conceded his demand.

But despite these contradictory disclosures, the last round of the JPC has clearly been able to corroborate the nexus between public sector units (PSUS), bankers and brokers; which had been the contention of the Janakiraman report.

But, despite the emergence of evidence that tenuously links politicians with the entire scam, their exact role has still to be established. Says JPC member Dipen Ghosh:

"The footprints of the political bosses have yet to be identified."

Also still to be identified is the end use of PSU funds in the stock-market. So far the JPC has used the Janakiraman report to trace the scam trail from the PSUS to the brokers, through banks. But since the report did not examine how the brokers finally used the funds in the market, the JPC would have to consider stock-market operations.

Next month, the committee will visit the Bombay Stock Exchange; have meetings with the Indian Banks Association, as well as clerical and officers' associations. As many JPC members have trade union links, they are expected to use them to ferret out details of stock-market transactions.

The committee may also scrutinise the computerised records of the stock exchanges to identify the big operators and the *vyaj-badla* operators. Vyaj-badla refers to transactions where a financier funds a speculative position taken by a market player.

Such an exercise may be imperative following the October 16 income tax raids on 14 Bombay brokers, including seven who happen to be in the list of notified persons of the custodian for scam-tainted shares.

Most of the brokers raided - Bhupen Dalal, Hiten Dalal, Abhay Narottam, Milan Dalal and J.P. Gandhi - are prominent members had dealings with Canfina. Although unaccounted assets worth Rs 8 crore were seized along with computer floppies and magnetictapes, bank lockers were sealed. But the raids were ineffective because most of those who were raided had been expecting them.

Moreover, getting off lightly in such raids is easy and considered normal practice. Usually, a settlement is reached between the brokers' lawyers and chartered accountants and the raiding authorities.

The modus operandi is simple: when the negotiations take place, brokers are asked to make a voluntary disclosure since there's no penalty on the amount.

Some undisclosed property is accordingly declared; and the final assessment order by the authorities is drafted out in such a manner that it leaves very little room for reopening it. Market sources say the current spate of raids might also end up in a similar manner.

However, to solve the stock-market end of the scam, it is imperative to crack this group as some of them are believed to have helped Bhupen Dalal in take-over coups, including the one by T.B. Ruia of Killick Nixon.

Front brokers are essentially used to avoid revealing the identity of the real corporate predators. Ruia, who had escaped the investigators' spotlight, on medical grounds, was also raided. He is amongst the prime accused in the FIR filed by Standard Chartered Bank.

Ruia had also borrowed a huge amount from Metropolitan Cooperative Bank. The bank, currently under liquidation, was involved in dubious transactions with Standard Chartered after the scam had surfaced.

Some of these brokers are also believed to have deployed a large amount of funds in vyaj-badla during the early 1992 boom. Funds from financial institutions were also placed in vyaj-badla to enable the generation of returns of up to 60 per cent on an annualised basis.

Even as the investigations on the Canfina brokers are underway, the stock-market anticipates a series of raids in the near future. On October 22, the CBI raided Pallav Seth and Shrenik Jhaveri, who were acknowledged brokers for Canbank Mutual Fund. The agency is also investigating their role in the alleged Fairgrowth fraud case.

As the JPC deadline draws closer, the committee expects to home in on the key players in the securities scandals. It also expects to establish the politicians-businessmen nexus. The secretariat has also begun work on the draft of the report.

Fatigued members, notching up more hours than they would in a year's attendance of other parliamentary committees, have begun work on the next round of examination, beginning October 28.

Many are looking to its timely culmination. But by then many more skeletons would hopefully have tumbled out, several heads, including that of some politicians, would have rolled and the shape of financial transactions in the country may have changed beyond recognition. [Source: INDIA TODAY – W.P.S. Sidhu - ISSUE DATE: Nov 15, 1992 | UPDATED: Aug 14, 2013 16:19 IST].

The JPC is a court where members continue to argue, the case hangs and Chairman Ram Niwas Mirdha, the judge, is in a hurry to close the files. "I may seek an extension if I choose to," says Mirdha, "but right now. No." For him the report must be filed by mid-May, before the current Parliamentary session closes. But steering his wobbly cart - of 30 politically motivated members belonging to nine different parties - is proving to be difficult.

The simmering political differences boiled over on the issue of drafting the report. Chairman Mirdha's attempts to get the committee's three study groups to start discussing the draft report failed. Then Mirdha got the JPC secretariat to thread the evidence together into a draft which is contested by the members and likely to undergo major changes by the time it is submitted. "This is a draft of the draft report." says T.N. Chaturvedi, the BJP Rajya Sabha member on the committee, "just a tentative summing up of evidence. The linkages are missing."

Apart from brokers and bank and public sector personnel - who were indicted by the Janakiraman Reports and the CBI anyway - the draft lets off the RBI with a brief reference to it for not taking notice of the irregularities in the annual review of banks. And, surprisingly, the committee holds the Finance Ministry responsible for the scam since it controlled most of the institutions involved in it.

The report begins by attributing the securities scam to a deliberate and criminal misuse of funds by select brokers, bank personnel and custodians of public sector funds. It puts the estimated amount of losses at Rs 4,024 crore, at least Rs 1.000 crore less than the CBI estimates. These observations set the tone for the rest of the report: concentration on dissecting the scam rather than presenting an overview of the collapse of the system.

Foreign banks particularly have got the fist in the face. These banks, the draft report says, behaved in an unbecoming manner even though they belong to advanced countries. And holds their top managers guilty.

But the indictment is based on flimsy evidence. Consider this statement: "...the magnitude of the irregularities is indicative of these being collective handiworks instead of isolated instances." As such, the report lacks authority.

The Goldstar deal and much of the evidence relating to the ministerial involvement has been left out. And this created a furore. "The report should pin responsibility on persons," says JPC member Gurudas Dasgupta of the CPI. An attitude which Congress (I) MP on the JPC Mani Shankar Aiyer deplores. "Members had a hypothesis on political culpability even before the committee started functioning," he says.

Also, the committee decided not to call in experts though it would have helped. "If I had more time I would have called experts, examined the role of the Securities and Exchange Board of India and that of the financial institutions much more thoroughly," Mirdha told INDIA TODAY.

And as a result, its recommendations run against those of experts. For instance, the JPC wants Bankers' Receipts (BRS) to be discontinued, though the Nadkarni Committee has suggested its continuance. Then, it wants a limit on foreign banks repatriating profits from security transactions. But elsewhere it says there is no way to figure this link.

But Mirdha had to concede one point from which he was flinching: calling ministers for deposition. The Left had threatened to file a dissent note if they were not called. The Congress (I) members wanted them to be called in as experts. The Opposition wanted them as witnesses to which Mirdha agreed. But allowed only three.

So Finance Minister Manmohan Singh, former petroleum minister B. Shankaranand and former finance minister Madhu Dandavate are going to depose. They have all filed replies to the JPC's queries. "The report may make or mar the JPC," says Janata Dal leader and JPC member Yashwant Sinha "but this will add credibility."

Though the real outcome will only be known after it is submitted, Mirdha's decision to get the secretariat to write out a draft report has had JPC members back at work. Members, who were staying away from the issue of a draft report, were marking out mistakes, raising queries and voicing differences. He was also able to get the unwilling members in a drafting committee that would formulate another draft report for final discussions. [Source: INDIA TODAY - SHEFALI BHIMAL - ISSUE DATE: May 15, 1993 | UPDATED: Aug 8, 2013 19:25 IST].

Apart from the nine brokers and 14 banks named by the JPC as being participants in the securities scam, some top government functionaries have also been accused. The following men came under the severest criticism but they have rejected the JPC's conclusions.

B. Shankaranand, former minister for petroleum and natural gas

CHARGE: The Oil Industry Development Board (OIDB) made disproportionate investments in Canfina and Syndicate Bank. Offers were entertained after the last date of submission of quotations in violation of norms governing prudent financial management. Worse, OIDB did not possess securities or stamped receipts for investments made.

Verdict:

The JPC rules that the assumption of responsibility for placement of funds by OIDB Chairman Shankaranand was uncalled for.

Defence: Says that all OIDB investments in nationalised banks were legally done under prescribed rules. Neither he nor his family derived any benefit from the OIDB decisions. Has made it clear that he does not feel any need to resign.

Rameshwar Thakur, former minister of state for finance

Charge: Received a file on Harshad Mehta's misdeeds from the Income Tax authorities in April '92 but sat on it for a month before passing it on to the finance minister by which time the scam had become public.

Verdict: The JPC expresses its unhappiness over the delay.

Defence: Says he was mostly on tour during the period mentioned and was involved in urgent official duties which included discussions with three foreign delegations. The Mehta file which came to him was not marked 'immediate' or anything else which would have indicated the need for quick action. There was also no reminder about this file from the Income Tax Department. All files relating exclusively to Mehta were cleared by his office without any delay.

S. Venkitaramanan, former Reserve Bank of India (RBI) governor.

Charge:

The RBI's blind eye to irregularities in transactions between July 1991 and April 1992 allowed brokers to play havoc. Treated foreign banks differently, delayed issue of the July 1991 circular that directed the Public Debt Office (PDO) to report bouncing of the Security General Ledger (SGL) to the banking department, recommended top appointments that became liabilities and took unusual interest in Harshad Mehta's accounts.

Verdict: As the RBI governor during this crucial period, he must be held responsible.

Defence: Disagrees with the JPC conclusions. His statement that the RBI should 'take care' when dealing with foreign banks was meant to alert his officials. The 1991 circular was delayed by his deputy Amitava Ghosh. The appointment of M.J. Pherwani as chairman of National Housing Bank (NHB) was not unnatural as he did not have any adverse record and already headed other government agencies. Took interest in Mehta's SBI account only to trace the source of the money.

Amitava Ghosh, former deputy governor, RBI

Charge: Ignored inspection reports prepared by RBI inspectors such as the Augustine Kurias report that pointed to irregularities in securities transactions way back in 1986, ignored the inspection reports of other banks and failed to take appropriate follow - up action. Did not take concerted action when SGL forms started bouncing in large numbers. [[Emphasis added]

Verdict: Held primarily responsible for the irregularities especially as he had held his post for more than 10 years.

Defence:

The deputy governor cannot look at each and every file. And the RBI cannot do a day - to - day monitoring of commercial banks. The Kurias report talked about two issues - irregularities in Portfolio Management Services and irregular transactions in securities through Bank Receipts. The RBI issued a circular in 1987 to commercial banks on the former and the latter was referred to the Secretary's department in the RBI for its comments. On receipt of the comments the note was disposed of with noting at the junior level. His suggestion to investigate foreign banks before sending the 1991 circular was not to delay but to gather more evidence against errant banks. (Ghosh resigned as chairman of the RBI's staff recruitment board last fortnight in protest against the conclusions and charges of the JPC report).

R. Janakiraman. Former deputy governor, RBI.

Charge: Janakiraman was in charge of the PDO which cautioned the chairmen of 11 banks and informed the Department of Banking Operations and Development (DBOD) of the RBI about the large number of SGL forms bouncing. But did not take follow up action. The goings on in both the SBI and the NHB, of which he was a director, clearly indicate a dereliction of duty* The SBI officially told the JPC that he did not caution the bank about irregularities in securities and banking transactions.

Verdict:

Gross dereliction of duty in the PDO and DBOD greatly contributed to the scam. The JPC regrets that the RBI nominees neither noticed the irregularities nor effectively discharged their role.

Defence: At no point was the bouncing of SGL forms brought to his notice. The subject of securities transaction did not come up in the only meeting held on December 2, 1991, of the NHB advisory board to which he was nominated by the RBI in October 1991. He became director of the NHB in April 1992 and not in 1991, as stated by the JPC in its report. Again, it was in April 1992 that the chairman of the SBI said that he had become aware of the irregularities a week earlier and that he (the chairman) had tried to take adequate steps to safeguard the bank's interest.

When the chairman and top executives of the SBI had no knowledge of irregularities it is unfair to expect an RBI nominee director to detect the fraud. [Source: INDIA TODAY – Shafali Bhimal, Dakshesh Parikh - ISSUE DATE: Jan 15, 1994 | UPDATED: Jul 2, 2013 14:50 IST].

The Securities Scam - In document <u>The Insider's View - Memoirs of a Public Servant - Javid Chowdhury</u> (Page 81-90)

The Securities Scam was a massive collapse of the financial regulatory system. This was the strongest temblor to have hit the financial system in the country's history. The scam was aided and abetted by gross and wilful negligence in the discharge of supervisory functions by the star mandarins of the Ministry of Finance and the RBI. Securities of various types were criminally diverted to generate funds to speculate in the stock market. The illicit gains from such transactions were either recycled into the stock market, or clandestinely transferred abroad through hawala. Some of the illicit foreign assets so accumulated abroad were in turn recycled into the country as remittances under the Immunity and Exemption Act, 1991, more commonly known as the Immunity Scheme. At the end of it the players in the scam were richer, both by way of illegal domestic funds and illicit foreign assets. In the early days after the exposure, there was much public outrage and demand for exemplary deterrent action. However, after that initial period of attention, the media tired of it, the general public gave up in despair, and the investigation of the criminal offences under different laws petered out. Out of the criminal cases filed by the CBI, only three have been finally decided, ending in a conviction. In the matters before the Directorate of Enforcement, criminal cases were filed and none has been finally decided. All the accused are out on bail. Four of the stars of the securities scam—Harshad Mehta; K.

Margabandhu, CMD of the UCO Bank; M.J. Pherwani, CMD, NHB; and B. Ratnakar, CMD, Canara Bank—have died natural deaths. This is the extent of progress in the criminal cases in a period of twenty years. In discharge of its responsibility of parliamentary scrutiny, the JPC submitted its report with 276 recommendations in December 1993. For many of these recommendations, particularly the more serious ones requiring recovery of losses, action is still pending. Till date, out of the total outstanding amount of Rs 11,323 crores, only Rs 292 crores has been recovered. From this it is clear that practically none of the criminals involved in the securities scam have been brought to book, nor has the financial loss been undone. One other aspect needs to be highlighted. The cases relating to the securities scam are principally based on documentary evidence. Unlike other types of crime, where eyewitnesses may turn hostile or die, weakening the prosecution's case, these can be called 'open-and-shut' cases. It would take very little time to conduct the trial in such cases. Despite all these favourable factors, if the cases are still making no progress, it must be because someone with the responsibility of pursuing the cases is holding them back.

The period immediately preceding the unravelling of the Securities Scam also highlighted how shallow the media is in assessing such developments. The media's reading of the situation was an astonishing display of lack of discernment and professional balance. In the month preceding the disclosure of the scam, the star of the TV screen was Harshad Mehta. The image of this 'fat cat' filled TV screens with his hyperbolic comments on the future of the Indian economy—'I am bullish about India'. And the TV anchors fawned over the banalities spewed by this semi-educated stock-broker from Palanpur. A few weeks later, the same channels repeated a clip hour after hour, showing Harshad Mehta under arrest, being transported in a bullet-proof police van. The commentary in the second clip was as high-pitched as it was when Harshad Mehta was making his profound prophecies.

Not one word was offered in explanation as to how the national icon of yesterday was now scurrying around in a wire-netted police van, like a trapped rat.

ACCOUNTABILITY

The Joint Parliamentary Committee (JPC) hearings on the securities scam began in mid-December 1992, two weeks after I took over in the Enforcement Directorate. At that stage, the investigations were in utter chaos. For one thing, the tsars of the economy were not particularly keen on having further skeletons disinterred. Also, as one can well imagine, the stock brokers in the line of fire were using all their money power and pre-invested goodwill to see that follow-up action in the Enforcement Directorate remained perfunctory.

In order to make a reasonable showing before the JPC, the first challenge was to rapidly internalize the basic facts relating to the cases that had been initiated. This was a Herculean task as these involved a mass of details. In the short time available, the basic facts that came to light showed that most of the transactions under investigation were indefensible. One could only give the Committee an assurance that the offences would be investigated earnestly, and the case would be taken to a conclusion.

Quite often, the handling of even an unholy mess provides a unique experience. In retrospect, it is now clear to me that to have witnessed those events was a once-in-a-lifetime experience. The position taken by the stars in the course of the hearings revealed the mindset of the bureaucratic elite.

The Finance Ministry team was led by K.P. Geetakrishnan, Finance Secretary and included the Secretary, Department of Economic Affairs, Montek Singh Ahluwalia. K Srinivasan, Chief Vigilance Officer of the Ministry of Finance and I completed the team as the extras.

The hearing began with a short opening statement by Geetakrishnan. It was a masterpiece of understatement—short, succinct, giving only facts that were already in the public domain, and remaining entirely silent on the question of constructive culpability for the magnitude of the fraud perpetrated. Geetakrishnan concluded by saying that the banks and the stock exchange, which were the institutions involved in the irregularities, came under the jurisdiction of the Department of Economic Affairs, and that his colleague Montek Singh Ahluwalia, Secretary, Department of Economic Affairs, would give the position of the Government of India in greater detail.

The Committee was, no doubt, a little taken aback by the brevity of the statement, but let it pass. It was brilliant strategy on the part of Geetakrishnan as he made a non-controversial and bland statement and yielded the floor to Montek Singh to face the flak. It also tickled Montek's ego to spearhead the defence for the government, as Montek is known to be happiest when holding forth before an audience. At the request of Geetakrishnan, the Chairman of the Committee gave the floor to Montek. He more than made up for Geetakrishnan's brevity.

Montek's performance was that of an excellent advocate with a very weak brief. In elegant language he went on the offensive. The episode had been an unfortunate 'systems failure'. The methods used by the stock market operators were, unfortunately, not congruent with the outdated economic laws, but were consistent with common 'market practice'. Further, he argued that, looking to the pace of developments in the post-reforms economy, the top managers of the banks were required to put in place certain regulatory safeguards, which they had failed to do. Montek's spiel was in general terms like a lecture on high finance and banking, but as the harangue continued, some of the members of the Committee started showing their unease; this was not what they had been looking for in the evidence of the Secretary of the ministry.

As the preliminary statement ended, pointed questions began to home in from different sides of the room. The Chairman was well briefed on the basis of the information that had been obtained by the Lok Sabha Secretariat; he also seemed to be privy to certain information available to private players in the financial market. Some of the other members of the Committee also seemed to have done their homework diligently. To specific questions on identified violations of procedures and regulations, Montek had a 'hold all' answer: rules and procedures were so outdated that all transactions would have ground to a halt if rigid compliance had been insisted upon by the RBI—the economy would have imploded. The Committee was not altogether docile: the Chairman, though a cultured and soft-spoken man, was extremely incisive in commercial matters. Some of the other MPs also, particularly from the Left Front, did not see these machinations of the stockbrokers and their colluders as a benign attempt to keep things afloat in the financial system, in furtherance of public interest. In the face of the attacks, Montek steered his defence with the swashbuckling confidence of an auto rickshaw driver in Chandni Chowk— swinging now to the left, then to the right, weaving and ducking his way through to avoid the missiles aimed at him by the Committee members.

But, the nature of the financial violations was brazen, and executed so obviously in furtherance of the private profit of certain select individuals that the defence arguments did not carry conviction.

One interesting issue discussed at length in the Committee is worth recounting.

Equity shares in certain public sector undertakings had at one point of time been disinvested in favour of public sector banks. The sale was subject to the condition that the banks would only 'on-sell' the shares, after the company was listed in the stock exchange. It is almost impossible to estimate in advance the market value of shares of fully state-owned public sector undertakings— obviously public sector companies' shares have a lot of locked-up value which can only be estimated through secondary market transactions. The government wanted an arrangement under which the full market value of the disinvested shares went to a public sector entity. The condition of listing in the stock exchange prior to 'on-sale' was obviously to forestall any collusive deals between the banks and the down-the-line private purchasers. The conditions of disinvestment were openly flouted by many of the banks. Many banks did not bother to wait for the shares of the public sector undertakings to be listed in the stock exchange. Some of the purchasing banks had entered into previous 'back-to-back' sale agreements with private purchasers at a fixed price, much before they had acquired the shares from the disinvesting public sector undertakings. In other words, it is not as though these banks *violated the condition after they had acquired the shares, out of compulsion on account of some force majeure circumstances. On the date the banks acquired the shares of the public sector undertakings,* they already had pre-existing contracts for 'on-selling' in violation of the terms of sale of these shares.

As ordinary human beings would understand it, the violation of the conditions was intentional and premeditated. A less courageous samurai than Montek would have conceded that there had been a deliberate violation of the disinvestment condition, and would have assured the Committee that responsibility would be fixed and action would be taken against the defaulters. But Montek is not an economist of the ordinary kind. Each time the Chairman tried to pin down his reply, Montek would come out with some circumlocutory argument to claim that the prior listing in the stock exchange was not a condition placed by the Cabinet when the Ministry of Finance put up the disinvestment proposal.

This was a specious argument, contrived as an afterthought. The Ministry of Finance note had mentioned in passing that the banks would be entitled to trade the shares, though it is nowhere mentioned that this would be in relaxation of the condition placed by Department of Public

Enterprises for prior listing in the stock exchange. Also, the Ministry of Finance had not sought explicit Cabinet approval to any such relaxation of the condition of prior listing. The Chairman's enormous patience was wearing thin with each passing minute. The simplest and most straightforward question fetched a circumlocutory reply. The Chairman was getting increasingly exasperated with these tactics. Finally, in despair the Chairman said: 'Mr Secretary you have been taking me round and round for too long now. We are already late for our tea break. One last time Mr Secretary, tell me in one word whether the 'on-sale' of shares by the banks before listing in the stock exchange, was in violation of the disinvestment conditions. Mr Secretary, I want your answer in a yes or no.' For once Montek did not have an instant response. He leaned back in the chair, thought for a few moments and then slowly said: 'Yes, Sir, but …' The Chairman sprang at his words with uncharacteristic alacrity:

'Thank you, Mr Secretary, I have your answer, thank you … and now we break for tea!'

We went into the tea break amidst a surcharged atmosphere. The members of the Committee milled around the tables, picking up their tea and nibbles. The bit players—Srinivasan and I—hung around the sidelines. The Chairman picked up his cup and seeing us standing alone, detached himself from the group of other members and came towards us: 'Are you not taking?' We assured him that we would help ourselves, and then just to create some conversation, I said: 'It's been a gruelling session, Sir.'

It was clear to us that, despite his exceptional forensic skills, Montek had screwed it up.

The overall impression that relative juniors like Srinivasan and I got from observing the Committee's proceedings was that the government considered it fit to brazenly defend the illegalities in the universe of securities and banks. There was not the slightest tinge of introspection or remorse—there was only an absolute confidence of talking one's way out of the crisis. The attitude was that if laws had been violated, the laws were wrong—because they understood economics, and therefore what they say should be the law!

It was in that period that Montek gave us Indians the mint-fresh expression—'systemic failure'. It became the ready alibi for any otherwise indefensible action in the decades that followed. The expression implied that the fault lay not with the civil servants, nor even with the Almighty, but at the door of the formless conceptual entity, 'the system'. The smart phrase ignores the obvious, that the system is created by civil servants and operated by civil servants; and if it fails, the responsibility is squarely theirs. It is only in a freak situation that a set of circumstances arise that could never have been anticipated at the time of the creation of the system. And, it is only in that rare instance that the causes for failure of the 'system' provide some measure of extenuation for the lapse. Save for that, the expression is only a cover for mala fides or lack of due diligence in the discharge of one's functions.

In that stormy period spanning about two weeks of hearings of the JPC, Srinivasan and I frequently discussed how a responsible government would defend itself in the face of such a crisis. It would be naïve to expect that every time a government department was called to account by a parliamentary committee or by the Comptroller and Auditor

General, they would immediately admit a mistake. The government's positions are often, at least partially, defensible; in many cases the circumstances surrounding a mistake, provided a mitigating circumstance. The government department under examination naturally makes the best defence possible, even in circumstances in which it was clear that a lapse had occurred. In fact, the standing tradition of the civil service is that the defence of a decision is most diligent when the decision under attack was that of a predecessor-in-office.

However, it is also equally true that no defence should reach a stage when it could not be treated as bona fide. Both of us felt that the Securities Scam, because of the circumstances and magnitude, was one case which admitted no bona fide defence. The culpability of individual players would, of course, depend on the attendant circumstances. However, a full-blooded, frontal defence—that such mishaps can occur in advanced financial systems—could only be treated as bad faith. In any area of governance, whether the swaggering financial sector, or the withering social sector, there is always a need for a trace element of public ethics. One cannot in good faith argue against the essentiality for this trace element. As I write these memoirs, after the collapse of the global financial system in the wake of the US sub-prime housing crisis, this universal truth stands reinforced. Using the language of modern-day management, there are certain processes and products in a modern socio-economy, the adoption and creation of which must be considered unpardonable in public interest, regardless of all other circumstances. Such methods in the financial sector are unacceptable in all circumstances.

Period. The modus operandi used in the securities scam was one such instance. In this backdrop, I would conclude that the sharpshooting defence of the Ministry of Finance in the course of the JPC hearings was a comprehensive failure. The final Report of the JPC is abruptly dismissive of all the smart wordplay, and is bluntly damning in its conclusions in respect of the illegalities.

HIT BY A RICOCHET BULLET

While the characters at the centre of the securities scam lead normal lives because their cases have not been decided, ironically, there are others who had only a peripheral role, but have suffered severe collateral damage. One such interesting tale is of Niranjan Shah. He was himself not involved in the securities scam; he was the hawala dealer for many of the principal players in the securities scam. Also, he was into drug trafficking for which he was using the hawala channels. When the securities scam was being investigated, the accounts threw up Niranjan Shah's case. Initially, he was arrested by the CBI, but finding only evidence of hawala transactions, he was released on bail without the Enforcement Directorate being informed. By the time the relevant documents were transferred to the Enforcement Directorate, Niranjan Shah had fled the country; he could be deported back from Dubai only after fifteen months. On his return, he was promptly put in preventive detention under the Conservation of Foreign Exchange and Prevention of Smuggling Act (COFEPOSA).

Niranjan Shah and his wife Roma Shah were drug smugglers sending narcotics to Canada and the US. Their consignments were wrapped in packets of Indian spices, so that the strong aroma masked the smell of the drug. In this way, they were able to get past the sniffer dogs routinely deployed at. [https://1library.net/article/securities-scam-insider-memoirs-public-servant-javid-chowdhury.z32e068q]

SUPERVISION OF RBI WAS THE NEED OF THE HOUR:

The main thrust of reforms in the financial sector was on the creation of efficient and stable financial institutions and markets. Reforms in respect of the banking as well as non-banking financial institutions focused on creating a deregulated environment and enabling free play of market forces while at the same time strengthening the prudential norms and the supervisory system. In the banking sector, the particular focus was on imparting operational flexibility and functional autonomy with a view to enhancing efficiency, productivity and profitability, imparting strength to the system and ensuring financial soundness. The restrictions on activities undertaken by the existing institutions were gradually relaxed and barriers to entry in the banking sector were removed. In the case of non-banking financial intermediaries, reforms focussed on removing sector-specific deficiencies. Thus, while reforms in respect of DFIs focussed on imparting market orientation to their operations by withdrawing assured sources of funds, in the case of NBFCs, the reform measures brought their asset side also under the regulation of the Reserve Bank. In the case of the insurance sector and mutual funds, reforms attempted to create a competitive environment by allowing private sector participation.

It has also been argued by some that various markets are still segmented. With blurring of boundaries among providers of various financial services, the issue as to what should be the appropriate supervisory framework for regulating them has also arisen.

The RBI supervises and is responsible for managing the operation of the Indian financial system. In addition to issuing regulations and guidelines for banking operations, it also administers the provisions of the RBI Act, the BR Act and FEMA. It has wide discretionary powers and is authorised to inspect and investigate the affairs of banks and to impose penalties in the event of non-compliance.

Each year, the RBI conducts an on-site financial inspection of a bank's books of accounts, loans and advances, balance sheet and investments. Following this, the RBI issues supervisory directions to banks highlighting the major areas of concern. Banks are then required to draw up an action plan and implement corrective measures to comply with the inspection findings.

The RBI also monitors compliance on an ongoing basis by requiring banks to submit detailed information periodically under an off-site surveillance and monitoring system. Based on this, the RBI analyses the financial health of banks between two on-site inspections and identifies banks that show financial deterioration that thereby require closer supervision.

The RBI issues directions from time to time to ensure compliance with the banking statutes and rectify non-compliance, if any. In the case of non-compliance with regulatory requirements, the RBI may impose a variety of sanctions, including fines, orders for the suspension of a bank's business and cancellation of the bank's banking licence.

Financial regulation and supervision are the two important functions of the RBI. Though the RBI is known for its function of monetary policy implementation, financial regulation and supervision are more effort taking as well as sophisticated functions. Supervision helps the RBI to continuously check to assess the health and stability of the financial system. Without effective supervision, the financial system may face crisis.

Regulation is just stipulating rules in accordance with the laws framed by the government for the effective control over the financial system. There is the Banking Regulation Act to regulate banks.

Supervision is different from regulation. Here, the RBI goes to the headquarter of the bank to check whether the bank's balance sheet is good. Objective of supervision is to ensure that banks remains healthy and stable.

Several norms are there for effective supervision. Supervision requires onsite surveillance of banks. Since the RBI is the regulator for most of the money market institutions including banks and Non-Banking Financial Institutions, there need a separate entity. The RBI has constituted a separate unit for supervision and it is called Board for Financial Supervision (BFS). The convention in central banking is that regulation and supervision should not be done by the same entity.

Board for Financial Supervision

The Board for Financial Supervision (BFS) was constituted in November 1994 to supervise the money market institutions in the country. The BFS has been constituted as an autonomous body under the RBI.

Board is drawn from the members of the Central Board of the Reserve Bank with the Governor as Chairman and one of the Deputy Governors as full time Vice-Chairman. The Board exercises the powers of supervision and inspection under the RBI Act, 1934 and the Banking Regulation Act, 1949 in relation to the different sectors of the financial system.

The BFS was initially given the mandate for supervision of commercial banks, Financial Institutions and NBFCs. Later, urban cooperative banks and primary dealers were also brought under the purview of the BFS. Since its formation, the BFS which meets every month, conducting on-site supervision of banks and off-site monitoring, based on quarterly reporting system.

Press Information Bureau - Government of India - Ministry of Finance - Powers of Reserve Bank of India (RBI) - 08 JAN 2019 5:24PM by PIB Delhi

"The Reserve Bank of India (RBI) regulates and supervises Public Sector and Private Sector Banks. Under the provisions of the Banking Regulation Act, 1949, it can, *inter alia*—

i. Inspect the bank and its books and accounts (section 35(1) *ibid.*);
ii. Examine on oath any director or other officer of the bank (section 35(3) *ibid.*);
iii. Cause a scrutiny to be made of the affairs of the bank (section 35(1A) *ibid.*);
iv. Give directions to secure the proper management of the bank (section 35A *ibid.*);
v. Call for any information of account details (section 27(2) *ibid.*);

vi. Determine the policy in relation to advances by the bank (section 21 *ibid.*);

vii. Direct special audit of the bank (section 30(1B) *ibid.*); and

viii. Direct the bank to initiate insolvency resolution process in respect of a default, under the provisions of Insolvency and Bankruptcy Code, 2016 (section 35AA *ibid.*).

Further, in respect of nationalised banks and the State Bank of India (SBI), under the provisions of the Banking Companies (Acquisition and Transfer of Undertakings) Acts of 1970 and 1980 ("Bank Nationalisation Acts") and the State Bank of India Act, 1955 ("SBI Act") respectively, *inter alia*—

1. RBI's nominee Director is a member on—

   i. the nationalised bank's Management Committee of the Board, which exercises the powers of the bank's Board with regard to credit proposals above specified threshold (section 9(3)(c) of the Bank Nationalisation Acts, and paragraph 13 of the Nationalised Banks (Management and Miscellaneous Provisions) Schemes of 1970 and 1980 made by the Government under the Bank Nationalisation Acts), and

   ii. the Executive Committee of the Central Board of SBI, which may deal with any matter within the competence of the Central Board subject to SBI General Regulations, 1955 and Central Board's directions (sections 19(f) and 30 of SBI

     Act, and regulation 46 of SBI General Regulations, 1955);
iii. RBI approves the appointment and fixes the remuneration of the bank's auditors (section 10 of the Bank Nationalisation Acts, and section 41 of the SBI Act); and
iv. RBI can appoint additional Directors on the nationalised banks' Boards and State Bank of India's Central Board (section 9A of the Bank Nationalisation Acts, and section 19B of the SBI Act).

In addition, whole-time Directors of nationalised banks and State Bank of India are appointed in consultation with RBI.

RBI has powers under other laws as well, which include, *inter alia*, the power under section 12 of the Foreign Exchange Management Act, 1999 to inspect for compliance with the Act and rules etc. made there under.

RBI also maintains the Central Repository of Information on Large Credits (CRILC) on aggregate fund-based and non-fund-based exposures of Rs. 5 crore and above of all banks. Further, RBI maintains the Central Fraud Registry and banks report all frauds involving amount above Rs. 1 lakh to RBI. In addition, RBI's Master Directions on Frauds lay out guidelines on categorisation, reporting and review of frauds, along with norms for consequent provisioning.

The powers of RBI are wide-ranging and comprehensive to deal with various situations that may emerge in all banks, including public sector banks. No proposal with regard to change in RBI's powers in respect of public sector banks is presently under consideration/

consultation. Improvement in regulatory functioning being an ongoing process, Government engages with stakeholders, including RBI, and discusses issues as they evolve.

This was stated by Shri Shiv Pratap Shukla, Minister of State for Finance in written reply to a question in Rajya Sabha today."

RBI thus having been backed up with all kinds of supervisory powers under the RBI Act, 1934 and the Banking Regulations Act 1949, question that arises in the context is why the regulator did not supervise the performance of the PSBs in those days and pinpoint the omissions and commissions to them timely when their every information was reaching the regulator as a matter of regulatory requirement. Based on the information made available by the PSBs, the regulator was fully competent under the law that has created it and under the Banking Regulation Act, 1949 to make close and strict scrutiny and to advise them directly and indirectly to the central government how the working of the PSBs has been deteriorating and measures needed to make them up. That did not happen, if happened, it was considered as routine part of the system with no special or particular attention needed from the supervisory body. It is not denied that the PSB officers and staff also would have been party in some cases but they would not have dared to do it of their own and would have done when they stood as witness to the pressures and influences that were pouring upon them from the sources stated before that showed deeper involvement of high level influential people that rather would have bolstered doing wrong things, if there were such cases.

What I submitted at the start of Part 01 of this book that Multimillion financial frauds and scams are not the acts of one or two person[s] but are made through illicit relationship and collusion built among the Interest Groups over a period of time that include political leaders, bureaucrats, Bankers' Bank, Banks and Brokers secretly & systematically until blown up making innocents the victims and the indicted the victorious. The Interest Groups sit silently and watch the developments to safeguard themselves against any accusations; yet they having killed their Conscience having done wrong things hardly feel the upheavals within because that is passed on to the scapegoats. That is the sum of the scam, holds the truth in its sense after the readers had the benefit of going through my submissions in Part 01 and Part 02 [this Part] that those who played active role in bolstering the scam have been exposed in the Janakiraman Committee Reports and the JPC Report. The Janakiraman Committee howsoever its integrity could have been had endeavored its best to cover up the roles played by the RBI officers and staff in so far as bouncing Subsidiary General Ledger [SGL} among the inter-bank operations. Whether it was accidental or intentional is a different but the circumstances under which it happened leads one to believe that it was deliberate collusion.

More curious aspect was that way back in 1986, the RBI Auditors had come across during their audit of the banking transactions of the Syndicate Bank and the Andhra Bank the use of Bank Receipt [BR] [presumed to be the origin of the concept of BR] and this fact was well within the knowledge of the RBI thereby as also in the knowledge of the Janakirman Committee Members but the Committee did not pinpoint why the RBI, having come to know the use Bank Receipts[BRs] by the commercial banks and foreign banks did not act forthwith against such inter-banks dealings, it having been vested all the powers to prevent the misuse of the operational considerations by the banks. More importantly, without the need for going through rigors of the Janakiraman Committee Reports, the RBI itself could have acted instantly when it had come to its knowledge of the fact of the use of BRs by the commercial banks through its own auditors. Had this been given due consideration by the RBI at that time and penalized the commercial and foreign banks, rather I submit, should have banned the use of BRs, the catastrophe of the financial scam would not have been there. Why it could not be done rather encouraged to be effectively used by the commercial and foreign banks can be best explained by the RBI itself. Fact, however, remains that the lapse was serious jeopardizing entire banking operational system in the country through the active participation of the leading brokers who had, as one could understand from the questions made by the JPC and the answers given by the high profiles, were the comfort of these high profiles.

More saddening part of the entire scam was that the investigating agency entrusted with the investigation of the crimes of the securities scam kept itself at distance to book the high profiles who were questioned by the JPC as accused and indicted them in its verdicts; why it did so is also a matter that could be best explained by the investigating agency itself. It did pounce upon the senior banks officers and the staff and the officers and staff of the PSUs, in some cases, there was not even so much provocation as to warrant criminal proceedings against such officers and staff but that was found to be necessary to keep the high profiles safe in the room duly locked up and explode the small fries associated with the securities transactions as part of functional duties, many of whom were innocents but that hardly mattered to the investigating agency because it was habituated to act that way to safeguard and protect the interests of its own officers, more so, high officers from the political backlash on them. Then, was there anyone else who could have given special attention on the need pursuing the verdicts of the JPC against the high profiles? None, to the best of my understanding. "If you see fraud and do not say fraud, you are a fraud" - Nassim Nicholas Taleb. "Our ability to manufacture fraud now exceeds our ability to detect it." - Al Pacino. That is what could be attributed to deafness on the part of the investigating agencies with respect to not initiating the prosecution process against the high profiles. That is where we ended up in the securities scam of 1992 where the ants were caught while the elephants were allowed to escape.

The prosecution proceedings launched by the investigating agency against those considered to be involved in the securities scam 1992 made a distinct difference between those who belonged to the lower rungs and the high profiles as could be discerned from what is submitted before. It seems the investigating agency have self-empowered powers to deal with lower and middle rung officials of the government bodies such as banks, PSUs, FIs etc. but that is not so in the case of high level politicians, the bureaucrats and high level officers in other bodies such as RBI. Their contributory cumulative circumstances found both in the Janakiraman Committee [except in the case of

RBI] and the JPC Report that would have been sufficient reasons to also include the politicians, bureaucrats and the RBI officers within the ambit of prosecution for the lapses that have been exposed or admitted in the above reports. But the investigating agency preferred to pick up on the middle and lower level officers and postpone or abandon the politicians, bureaucrats and officers of RBI for initiating criminal proceedings knowingly well that without the influence and pressure from the latter category of people, the former category of people would not have dared to enter the areas beyond their entrusted duties and functions. This comes crystal clearly from both the reports stated before but the investigating agency has, as it seems, its own discretionary powers to prosecute the one but the not the other.

The fundamental rights as regards non-discrimination available also to the accused person in criminal cases have no meaning to the investigation agency. This view is submitted based on the manner and method the investigating agency choose to adopt for prosecuting an ordinary citizen and the high profile political and bureaucratic persons, in both the cases, there being an element of similarity in the accusations of having committed criminal acts such as those as indicted by the JPC in its verdicts against the high profiles stated before just because the investigating agency gets itself mired into political pressures and influence that it doesn't want to cross over. In doing so, it doesn't realize the essence of non-discrimination approach between the ordinary citizens and the high profiles laid down under the fundamental rights which is the weakest corner of consideration by the investigating agency in dealing with the ordinary citizens and the high profiles in the matter of crimes. The ordinary citizens are made to come to the table of understanding as worked out by the investigating agency that goes even to patching up, twisting the arms of the witnesses and stitching up the cases otherwise non-existing thus transforming the innocent citizens into scapegoats to save the honour and dignity of the high profiles. This point is not legally combatable by the ordinary person for; the Hon'ble courts of law are not inclined to go into that area and confine themselves to the extent of the criminal allegations against ordinary citizen.

The judicial system does not go into these considerations. It is concerned and confined to the extent of the persons against whom the criminal proceedings have been launched and whether such proceedings are justified or not is to be pondered over by the judicial system and its order handed over. The person who is a made criminal has no right whatsoever to submit any complaint as to why he was being prosecuted while the higher ups whose contribution was more than his in the commission of the alleged crime. Such criminal is left with sole choice to defend himself or herself against the allegations made out in the Charge Sheet according to the internal decision of the investigating agency. The investigating agency cannot afford to adopt such approach against the high profile people which prescribes directly or indirectly the barriers to be crossed in the case of such people. The barriers are none other than pure political considerations rather than the available facts. This is the practice permanently stands established which the investigating agency finds cumbersome to go through leave alone crossing it over.

This is the scenario that comes out from the securities scam 1992 where who are accused have to undergo the trial for years together, the factor of innocence or otherwise having had to be considered by the judicial system on the basis of available material and evidence on record. The need and necessity for expeditious processing the case is not the concern of the investigating agency. The criminal case pending since long period stretching over 25-35 years has nothing to do anything either with the investigating agency or the judicial system. Basically, there is no window for the accused persons in such cases and, if there is one, that is knocking the doors of the higher courts that entails additional expenditure, physical and mental stress, not being sure of outcome. Such procedure is there under the laws but is considered by most of the accused as unaffordable. What is the legal remedy available to such accused persons? None has thought over this so far nor there is any assurance or certainty of doing something in such case in the near future. So, let us stop here any further discussion thereon.

The inordinate and unexplainable delays in completion of the trials pending over 30 years drives the innocent accused persons sometimes to become mentally upset including even a stage that may come to such persons when they may have to be admitted in the Lunatic Home, the prosecution and the judicial system having no sympathy and humanitarian consideration. The prosecution would be too eager to admit such accused persons in a Lunatic Home, if the Hon'ble Trial Court permits it do so, immediately because that would become unquestionable cause for further delay in the case, the accused person having become lunatic. Where do the Fundamental Rights of the accused persons guaranteed under the Constitution of the country stand in such cases? Or should we say the Fundamental Rights have no relevance to the prosecution and trial courts for long over hanging of the cases against the innocent accused persons? The process of establishing whether the accused person is innocent is itself a long drawn battle and, if after completion of the trial over a period of 30-35 years, if the accused person is found innocent; does it amount to justice or injustice? If the Charge Sheet itself discloses and speaks the innocence of an accused person; for example, in the case of the trial under the Anti-Corruption Law, if the Charge Sheet does not make any allegation against an accused person that there is no recovery from him or his family members or relatives or there is no financial loss caused to the organization he or she belongs, can't the Hon'ble Trial Court exercise its powers to deem such accused person as innocent at the stage of taking cognizance of the charge sheet instead of finding so after a prolonged period of over 30 years?

"IT'S TOO EASY TO CRITICIZE A MAN WHEN HE'S OUT OF FAVOUR, AND TO MAKE HIM SHOULDER THE BLAME FOR EVERYBODY ELSE'S MISTAKES." ~ LEO TOLSTOY

A scapegoated person suffers the worst in life which when prolonged, he or she starts hitting his or her head against the wall, bleeding soaks the clothes on the body, that continues as long as he or she has blood in the body; thereafter, collapses on the ground. The people around are afraid of touching him or her out of their own fear. Thus dies the scapegoat when everyone around expresses his or her sympathies. The case comes to end with remarks 'deceased' recorded in the Hon'ble Trial Court file.

PART 03
BANK RECEIPT - LEGALITY

The Bank Receipts [BR] used in the securities scam 1992 was not normal bank receipt used by the banks in the ordinary course of their banking business. Such ordinary receipt had no value in scams. All these bank receipts have their legality having been legally prescribed by the banks and considered cognizable in law when disputes arise between the bank and the customer. The BR used in the scam not being a normal bank receipt, the inference would be that it was an 'abnormal' receipt specially made and used in the scam, whether or not it was legally prescribed and had legal validity is a matter that doesn't apply in financial scams. The scams are born through new inventions from top to bottom including the Bank Receipt [BR]. These inventions are made when there is need to depart from the established banking system that happens in the scams, whether or not those involved in the scams are highly learned ones, half learned ones or unlearnt ones. The combination of these factors search for the scams signalled by the politicians, the bureaucrats and high level bankers. The scamsters are the instruments to follow the instructions of high politicians and officials and fulfil their desires that give them strength to self-rise against all the odds, the greatest art only they consider much useful for maintaining professional career and to the politicians, amass wealth for their political parties for illegal use in the elections. Every scam, if one swims through, reveals the same story. So also the scam struck in 1992. The legality takes the back seat when only the illegality can be put forward for operation. The cyclone in the sea sweeps everyone in the sea but the sharks and whales somehow manage to reach the shore. It is said that 'the larger the sea creature, the better their chances are of survival during an impending hurricane. For example, a shark or whale can swim at a fast enough speed to elude storms, in addition to being developed enough to detect pressure changes in the water that give them an indication that evacuation is necessary.' That is what happened also in the cyclonic like financial scam of 1992. Let us see it now through the legal/regulatory eyes.

WHAT IS A BANK RECEIPT?

Bank Receipt is not defined either under the Banking Regulations Act, 1949 or under the Reserve Bank of India Act, 1934 or under the Securities Contract Regulations Act, 1956. Then, wherefrom authority was derived by the RBI, the commercial banks and even the Indian Banks Association [IBA] to talk about the Bank Receipt? There is no explanation or clarification available in this regard in the public domain. If we were to accept such practice as the normal practice followed by the banks, days are not far when the commercial banks and brokers could continue to play havoc in the securities both in the government securities and the public sector bonds or any new types financial instruments to come in future, as and when the opportunity stands before them. This cannot be ruled out as the securities scam of 1992 was not ruled out when several such scams and frauds had taken place thereto before. To understand the definition of the Bank Receipt, the following statement available on the Website is given:

"A bank receipt contains detailed information about a **financial transaction** conducted at a bank. The transaction receipt generally includes the amount of the transaction, the date it occurred, and the employee number of the bank employee who conducted the transaction. Aside from transactions involving deposit accounts, bank receipts are also given to customers who make loan payments, **credit card** payments, and conduct other similar types of transactions. Banks provide account holders with a copy of the bank receipt and the bank also maintains its own records of all transactions.

Financial institutions issue receipts to customers to avoid disputes relating to the details of transactions. Immediately after taking possession of the bank receipt, the account holder has the opportunity to dispute any information that is incorrectly recorded on the receipt. If an error occurs after an account holder leaves the bank and funds are deposited into the wrong account, the customer can use the bank receipt as a means of having the transaction corrected and funds deposited into the correct account.

Banks encourage account holders to use their transaction receipts to balance their accounts at least once a month. Many people review their monthly bank statement and compare the amounts and transaction dates of items listed on the statement with their own bank receipts. Businesses typically keep bank receipts until the end of the year so that the receipts can be used for tax preparation purposes. Individuals who claim tax deductions for certain kinds of expenses must also keep copies of bank receipts to prove that they qualify for deductions related to banking transactions, such as interest charges on mortgages.

Only an account holder can usually make a withdrawal from a deposit account, but anyone can make a deposit into an account. To protect the privacy of depositors, banks typically do not print account numbers on bank receipts in case the person making the deposit is not the actual account owner. Banks normally do not print account balances on receipts, although customers can request to have the balance printed if they can establish their identity at the time they make a request.

Historically, bank receipts were paper slips. In recent years, many banks have begun to offer online receipts. These receipts are normally sent to the account holder via e-mail. Using online receipts rather than paper receipts enables the bank to save on printing costs and also provides convenience for account holders who no longer have to keep track of numerous paper receipts." [Source: Smart Capital Mind Website – April 06, 2023]

Summary of Instructions Issued by Reserve Bank of India on Repos [Annexure VI] posted on the Website as also referred to before provide: [Relevant Excerpts]

In April 1987, banks were advised to follow the guidelines given hereunder in respect of their buy-back arrangements with banks and others:

"1. Ready Forward (buy-back) deals in4Government and other approved Securities:

1.1 In April 1987, banks were advised to follow the guidelines given hereunder in respect of their buy-back arrangements with banks and others2. Need to hold the security before sale.

2.1 <u>In July 1991, banks were advised inter alia, that it was observed that certain banks were resorting to buy-back deals in Government Securities amongst themselves</u>

without actually holding sufficient securities either in physical form or in their Subsidiary General Ledger (SGL) account (resulting in substitution of Bank Receipts (BRs)/ return of SGL forms for want of sufficient balance), at rates which had no relevance to market, with a view to window-dressing their profitability/ maintenance of SLR requirement, with the tacit understanding with the counter party banks. Some of the banks appeared to be taking outright oversold position in securities and in their desperate bid to cover the oversold position in a particular security/ies they had entered into double Ready Forward deals and other banks had obliged them in the matter.
[Emphasis added]

Indian Bank Association [IBA] communication No. OPR.C/52-20/1039 6th May. 1991 to the PSBs:

STANDARDISED FORMAT OF BANK RECEIPT (BR}

In the inter-bank market, large number of transactions in securities is concluded by means of BR deliveries, particularly when the *selling bank is not in a position to effect physical delivery of scrips for various reasons. It is common practice among banks to issue BRs which acknowledge receipt of funds for· the securities sold and undertake to hold the same in trust, until these are physically delivered.* [Emphasis added]

The above communication suggests It was not the type of Format of Bank Receipt [BR] being used by commercial banks and the brokers until May, 1991. That also suggests that the formats of BR used thereto before were left to the discretion of the operating banks. RBI was aware of the BR being used between two nationalized banks since 1986; it pointed out the same as irregular practice without any further action thereon.

It seemed that it was considered necessary to devise a standard format of BR and frame rules therefor for uniform adoption by member banks, financial institutions, public sector undertakings and other IBA/RBI specified institutions. Accordingly, the standardised formats etc. for the above evolved by Investment Dealers Club and reviewed by the IBA Committee on funds and lnvestmems (COFI) were placed before the Managing Committee of the IBA in its meeting on 23rd April, 1991 for approval.

The Managing Committee approved the standard format of the BR. BR Rules and monthly statement of BRs held and issued and recommended these for uniform 'adoption by member banks, financial institution like IDBI/IFCI/ICJCI/NABARD/UTI/GIC/LIC, public sector undertakings and other IBA/RBI specified institutions. At present, different BR formats are being accepted by the IBA non-member institutions; there should therefore be no difficulty in their accepting the uniform BR· format which is being recommended now. The RBI is being informed and requested to consider the eligible institutions from its end also. Member banks may adopt standard format of BR, BR Rules and monthly statement of BRs held and issued, the specimen of which are enclosed.[Reproduced below]:

BANK RECEIPT RULES:

1. The Bank Receipt should be issued in the prescribed format only. Receipt issued in any other format will not be accepted.
2. Normally no BR should be issued where SGL facility is available. In any other cases the

scrips shall be delivered to the buyer as soon as possible except for R/F transactions.
3. A separate BR should be issued for each type of security.
4. BR is non-transferable.
5. Banks should issue BRs serially numbered on Security Paper.
6. BR must be exchanged with actual scrips as early as possible, and in any case within 90 days of issue. <u>However, it would be open-for banks to issue fresh receipt in the event BRs are not discharged within 90 days and the reason for the same should be mentioned in the renewed BR. [Emphasis added]</u>
7. BR should be signed by two authorised signatories whose signatures should be registered with the buyer bank to verify the signatures.
8. BR can be accepted from any of the following institutions.
   a) All member banks of the IBA.
   b) Financial institutions like IDBI, IFCI, ICICI, NABARD, UTI, GIC, LIC.
   c) Public Sector Undertakings
   d) Any other institution specified by the IBA/RBI.

[Author's Note: BR Format not attached with the communication posted on the Website]

The above communication issued by IBA in May, 1991 was addressed to the CEOs of the PSBs. It was not endorsed to the other institutions mentioned above including the PSUs though the rules state BR can be accepted from any of the institutions named at (b) and (c) it could be, inferred that the Format and its governing rules were not in the knowledge of those institutions. This was a gap that made the other institutions stated before being unaware of the operational aspects of the BR.

This was for the first time that the BR in the specific Format along with its governing Rules was officially circulated to the PSBs specific to interbank sale and purchase of government securities and public sector bonds.There was no such formatted BR being used by the PSBs prior thereto. The BRs used by PSBs, in the normal course thereto before were intended to be in the ordinary course of their banking operations and the formats varied from bank to bank as noted before. It is understood that the RBI itself also forwarded the IBA Format of BR and its governing rules to the PSBs. This indicates that the RBI had consented to the use of the IBA BR Format and its governing rules which, however, was whether the technical or statutory approval is the matter that still remains open.

This is so because the statutory approval implies the written approval of the RBI while the technical approval amounts to just acceptance on the face of it. The statement that the Managing Committee of IBA approved the BR Format and its governing Rules was to fulfil compliance of its internal rules but IBA having had no locus standi under the RBI Act, 1934 or the BR Act, 1949, BR Format and its governing rules so circulated also were supposed to be approved by the RBI or the BOD/COD of PSBs individually in order to give it legal effect though there may not be specific provisions of such requirement in the said Acts but the need for such approval deemed to be vested under the powers of the RBI or the BOD/ COD of PSBs considering the serious implications of the BR as became evident during the scam.. Further, IBA being an unincorporated body and, as such, had no legal status. It was formed to facilitate the PSBs and others as a voluntary body but its services were not intended to be considered as legally operative as admitted by IBA.

In the *RK Jain versus Indian Banks' Association* case, the Central Information Commission considered whether the IBA comes under the RTI Act. The Commission, in its order of November 13, 2017, said: "Taking into account that the IBA performs functions as state agency and its majority control vests in Government of India-appointed Managing Directors of public sector banks, the IBA qualifies to be a public authority under the RTI Act, 2005. The Commission, therefore, directs the IBA to designate an official of the IBA as the CPIO at the earliest as per provisions of Section 5 of the RTI Act, 2005 and also to comply with Section 4 of the RTI Act, 2005 within four weeks of the receipt of the order of the Commission."

Further, the Commission held: "So far as control part of appropriate government is concerned, it is noted that the IBA is an agency or instrumentality of the state. The appropriate government controls it as majority of Managing Committee members are Managing Directors of public sector banks, who in turn are Government of India employees..."

COURT STAYS ORDER

The IBA filed a writ petition before the Delhi High Court (WP No 11046/2017), and on December 13, 2017, the High Court stayed the CIC order. While granting the initial stay, the court observed the following (among other observations): "The short question involved in the present case is whether the petitioner is a public authority within the meaning of Section 2(h) of the Right to Information Act, 2005. It is stated that the petitioner is an association of banks. It has 241 members and only nine members are public sector banks." The latest status is not known.

The operational requirements of the Government Securities including inter-bank transfers etc. are governed by the Depository Participant Operations Manual for Government Securities. The Subsidiary Ledger Account [SLA] transfer form and operational requirements are covered under the said manual.

The Bank Receipt in the ordinary parlance is the receipt used by the banks and the financial institutions in the ordinary course of conduct of their business, the definition of which is stated before. The other point to be noted here is that the Bank Receipts and Transactions Receipts followed by the banks are not in the standardized form and are; therefore, their formats differ from bank to bank.

The format of the Bank Receipt {also called BR} used by the commercial banks and the brokers under the securities scam, 1992 is the one prepared and circulated by the Indian Banks Association [IBA] in May, 1991. BRs were being used by the commercial banks since 1986. It is not ascertainable which type of BR Format was being used by the commercial banks and the brokers before the IBA circulated the standard form and its governing Rules.

IBA has no locus standi either under the Banking Regulations Act, 1949 or under the Reserve Bank of India Act, 1934, the principal Acts that govern the functioning and operational aspects of the Banks though RBI Act, 1934 covers wide range of powers for being exercised over the banks established under the said Act, the Non-Banking Financial Institutions/Companies, Cooperative Banks and the Public Financial Institutions.

The various forms including the form of the bank receipt defined before, the deposit and withdrawal slips adopted by the banks and used by the customers supposed to have been standardized varying from bank to bank but the crucial consideration in all these cases is that the bank adopts a form or slip or a format of the receipt as prescribed by its Head Office implying such forms have the approval of the competent authority designated in the Head Office. This is so to establish the legal identity and acceptance by the general public, more so, the customers and a binding thread between the banks and their customers in the event of any dispute or question of law arises challenged either by the banks or the customers.

The legal sanctity of the forms and formats and their governing conditions or rules has to be considered as a necessity. This was not so in the case of the Bank Receipts [BR] used by the commercial banks and the brokers in the scam under consideration. Even, according to rules governing the BR as laid down by the IBA provides for safeguards including that it should be signed by at least two authorized signatories of the bank concerned but the further question that arises is whether or not such format [BR] and its governing rules had the legal sanctity at all. There is no information on Website as to approval of the BR format by the BOD of the Bank or any other competent authority in the Bank.

That suggests the banks had not complied this legal requirement and rendered the BR and its governing rules so as to have made it legally tenable. Given this status, BR used becomes questionable as to its legality. This aspect has not at all been given any consideration, as the available information on Website shows, either within the bank or by the investigating agency or before any trial court of law. However, the PSUs which invested their surplus funds in the secondary market through the commercial banks considered the BR as legally prescribed by the competent authority under the RBI Act, 1934 or the BR Act, 1949.There was, therefore no need for them to go further into this aspect. That was precisely the status of understanding by the PSUs when they accepted the BR system adopted by the commercial banks. The BR, on the other hand, formed crux of the entire scam. How to deal such situation could be best left to the legal pundits and the Hon'ble Courts of Law. This lacuna, however, in my opinion, left behind a serious question of law unanswered during the scam period or during the trials in the Hon'ble Courts of Law. I refrain myself from going into that aspect.It, however, remains a question to be answered by some competent authority such as RBI in order to establish its legality, the same having been used in the scam. scam.. It was noted that the BRs were used for issuing fresh BRs in respect of the existing investment instruments held. It is relevant to refer to the Rule No. 6 of the IBA Rules governing the BR, according to which, 'BR must be exchanged with actual scrips as early as· possible, and in any case· within 90 days of issue. However, it would be open-for banks to issue fresh receipt in the event BRs are not discharged within 90 days and the reason for the same should be mentioned in the renewed BR.

One may ask what the legal back up has to do with the BR when the fact remains that the BR system was used in the scam and the RBI and the PSBs accepted the same. I wish to submit that the legal back up to the document establishes its legal credibility and protection where its enforcement is called for. If we consider that legal back up is not necessary for a document, then identical document can be fabricated and used and until it is proved it is fabricated, the legality is not established because fabrication stands proved once it fails to satisfy the legal back up. In the case of a document that is used in large scale, its legality has to be proved first before it is put to use. If we say that it is not so required, then we are opening up the field for the miscreants to fabricate as many as documents which continue to be operative unless and until it is proved beyond doubt that the document is fabricated because it did not have the legal sanction or back up.

That is what happened in the present scam. Every bank and every broker started using the BR, whether it was the same as in the legally approved form, was not subjected to verification rather there was no legally approved format and its operational method that would have enabled to differentiate which was legal format and which was illegal format until the time the one prescribed by the IBA. That was not done by anybody anytime during the scam or during the investigation or trial. BR Format acquired its official status only when IBA laid down the Format with its governing Rules but the format as well as the rules lacked their legal sanction, the same not having been approved by the competent authority that is, either by the RBI or by the

BOD/COD of PSBs although they were accepted for use On the other hand, fake BR means the BR used without any back up securities and continued to be operated in the secondary market which happened for want of a prescribed format with the governing conditions approved by the competent authority

Fact of use of Bank Receipt by two nationalized banks in lieu of the physical possession of the securities way back in 1986 was known to the RBI through its Auditors who examined the accounts of those two banks. RBI remained silent. RBI itself admits that the prescribed forms for the interbank sale and purchase of government securities through the SLA operational manual was not insisted upon and followed by its PDO rather it allowed the BR to be used by the participating banks, as noted before. This gave a spontaneous impetus to the banks to continue to indulge in the use of BR recklessly in their securities transactions without in possession of the securities.

It is surprising as to why the management of the banks overlooked the above consideration and why RBI which had come to know of the use of the BR in lieu of physical possession of the securities in the securities transaction between the two nationalized bank as early as 1986 did not initiate action forthwith or order for further inquiry which, not only would have corrected the irregular practice and also would have extended the investigation through such inquiry whether similar irregularities were being committed by other banks and to have ensured complete prevention of such irregularities in future.

That didn't happen and the scam struck when RBI woke up and constituted a high level committee known as Janakiraman Committee to go into all the aspects of the irregularities with wider terms of reference. The common saying that 'prevention is better than cure' didn't seem to strike to banks management and the RBI. There is also another saying 'what you done if you have woken up after the damage is done which was like what you done by burning lamp in sun the oil therein dried up by the time the night set in.'

How could PSUs know what things were happening among and in between the banks and the brokers. PSUs had in hand the BRs which were considered as surety and comfortable evidential document about the existence of the securities specified in the BRs without insisting for the physical possession of the securities involved and believed that to be the normal banking practice in the interbank sale and purchase of securities. It has to be presumed, in the circumstances, that both the RBI and the MOF were in know of the BR system taking place among the commercial banks dealings in the secondary market much earlier than the official format that was circulated by IBA in May, 1991. The guidelines and master circulars being issued by the RBI were not being endorsed to the PSUs, the same being outside the jurisdiction of the RBI thereby they remained in dark about them.

PSUs believed in the authenticity and genuineness of the BR. PSUs were left with no other choice in the given circumstances and had to adhere to the instructions issued by the MOF. Sadly, this was construed by the investigating agency as conspiracy between the PSUs, the commercial banks and the brokers. Was that all happened submitted before suggests there having been any conspiracy as assumed by the investigating agency? PSUs officers were discharging their given duties and in compliance with the government instructions.

Let me give an example. I go to a public sector bank and express my desire to invest certain amount in the FD, the bank welcomes the offer, provides me the form to be completed and I comply with that requirement and submit the same to the bank along with the cash for the intended investment. The bank asks me to wait for few minutes and delivers to me there itself the FDR. I feel great happy and return to home with that FDR. That is my jurisdiction up to which I have the permission of the bank to enter into. Thereafter, it is not my business to follow up how the bank is using that investment or what it is doing with that investment nor I have any legal right to do that having no accessibility under any rule or law or any need for any such necessity. I keep the FDR till its maturity date and on the maturity date go to the Bank and present the FDR with filled up and duly signed Form and get back my investment along with interest amount at specified rate therein. The matter ends there.

What I have explained above is discernable from the proceedings before the JPC as have been submitted before as well as the Action Taken Reports placed before the Parliament in instalments from time to time, the last one being in 2018 which are posted on Website but are not reproducible but the details of those have been given before. The JPC questioned select high profiles as accused, given its verdict and also heard their defense. What had come out of such questions has been presented in the earlier part of this book. The investigating agency which also had the opportunity of going through these questions and answers did not consider it necessary to initiate action in respect of those who were indicted by the JPC in its verdicts.

They believed it better and easier to spread their own net to catch the small fries and make their life miserable. It did not place the floppies and magnetictapes seized from the office premises of the brokers before the JPC while the bureaucrats, on the specific question/instruction of JPC, placed before the JPC the list of names of their children who were employed in the foreign banks. When the bureaucrats could do so, why the investigating agency could not place before the JPC the floppies and the magnetictapes that contained information about the investment deals by the high profiles? In all such cases, the answer is to keep distance from the high profiles.

BRs could not be issued for Government securities, but could only be issued only when PSU bonds or mutual funds unit are traded. The record of Government securities held by Banks is maintained by RBI's Public Debt Office through SGL (Subsidiary General Ledger). When a Bank wanted to sell Government securities, it only had to give a SGL transfer form to the PDO, which would then credit the securities to the buyer's account and debit the seller's Bank's securities account. BRs were valid up to 90 days. Interestingly, a Bank would be holding a BR yet to receive delivery of the securities would trade in those securities with a third Bank, and issues another BR. In fact, BRs were issued with BRs without underlying securities. As per RBI inspection report in October 1986, Andhra Bank and Syndicate Bank had issued BRs without having underlying securities. It is relevant to recall in this regard what Rule No. 6 of the IBA BR Format governing rule stated before.

BANK RECEIPT SCAM

In a ready-forward deal, the borrower (seller of securities), gives the buyer of the securities a bank receipt (BR). There were no securities moved back and forth in reality. The BR is a receipt from the selling bank, and it guarantees that the buyer will receive the securities they have paid for at the end of the term. Some banks, on the request of the brokers issued fake BRs that are not backed up by securities. Once these fake BRs were issued, they were passed on to other banks and the banks gave money to the brokers, on the assumption that they were lending against the securities.

The scenario that was glaring at the PSUs and its officials was so painful as if pushing the herd of sheep and goats into the mouth of the wild animals such as lions and tigers so that those are within the grip of the jaws of the wild animals, their fate would be the death; thereafter the pending case comes to an end and stands closed. That gives tranquillity to the investigating agency and distress to the surviving members of the family of such persons. Oh! Why to think of such scenario when there is no one to protect such persons from the criminal jaws. Better to leave Mother Earth with peace of mind that is what the innocents considered more appropriate.

RBI vide its Master Circular No. RBI/ 2009-10/20

DBOD No. BP. BC.3 / 21.04.141 / 2009-10 dated July 1, 2009 addressed to all Commercial Banks [excluding Regional Rural Banks] regarding Prudential norms for classification, valuation and operation of investment portfolio by banks, specified the following conditions in regard to the use of Bank Receipt [BR]. This is cited here for sake of information and record since what was to happen had already happened. The above Master Circular, at best, can be considered as intended for future compliance by the commercial banks.

"1.1.3 Use of Bank Receipt (BR)

The banks should follow the following instructions for issue of BRs:

a) No BR should be issued under any circumstances in respect of transactions in Govt. securities for which SGL facility is available.

b) Even in the case of other securities, BR may be issued for ready transactions only, under the following circumstances:

(i) The scrips are yet to be issued by the issuer and the bank is holding the allotment advice.

(ii) The security is physically held at a different centre and the bank is in a position to physically transfer the security and give delivery thereof within a short period.

(iii) The security has been lodged for transfer / interest payment and the bank is holding necessary records of such lodgements and will be in a position to give physical delivery of the security within a short period.

c) No BR should be issued on the basis of a BR (of another bank) held by the bank and no transaction should take place on the basis of a mere exchange of BRs held by the bank.

d) BRs could be issued covering transactions relating to banks' own Investments Accounts only, and no BR should be issued by banks covering transactions relating to either the Accounts of Portfolio Management Scheme (PMS) Clients or Other Constituents' Accounts, including brokers.

e) No BR should remain outstanding for more than 15 days.

f) A BR should be redeemed only by actual delivery of scrips and not by cancellation of the transaction/set off against another transaction. If a BR is not redeemed by delivery of scrips within the validity period of 15 days, the BR should be deemed as dishonoured and the bank which has issued the BR should refer the case to the RBI, explaining the reasons for which the scrips could not be delivered within the stipulated period and the proposed manner of settlement of the transaction.

g) BRs should be issued on semi-security paper, in the standard format (prescribed by IBA), serially numbered and signed by two authorised officials of the bank, whose signatures are recorded with other banks. As in the case of SGL forms, there should be a control system in place to account for each BR form.

h) Separate registers of BRs issued and BRs received should be maintained and arrangements should be put in place to ensure that these are systematically followed up and liquidated within the stipulated time limit.

i) The banks should also have a proper system for the custody of unused B.R. Forms and their utilisation. The existence and operations of these controls at the concerned offices/ departments of the bank should be reviewed, among others, by the statutory auditors and a certificate to this effect may be forwarded every year to the Regional Office of Department of Banking Supervision (DBS), RBI, under whose jurisdiction the Head Office of the bank is located.

j) Any violation of the instructions relating to BRs would invite penal action, which could include raising of reserve requirements, withdrawals of refinance facility from the RBI and denial of access to money markets. The RBI may also levy such other penalty as it may deem fit in accordance with the provisions of the Banking Regulation Act, 1949.

1.1.4 Retailing of Government Securities

The banks may undertake retailing of Government securities with non-bank clients subject to the following conditions:

i) Such retailing should be on outright basis and there is no restriction on the period between sale and purchase.

ii) The retailing of Government securities should be on the basis of ongoing market rates/ yield curve emerging out of secondary market transactions.

1.1.5 Internal Control System

The banks should observe the following guidelines for internal control system in respect of investment transactions:

(a) There should be a clear functional separation of (i) trading, (ii) settlement, monitoring and control and (iii) accounting. Similarly, there should be a functional separation of trading and back office functions relating to banks' own Investment Accounts, Portfolio Management Scheme (PMS) Clients' Accounts and other Constituents (including brokers') accounts. The Portfolio Management service may be provided to clients, subject to strictly following the guidelines in regard thereto (covered in paragraph 1.3.3). Further, PMS Clients Accounts should be subjected to a separate audit by external auditors.

(b) For every transaction entered into, the trading desk should prepare a deal slip which should contain data relating to nature of the deal, name of the counter-party, whether it is a direct deal or through a broker, and if through a broker, name of the broker, details of security, amount, price, contract date and time. The deal slips should be serially numbered and controlled separately to ensure that each deal slip has been properly accounted for. Once the deal is concluded, the dealer should immediately pass on the deal slip to the back office for recording and processing. For each deal there must be a system of issue of confirmation to the counterparty. The timely receipt of requisite written confirmation from the counterparty, which must include all essential details of the contract, should be monitored by the back office.

(c) With respect to transactions matched on the NDS-OM module, since CCIL is the central counterparty to all deals, exposure of any counterparty for a trade is only to CCIL and not to the entity with whom a deal matches. Besides, details of all deals on NDS-OM are available to the counterparties as and when required by way of reports on NDS-OM itself. In view of the above, the need for counterparty confirmation of deals matched on NDS-OM does not arise. However, all government securities transactions, other than those matched on NDS-OM, will continue to be physically confirmed by the back offices of the counterparties, as hitherto.

(d) Once a deal has been concluded, there should not be any substitution of the counter party bank by another bank by the broker, through whom the deal has been entered into; likewise, the security sold/purchased in the deal should not be substituted by another security.

(e) On the basis of vouchers passed by the back office (which should be done after verification of actual contract notes received from the broker/ counterparty and confirmation of the deal by the counterparty), the Accounts Section should independently write the books of account.

(f) In the case of transaction relating to PMS Clients' Accounts (including brokers), all the relative records should give a clear indication that the transaction belongs to PMS Clients/ other constituents and does not belong to bank's own Investment Account and the bank is acting only in its fiduciary/ agency capacity.

(g) (i) Records of SGL transfer forms issued/ received, should be maintained.

(ii) Balances as per bank's books should be reconciled at quarterly intervals with the balances in the books of PDOs. If the number of transactions so warrant, the reconciliation should be undertaken more frequently, say on a monthly basis. This reconciliation should be periodically checked by the internal audit department.

(iii) Any bouncing of SGL transfer forms issued by selling banks in favour of the buying bank should immediately be brought to the notice of the Regional Office of Department of Banking Supervision of RBI by the buying bank.

(iv) A record of BRs issued/ received should be maintained.

(v) A system for verification of the authenticity of the BRs and SGL transfer forms received from the other banks and confirmation of authorised signatories should be put in place.

(h) Banks should put in place a reporting system to report to the top management, on a weekly basis, the details of transactions in securities, details of bouncing of SGL transfer forms issued by other banks and BRs outstanding for more than one month and a review of investment transactions undertaken during the period.

(i) Banks should not draw cheques on their account with the RBI for third party transactions, including inter-bank transactions. For such transactions, bankers' cheques/pay orders should be issued.

(j) In case of investment in shares, the surveillance and monitoring of investment should be done by the Audit Committee of the Board, which shall review in each of its meetings, the total exposure of the bank to capital market both fund based and non-fund based, in different forms as stated above and ensure that the guidelines issued by RBI are complied with and adequate risk management and internal control systems are in place;

(k) The Audit Committee should keep the Board informed about the overall exposure to capital market, the compliance with the RBI and Board guidelines, adequacy of risk management and internal control systems;

(l) In order to avoid any possible conflict of interest, it should be ensured that the stockbrokers as directors on the Boards of banks or in any other capacity, do not involve themselves in any manner with the Investment Committee or in the decisions in regard to making investments in shares, etc., or advances against shares.

(m) The internal audit department should audit the transactions in securities on an on-going basis, monitor the compliance with the laid down management policies and prescribed procedures and report the deficiencies directly to the management of the bank.

(n) The banks' managements should ensure that there are adequate internal control and audit procedures for ensuring proper compliance of the instructions in regard to the conduct of the investment portfolio. The banks should institute a regular system of monitoring compliance with the prudential and other guidelines issued by the RBI. The banks should get compliance in key areas certified by their statutory auditors and furnish such audit certificate to the Regional Office of DBS, RBI under whose jurisdiction the HO of the bank falls.

1.1.6 ENGAGEMENT OF BROKERS

i) For engagement of brokers to deal in investment transactions, the banks should observe the following guidelines:

(a) Transactions between one bank and another bank should not be put through the brokers' accounts. The brokerage on the deal payable to the broker, if any (if the deal was put through with the help of a broker), should be clearly indicated on the notes/memorandum put up to the top management seeking approval for putting through the transaction and separate account of brokerage paid, broker-wise, should be maintained.

(b) If a deal is put through with the help of a broker, the role of the broker should be restricted to that of bringing the two parties to the deal together.

(c) While negotiating the deal, the broker is not obliged to disclose the identity of the counterparty to the deal. On conclusion of the deal, he should disclose the counterparty and his contract note should clearly indicate the name of the counterparty. It should also be ensured by the bank that the broker note contains the exact time of the deal. Their back offices may ensure that the deal time on the broker note and the deal ticket is the same. The bank should also ensure that their concurrent auditors audit this aspect.

(d) On the basis of the contract note disclosing the name of the counterparty, settlement of deals between banks, viz. both fund settlement and delivery of security should be directly between the banks and the broker should have no role to play in the process.

(e) With the approval of their top managements, banks should prepare a panel of approved brokers which should be reviewed annually or more often if so warranted. Clear-cut criteria should be laid down for empanelment of brokers, including verification of their creditworthiness, market reputation, etc. A record of broker-wise details of deals put through and brokerage paid, should be maintained.

(f) A disproportionate part of the business should not be transacted through only one or a few brokers. Banks should fix aggregate contract limits for each of the approved brokers. A limit of 5% of total transactions (both purchase and sales) entered into by a bank during a year should be treated as the aggregate upper contract limit for each of the approved brokers. This limit should cover both the business initiated by a bank and the business offered/ brought to the bank by a broker. Banks should ensure that the transactions entered into through individual brokers during a year normally do not exceed this limit. However, if for any reason it becomes necessary to exceed the aggregate limit for any broker, the specific reasons therefor should be recorded, in writing, by the authority empowered to put through the deals. Further, the board should be informed of this, post facto. However, the norm of 5% would not be applicable to banks' dealings through Primary Dealers.

(g) The concurrent auditors who audit the treasury operations should scrutinise the business done through brokers also and include it in their monthly report to the Chief Executive Officer of the bank. Besides, the business put through any individual broker or brokers in excess of the limit, with the reasons therefor, should be covered in the half-yearly review to the Board of Directors/ Local Advisory Board. These instructions also apply to subsidiaries and mutual funds of the banks.

[Certain clarifications on the instructions are furnished in the **Annexure II**.]

[Author's Note: Annexure II not attached with this Master Circular posted on the RBI Website].

ii) Inter-bank securities transactions should be undertaken directly between banks and no bank should engage the services of any broker in such transactions.

Exceptions:

Note (i) Banks may undertake securities transactions among themselves or with non-bank clients through members of the National Stock Exchange (NSE), OTC Exchange of India (OTCEI) and the Stock Exchange, Mumbai (BSE). If such transactions are not undertaken on the NSE, OTCEI or BSE, the same should be undertaken by banks directly, without engaging brokers.

Note (ii) Although the Securities Contracts (Regulation) Act, 1956 defines the term `securities' to mean corporate shares, debentures, Govt. securities and rights or interest in securities, the term `securities' would exclude corporate shares. The Provident / Pension Funds and Trusts registered under the Indian Trusts Act, 1882, will be outside the purview of the expression `non-bank clients' for the purpose of note (i) above."

The Fire Brigade Team caught up in traffic jam; however, by the time it reached the Site, the house was completely burnt including serious casualties that are what could be said about the RBI Circular of 2009 dealt with above.

Those who believe in GOD and have certain comprehensions of GOD think twice before harming others while those who also believe in GOD and doubt the comprehension of GOD find no time to think before harming others. That is the process of one's life on Mother Earth for; the humans consider most dominating and commanding compared to helpless ones and other Living Beings.

PART 04
SUMMATION

Harshad Mehta was an Indian stockbroker and is alleged to have engineered the rise in the BSE stock exchange in the year 1992. Exploiting several loopholes in the banking system, Harshad and his associates siphoned off funds from inter-bank transactions and bought shares heavily at a premium across many segments, triggering a rise in the Sens*x. When the scheme was exposed, the banks started demanding the money back, causing the collapse. He was later charged with 72 criminal offenses and more than 600 civil action suits were filed against him. He died in 2002 with many litigations still pending against him.

In 1981 he became a sub-broker for stock brokers J.L. Shah and Nandalal Sheth. After a while he was unable to sustain his overbought positions and decided to pay his dues by selling his house with consent of his mother Rasilaben and brother Ashwin. The next day Harshad went to his brokers and offered the papers of the house as guarantee. The brokers Shah and Sheth were moved by his gesture and gave him sufficient time to overcome his position.

After he came out of this big struggle for survival he became stronger and his brother quit his job to team with Harshad to start their venture Growmore Research and Asset Management Company Limited. While a brokers card at BSE was being auctioned, the company made a bid for the same with financial assistance from Shah and Sheth, who were Harshad's previous broker mentors.

He rose and survived the bear runs, this earned him the nickname of the Big Bull of the trading floor, and his actions, actual or perceived, decided the course of the movement of the Sens*x as well as scrip-specific activities. By the end of eighties the media started projecting him as "Stock Market Success", "Story of Rags to Riches" and he too started to fuel his own publicity. He felt proud of this accomplishment and showed off his success to journalists through his mansion "Madhuli", which included a billiards room, mini theatre and nine-hole golf course, and a fleet of imported cars including a custom built Lexus luxury sedan, a rarity in India in those days. During his heyday, in the early 1990s, Harshad Mehta commanded a large resource of funds and finances as well as personal wealth.

In April 1992, the Indian stock market crashed, and Harshad Mehta, the person considered the architect of the Bull Run was blamed for the crash. He had manipulated the Indian banking systems to siphon off funds from the banking system and used the funds to build large positions in a select group of stocks. When the scam was exposed, he was called upon by the banks and financial institutions to return the funds. This necessitated the liquidation of the stock holdings and an exit from the positions which he had built in various stocks. The selling brought about a severe market downturn, creating a selling panic, and the stock market crashed within days. He was arrested on June 5, 1992 for his role in the scam.

Harshad Mehta had been buying shares heavily since the beginning of 1990. The shares which attracted attention were those of Associated Cement Companies (ACC). The price of ACC shares was bid up to Rs 10,000. Mehta justified by the "Replacement cost theory" which argues that "Old companies should be valued on the basis of the amount of money which would be required to create another such company".

Through the second half of 1991, Mehta was the darling of the business media and earned the sobriquet of the 'Big Bull', who was said to have started the Bull Run. But nobody in the market could figure out the source of money for Mehta's investment.

The crucial mechanism through which the scam was effected was the Ready Forward (RF) deal. The RF is in essence a secured short-term loan (typically 15-day) from one bank to another. Crudely put, the bank lends against government securities just as a pawnbroker lends against jewellery. The borrowing bank actually sells the securities to the lending bank and buys them back at the end of the period of the loan, typically at a slightly higher price." It was this ready forward deal that Harshad Mehta and his cronies used with great success to channel money from the banking system.

A typical ready forward deal involved two banks brought together by a broker in lieu of a commission. The broker handles neither the cash nor the securities, though that wasn't the case in the lead-up to the scam. "In this settlement process, deliveries of securities and payments were made through the broker. That is, the seller handed over the securities to the broker, who passed them to the buyer, while the buyer gave the cheque to the broker, who then made the payment to the seller. In this settlement process, the buyer and the seller might not even know whom they had traded with, either being known only to the broker."

This the brokers could manage primarily because by now they had become market makers and had started trading on their account. To keep up a semblance of legality, they pretended to be undertaking the transactions on behalf of a bank. Another instrument used in a big way was the Bank Receipt (BR). In a ready forward deal, securities were not moved back and forth in actuality. Instead, the borrower, i.e. the seller of securities, gave the buyer of the securities a BR. A "BR" confirms the sale of securities. It acts as a receipt for the money received by the selling bank. Hence the name - bank receipt. It promises to deliver the securities to the buyer. It also states that in the meantime, the seller holds the securities in trust of the buyer.

Having figured this out, Mehta needed banks, which could issue fake BRs, or BRs not backed by any government securities? "Two small and little known banks - the Bank of Karad (BOK) and the Metropolitan Cooperative Bank (MCB) - came in handy for this purpose. These banks were willing to issue BRs as and when required, for a fee," ....

Once these fake BRs were issued, they were passed on to other banks and the banks in turn gave money to Mehta, obviously assuming that they were lending against government securities when this was not really the case. This money was used to drive up the prices of stocks in the stock market. When time came to return the money, the shares were sold for a profit and the BR was retired. The money due to the bank was returned.

The game went on as long as the stock prices kept going up, and no one had a clue about Mehta's modus operandi. Once the scam was exposed, though, a lot of banks were left holding BRs which did not have any value - the banking system had been swindled of a whopping Rs 4,000 crore (close to $ 1 billion)

The Harshad Mehta induced security scam, as the media sometimes termed it, adversely affected at least 10 major commercial banks of India, a number of foreign banks operating in India, and the National Housing Bank, a subsidiary of the Reserve Bank of India, which is the central bank of India.

A number of people holding key positions in the India's financial sector were adversely affected, which included arrest and sacking of K. M. Margabandhu, then CMD of the UCO Bank; removal from office of V. Mahadevan, one of the Managing Directors of India's largest bank, the State Bank of India.

The Central Bureau of Investigation which is India's premier investigative agency was entrusted with the task of deciphering the modus operandi and the ramifications of the scam. Harshad Mehta was arrested and investigations continued for a decade. During his judicial custody, while he was in Thane Prison, Mumbai, he complained of chest pain, and was moved to a hospital, where he died on 31 December 2001.

His death remains a mystery. Some believe that he was murdered ruthlessly by an underworld nexus (spanning several South Asian countries including Pakistan). Rumour has it that they suspected that part of the huge wealth that Harshad Mehta commanded at the height of the 1992 scam was still in safe hiding and thought that the only way to extract their share of the 'loot' was to pressurize Harshad's family by threatening his very existence.[citation needed] In this context, it might be noteworthy that a certain criminal allegedly connected with this nexus had inexplicably surrendered just days after Harshad was moved to Thane Jail and landed up in imprisonment in the same jail, in the cell next to Harshad Mehta's. [Source: CAclubindia – Harshad Mehta Scam - CA Manish K Dhoot (CA, B. Com, NCFM, CPCM) (5015 Points – 15 August, 2010.

Events that happened in seriatim in 1987-90, the period during which large funds were flushing with the PSUs, having mobilized them in large scale through issue of tax free bonds facilitated by the government policy of 1986 permitting the PSUs to mobilize their financial resources, there having been a cut in the budgetary support to them for their various development projects undertaken, to make up the gap to the extent possible. Funds so mobilized were found to be surplus with the PSUs due to there being no immediate necessity of capital expenditure. These funds caught the attention of the Ministry of Finance [MOF]. Hitherto, the surplus funds available with the PSUs were to be invested in Fixed Deposits [FDs] in the SBI and its then Associates and the nationalized banks as per the then prevailing policy of the government. This was continuing since long time.

Sometime in December, 1987, the MOF issued fresh instructions to the PSUs permitting them to invest their surplus funds in the government securities, public sector bonds and as deposit with the government. This was followed by another instruction in February, 1988 that specified what constituted the surplus funds with PSUs and allowing the PSUs to invest their surplus funds in the above financial instruments through the secondary market. The secondary market means, as noted in Part 01 of this book, the secondary securities sale and purchase mainly operated between the commercial banks and the recognized brokers. RBI issued new instructions in April, 1987 covering the changes in the matter of investments including entering into Ready Forward Deals and its working procedure.

The changes that thus took place in seriatim whether could be termed as prompting, tempting or coincidental in the circumstances is a matter best left to the MOF and RBI. The aftermath of those changes suggests they were of more tempting nature to the commercial banks, brokers and the Interest Groups actively associated with in the stock exchanges investments that were taking place. What is Interest Group has already been clarified before. The Stock Exchange Index suddenly started shooting up during 1989-91. The brokers were struggling for funds for their operation in the Stock Exchanges as the value of the shares continued to shoot upward. So also was the case of Interest Groups. This pressure was slowly building up on the brokers which lead the brokers to move fast in search of the additional funds for further firing up the stock exchange to create temptation to corporate and individual investors.

Once the commercial banks and brokers learnt about the relaxations made by the MOF in investment of surplus funds available with the PSUs in the instruments stated before, they spread out like birds in the sky and started reaching the doors of the PSUs having huge surplus funds. The brokers met top management people in the PSUs but the PSUs were found hesitant to accede to the suggestions/proposals of the brokers rather they were reluctant to deal with the brokers direct. The brokers having sensed this, moved fast to meet the bureaucrats and the politicians in position with a view to influencing the PSUs to associate with the brokers specialized in the secondary market while the PSUs had no experience, least the specialized knowledge, to deal in secondary market, Brokers interacted with the commercial banks to act in the front to enable them to secure the surplus funds from the PSUs so that they could facilitate the banks acting as their official brokers/agents. This was a midway the commercial banks and brokers found more appropriate in the circumstances.

Brokers convinced the bureaucrats and the politicians that the investment of the surplus funds with the PSUs could be done through the commercial banks [SBI and its then Associates and nationalized banks] including through the foreign banks. They succeeded in this and the PSUs were made to change their mind in favour of such investment process. PSUs had the powers according to their internal rules to deal with the brokers direct but except few, most of them did not opt for this and preferred to go through commercial banks. That was how the PSUs and their officials were caught in the spider web of the scam. The order of events is as given below:

In sum:

a. Brokers wanted to make deals with the commercial banks without the need for interchange of the securities held for obtaining loans.

b. Two nationalized banks introduced of their own the Bank Receipt [BR] system in place of securing the securities physically in 1986. This method stated to be the brain child of two former top executives of the Banks who died, first in 1991 and the second in 1992.

c. This started slowly expanding its wings among the other state owned banks.

d. RBI Auditors in the course of audit of the accounts of the two nationalized banks stated before found BR system as irregular pursuant to the RBI instructions to the Banks which provided for physical possession of securities.

e. Thus, such system prevailing among the commercial banks was in the knowledge of the RBI.

f. RBI also found that its own Public Debt Office [PDO} was entertaining the BR system in place of prescribed Subsidiary Ledger Form for interbank sale and purchase of government securities.

g. RBI made it clear in its instructions to the commercial banks that they must make interbank sale and purchase of government securities only through the prescribed SLA Form.

h. RBI also knew that there is no provision either under RBI Act, 1934 or the Banking Regulations Act, 1949 regarding the Bank Receipt [BR] used by the commercial banks and the brokers during the course of the securities scam, 1992.

i. RBI's permitting the use of BR as such was not in accordance with the provisions of the said Acts and, accordingly, the practice of using BR was irregular and in contravention of the provisions of the said Act. However, it could be said that the RBI had accepted the BR system under its deemed powers under the Act.

j. The commercial banks found it more convenient and comfortable to engage the brokers as intermediaries in the interbank sale and purchase of public sector bonds.

k. The commercial banks stated to have conveyed to the RBI their difficulty in the transfer of securities in physical terms for each interbank purchase and sale of the securities and wanted some other method that could be adopted while retaining the securities in physical form.

l. It was here that the RBI stated to have considered the matter and accepted the BR system being followed by the commercial bank and their brokers.

m. RBI also made it clear to them that the BR should be used only in the case of interbank sale and purchase of Public Sector Bonds.

n. RBI also stated to have informed the commercial banks and the Indian Bank Association [IBA] would be working out the format and its governing rules that needed to be adopted by the commercial banks.

o. The Indian Bank Association [IBA] worked out the standard BR Format together its governing Rules. Thus the format of BR and its governing rules were officialised.

p. The interbank sale and purchase of the public sector bonds were thus started taking place through BR system officially for interbank purchase and sale of public sector bonds through medium of the brokers of those banks.

q. The commercial banks and their official brokers started using the BR as the primary document in the interbank sale and purchase of public sector bonds and the need for possession of the bonds in physical terms was thus dispensed with.

r. The Brokers found it easy then to make the BR without in possession of the securities for obtaining loans and advances from the banks.

s. This method was tested by them first time with the Bank of Karad and Metropolitan Cooperative Bank functioning and operating in Maharashtra.

t. Such operational system was possible only after the brokers had made an implicit understanding with the high officials of the above banks, also with the understanding of compensating them for the same.

u. Brokers' stated to have maintained records of transactions of the beneficiaries in floppies and magnetic tapes including their names.

v. Stock Exchanges found dancing in the shares index shooting up day by day.

w. The investors in shares including the high profiles reaped the richness

x. The system so being followed exposed in the case of one large investment deal done between the SBI and Harshad Mehta.

y. Mehta defaulted in the deal.

z. This exploded through an article authored by an eminent journalist and published in the newspapers.

aa. That became the triggering point of the scam.

bb. The entire financial market in the country was jolted.

cc. The government ordered immediate investigation process by the investigating agency.

dd. The investigating agency raided the offices and premises of the brokers overnight and seized the incriminating documents including particularly the floppies and magnetic tapes maintained by them.

ee. These floppies and tapes as noted before had the details of shares made available to the high profiles through the contract notes but without any consideration being paid by them to Harshad Mehta and similarly to others.

ff. That seemed to have been the reason for the investigating agency to seize the floppies and the tapes immediately from the brokers' offices and premises.

gg. The whereabouts of the floppies and tapes not known, the same having not placed before the JPC.

hh. The names contained in the floppies were not placed before the JPC while all other documents and information sought for were complied with. This is based on assumption that there is no mention of the floppies and tapes having been placed during the JPC proceedings as no such information is available on the Website.

ii. That seemed to be the reason for the JPC to question some of the high profiles as accused and record its verdict, also allowing such high profile to submit his or her defense there itself. These have already been dealt in detail in other Part of this book.

jj. The investigating agency had the specialization in the investigating of the criminal cases but had no expertise in investigating financial frauds, scams and other nature of financial crimes.

kk. That being so, the investigating agency outsourced the services of the CAs and Financial Analysts in the examination of the investment transactions by the commercial banks, foreign banks and the brokers.

ll. RBI had wide powers to act upon the commercial banks but preferred to have remained silent as evident from the fact that it was in the know of the BR being used in 1986 and its use by the commercial banks in the later course of their operations including for interbank sale and purchase of government securities considered acceptable by its

Public Debt Office [PDO}, it did not act upon and, if acted upon, the course of the securities scam would have taken a different direction.

mm. The developments that were taking place were also in the knowledge of the government and the high profiles [as comes out during the questioning by JPC] who also preferred to remain silent.

nn. Perhaps it was thought by the government and the RBI that the developments in the stock exchanges would fizzle out of their own.

oo. They woke up when their silence turned into backfire in the financial market.

pp. The backfire reached its peak once the scam was exposed and made the individual investors to shiver and spend sleepless nights. They lost their fortune they built when the shares value was at the peak in the stock exchanges.

qq. There was no hue and cry as far as the high profiles that were holding shares which were gifted by the kingpin of the brokers and other brokers without any consideration.

rr. To assuage the investors' concerns and plight, RBI constituted a high level committee to go into all the aspects of the scam.[Janakiraman Committee].

ss. The outcry forced the government /parliament to constitute the Joint Parliamentary Committee.
tt. In this flood of scam, the innocents who were discharging their given duties in the PSUs and commercial banks were made front line victims of the scam.
uu. The top and middle level officers of the commercial banks who had links with the high profiles somehow managed to survive except few who were caught, criminal proceedings instituted and punished. Some of them meanwhile died. The process is still going on.
vv. There was not a single high profile consisting of bureaucrats and politicians against whom the investigating agency could take up the investigation let alone find any fault and they remained comfortable in their positions with whatever financial benefits they received.
ww. From the JPC proceedings that have been recaptured in the other Part of this book, one could see that not only the bureaucrats, also ministers were involved in the questioning by the JPC. That is self-explanatory about their possible involvement in the scam.
xx. Curiously, even those who were indicted by the JPC in its verdict remained untouched by the investigating agency.

yy. Some of the investors and accused innocents committed suicides leaving their families at the mercy of God.

zz. To the best of understanding, none of the officials of the RBI were subjected to criminal proceedings as no such information is available on the Website while the information about the criminal proceedings against the top management people of the government owned banks could be found on the Website.

aaa. The investigating agency registered the cases in the Hon'ble Courts with proceedings pending since more than thirty years that hardly mattered to the investigating agency.

bbb. The pending criminal cases against the innocent accused persons are now no body's concern.

ccc. There is none to feel the pinch and appreciate the physical, financial and mental agony of the innocent accused persons.

ddd. Who is innocent? One against whom there are no allegations in the Charge Sheet of the investigating agency registered in the Hon'ble Court of any recovery made during its raids of residential premises and the office premises of the accused or any of his or her family members or from his or her relatives. Nor, there is any allegation in the Charge Sheet of accused person having caused any financial loss to the organization he or she was serving.

eee. Most of the innocent accused persons died during the course of the trial.

fff. Those accused who are alive are in the age group of 75-87 years.

ggg. Their families and children are struggling for simple survival.

hhh. The innocent accused though living but they are livingly dead.

iii. Overall, the situation that was prevailing necessitating the scam was due to facilitation of the policies of the central government through the instructions issued on investment of surplus funds with PSUs, RBI lapses and officially using of the BR system.

jjj. RBI permitted the BR System in its Master Circulars which was contrary to the requirement of inter-bank sale and purchase of securities based on the physical possession, the only practice that was prevalent since long time and was valid in law.

kkk. RBI's oversight of the BR system was in contravention of the provisions of its own Act, the BR Act, 1949 and other applicable law such as the Contract Act, 1872.

lll. The lives of the innocent officers of PSUs who were unaware of the banking intriguing operational aspects were pawned with their career as property and continue to be held by the investigating agency until the judgment day.

mmm. It also suggests that the authorities maintained perceptible silence on the happenings in the financial market that encouraged both the banks and brokers to play the game as they wished.

nnn. Those responsible for the checking and controlling the onset of the scam did not timely act which was not only unfortunate but also signalled leniency on their part passing on the entire blame on the PSUs and commercial banks which was unfair on their part. Also known as 'blame game' which has been explained in the earlier part of this book?

ooo. This also could be perceivable in the questioning and proceedings of the JPC as reported in the newspapers as also incorporated in its Findings in the Report. The cover up seemed to be more dominant than action on the part of the authorities concerned.

ppp. This sums up and self-explains the officially initiated policy measures on investment of surplus funds of PSUs and introduction of the BR System were, if not direct but impacted indirect compulsions for the birth of the scam in the financial market making the PSUs, the commercial banks as the central point for shooting game.

qqq. No amount of efforts and technological advancements can change the banking and financial frauds and scams occurring recurrently unless the humans change in theirs heart; there is no such heart today in the humans who want to make hay while sun shines that covers all the spheres of life of humans including the self-greed, political greed, the corporate greed and institutional greed and above all the governance greed.

rrr. The frauds and scams will continue to be there in the life of a nation because the citizens involved or learning to involve in such crimes refuse to change themselves that happens when their Conscience dominates them in their life.

sss. The scams and frauds, as the history speaks, are the result of the political, bureaucratic and corporate games that act as necessary tool for their survival.

ttt. Let us stop talking about the scams and frauds and let us continue to analyse and assess the impact of the scams on the citizens and the economy after they have occurred, one after the other.

uuu. Why should we blame illiterate criminals who indulge in crimes of different nature when the highly literate people indulge in

vvv.   the financial frauds and scams having much larger impact as a whole?

vvv.   The high profiles [Interest Groups] are a distinct class in themselves and the Exceptions are considered as rule and under the relevant laws in their cases and are thus made to escape the process of criminal proceedings and punishment. Seen from this angle, the rule of law is a laughing stock for such people.

www.   Whereas, the rule of law is enforced in letter and spirit carefully reading the commas, semi-colons and full stops in the case of ordinary citizens and the interpretations are made on that basis to charge the person on one or the other excuse.

xxx.   This kind of treatment is no less than completely curtailing the Liberty of such person under the Constitution.

yyy.   It cannot be said that the Constitution has nothing to do with law of innocence under the criminal law.

That term the "Presumption of innocence" sometimes refers by the Latin words as Ei Incumbit probatio qui dicit, non qui negat(the burden of proof is on the one who declares, not on one who denies), it should be known as that one principle which considered innocent unless proven guilty. Or can say that the burden of proof is on the person who is proved guilty and we cannot say him guilty unless he should be proved. Up to that he/she is innocent. This type of principle has been seen in those countries where his executorial system is prevalent. In the European countries, the Inquisitorial principle or those principles which were based on the enquiry is not being followed. But contrary to our country India as per the Indian laws, many of the countries take his accused as an offender until he proved guilty. So, our country India having the executorial system, our country's laws are able to accept both of these principles.

"I PREFER A PRISON FULL OF CRIMINALS THAN A GRAVEYARD FULL OF INNOCENT PEOPLE." - JAIR BOLSONARO. This aptly applies to the innocent people who were deliberately converted to have committed the crime in the securities scam. The investigating agency must read this Quote to understand the in-depth sentimental feelings and insulting injuries to the innocent humans made to suffer all through their life.

The Securities Scam 1992 is history by now and many learned authors have authored books on this subject matter. Even the film series have recently been made. These series focussed on the kingpin of the scam that did not bring the hidden Truth because the film series makers did not make backward journey where the Truth was concealed. What the kingpin did was illegal but it was the culmination of the contribution made by other actors associated in the scam including the high profiles and the Interest Groups. This seems to have not been reminisced. I believe the film has refreshed the viewers' mind and most of them enjoyed the film. I extend my congratulations to the series makers for this achievement and wish them all the success in their future efforts. I wish if the film series on the scams and frauds also, apart from showing the real happenings in the nation, include in such film series that awaken the

Consciousness and Conscience of the citizens that have the capacity to control the scams and frauds. The positive part of anything can be appreciated only when the negative part and its effects become known.

"Education is a companion which no misfortune can depress, no crime can destroy, no enemy can alienate, no despotism can enslave. At home, a friend, abroad, an introduction, in solitude a solace and in society an ornament. It chastens vice, it guides virtue, it gives at once grace and government to genius. Without it, what is man? A splendid slave, reasoning savage." — Joseph Addison

Let the film series on scams and frauds bring what is said in the above Quote into the light while making the series that goes a long way in educating the people, the last call of humans to stop all kinds of crimes for; lack of education denies the basic needs of human life, the employment opportunities, self-earning capacity, self-security, self-respect and self-dignity - the ultimate cherishment of humans. Here, the education means not merely the acquiring of the qualifications and degrees; there are certain things which stand much higher than qualification and degrees, as integral part of the education system and one's life – dharma, values, virtues, conduct, character, honesty, integrity and many more but who cares for them today while imparting the artificially prescribed education system. The film makers and the electronic media have all the prerequisite credentials and means to cultivate the citizens to practice those values residing in Mother Earth but gradually being detached by the humans while all the other Living Beings are bound by their own conduct and character. Without these values, our democracy will continue to be on Rope Dancing not knowing when it would lose its balance.

Let us not blame the culture of democracy we are practising presently which is meanest in its every sense. This has been made so mainly by the political class and religious bodies whose business is to keep the blame games alive for self-survival and not for the survival of the democracy. One would know the difference between democracy and dictatorship if one had tasted the dictatorship. The fundamental rights including our liberty and freedom we boast today as a democratic country would have been buried beneath the ground if we were to experience the dictatorship. I touched here all this just to make understand what is the real value of education one should learn and earn for one's own survival with the self-respect and self-dignity. Education minus those values is equal to zero value. "…..Conscience is a person's considered and sincere judgment about right and wrong, and an enlightened constitutional regime would try to protect it from regulation' – Steven D. Smith. To understand this, one has to cultivate the values of life stated before as part of the education system. Bifurcation of the stated life values from the education system would make the human body a barren land.

The scam left behind blurs and scars on thousands of innocent people, an act not open to any excuse by the most suffered people while there was not even need for excusing, let alone criminal proceedings, against those who were involved in the scam [Interest Groups] rather even were responsible for necessitating scam.

The authorities and the investigating agency could take great pride in ultimately pinning down the scam but that was prejudicial not being based on the Truth and this will continue to chase one and all that associated and facilitated the scam, the others in the scam were bystanders but dragged into the scam. Many received rich dividend while many others lost what they had in hand with precarious future awaiting for them. The bygone days that inflicted intentional injuries on the innocent people will never die and will continue to confront the people who have done wrong.

Have SEBI, RBI, and IRDAI Been Effective Regulators?

31 years later, a few bitter facts about scams and financial markets remain relevant. The most important fact is that the average Indian continues to be extremely vulnerable to such scams and millions have lost almost all their savings to them.

Second, regulators like the Securities Exchange Board of India (SEBI), the Reserve Bank of India, and the Insurance Regulatory & Development Authority of India do play their role as watchdogs; but there is a big question mark over their effectiveness as regulators.

Third, the advent of Big Data, the Internet, Artificial Intelligence, and the like, will encourage scammers to become more active.

However, as it was important to have a regulator for the stock markets, SEBI was formed in January 1992, just a few months before the scam broke out. The scam led to SEBI announcing a series of measures to prevent such market manipulation by financial predators.

The question is: did regulators learn any lessons from the Harshad Mehta scam? Did SEBI succeed in its mission to prevent a repeat of such scams? Not by a long shot.

B3) Reasons for the Reoccurrence of Security Scam in 2001 Inspite of Guidelines Issued by RBI in 1992

The Committee did not have the benefit of a report on the lines of the Janakiraman Committee Report which was made available to the previous JPC on the scam in securities and banking transactions. Reliable evidence was difficult to find and took much time to cull. The Committee had to rely on a number of reports that dealt with specific and limited subjects. The enquiry reports of the regulators also displayed many gaps which had to be filled by securing answers to a very large number of questions asked by the Committee. The Special Cell constituted by the Ministry of Finance in June, 1994 to investigate the nexus between brokers and industrial houses in pursuance of the recommendation of the earlier JPC having gone defunct since May 22, 1995, without coming out with any tangible findings or recommendations for remedial action, is one of the examples of apathy on the part of different agencies and departments concerned. The Committee were informed by the Central Board of Direct Taxes that on May 19, 1995 the DGIT (Investigation), Bombay, who headed the Special Cell, had sought from CBDT adequate empowerment and administrative support for the Cell in the absence of which the Cell was unlikely to reach to any firm conclusions about the role of any one or more industrial houses in comprehensive manner but the Chairman, CBDT, in his response thereto had suggested that due to limited scope of task of the Special Cell no additional manpower was required. …………..

It is the considered view of the Committee [JPC 2001] that the lack of progress in implementing the recommendations of the last Joint Parliamentary Committee set up in 1992 to enquire into Irregularities in Securities and Banking Transactions emboldened wrong-doers and unscrupulous elements to indulge in financial misconduct. The Special Cell constituted by the Ministry of Finance in June 1994 to investigate the nexus between brokers and industrial houses in pursuance of the recommendation of the previous Committee having gone defunct since 22 May 1995, without coming out with any tangible findings or recommendations for remedial action, is one of the examples of apathy on the part of different agencies and departments concerned. The Committee express their concern at the way the supervisory authorities have been performing their role and the regulators have been exercising their regulatory responsibilities………..

B4) Mr R Janakiraman's (Ex Deputy Governor of RBI) views on the Reoccurrence of a Security Scam in India and Corporate Governance in this regard.

"New brains are out to circumvent rules in the system. Politicians and politics have a major role to play. There is a pressure in PSUs to hire every X, Y and Z and hence overstaffing and inefficiency. They have become more commercial in operations. These workers are also inefficient and have no incentive to work hard. As much as how good work is not rewarded so are mistakes not found out and corrected. While people in major banks are paid less they have no initiative to work hard. In order to prevent another scam from happening a more comprehensive set of guidelines have to be prepared. Master Circulars have to be made available to bankers so that they work honestly and efficiently. In India justice is so much delayed and people often fall into old ways without following guidelines

I have reproduced above article not to burden readers but to enlighten them how the scams erupt and the contributory factors therefor. A cursory perusal of the in-depth study, analysis and findings made in the article suggest that the scams do not happen one time but every time because they are made to happen; the basic actors and characterstics remain the same and the findings of the JPCs, filing of Action Taken Reports [ATRs] by the government have become perfunctory. This understanding comes out clearly from the observations of the JPC in 2001 that the government agencies and regulatory bodies hardly bothered to realize the lapses that occurred in the scam of 1992, the enormous efforts put by the JPC then constituted for that purpose to dig them out which called immediate implementation and making up the deficiencies in the governmental and regulatory systems. That was not done as it is borne out from the observations of the said JPC [2001] which, even went to the extent of noting that if the regulatory body acted timely on the findings on scam of 1992 would have avoided the scam of 2001. Does it suggest that there should be another higher body over the regulatory bodies to consider whether or not the findings of the Parliamentary Committees are effectively implemented? That is not possible because that is not the solution to the problem of partial or non-implementation of the fundamental findings of the parliamentary committee or, for that matter, the departmental committees. The irregularities in both cases were found to be similar which should not have happened if the findings of earlier committees had been duly implemented and overseen. That can be hoped for but doesn't happen, we having been cultivating and practising the frauds and scam as a matter of habit and the regulatory authorities are cultivating and practising advisory role and not ultimate role of action that is what comes out from the observations made by the JPC stated before.

"Ghosts don't haunt us. That's not how it works. They're present among us because we won't let go of them." - Sue Grafton

The scam was like inviting the wandering ghosts into the home for sumptuous dinner without thinking what the ghosts would do after the dinner is over that is what comes out of this book. Let the cat out of the bag that was the humble endeavour of this book.

The Bank Receipt [BR] was the epicentre of the scam and the devil in disguise that enriched some, worsened the wealth of some others, trapped and victimized the innocents into criminal cage. My salute to the efforts made by the investigating agency though it misleads itself in search of the truth.

The in-depth analysis that has been made and presented in the earlier parts and in this part of this book compels one to think that the scam was conceived one. When, where, how who conceived now emerges, based on what has been submitted so far in this book, as its conception was rooted in the seriatim events that took place in 1987 both at the MOF and RBI levels, opening and tempting the path for scam. This cannot be refuted, the statement being supported by the communications in writing. MOF cannot give up responsibility on its lapse to also have issued suitable guidelines to the PSUs on the operational aspects of the secondary market it permitted them to enter into from 1988 onwards knowing well that the PSUs had no expertize in that respect having been investing their surplus funds in the FDs thereto before also as per instructions of the MOF. For want of this, the PSUs had no option but depend upon the commercial banks that used the brokers. Just before that first set of BR transaction that took place between the two nationalized banks in 1986 was in the nature of a trial. RBI had come to know of it but did not act under the relevant provisions of its Act that sent a wrong message to the other commercial banks, the smell of which also spread among the brokers' community. It was further facilitated with the RBI issuing fresh instructions to the commercial banks on dealing with their investment portfolio including ready forward deals in 1987. Together, these events clearly point to the existence of some rapport among the concerned government authorities and the RBI officials that lead interactions with the leading brokers of the time. The allegations made by a leading broker against the then Prime Minister pepped up the need for instant action of revengeful nature against the brokers which also encircled the commercial banks and the PSUs.

It is worth noting here that the Ninth and Tenth National Elections were held in 1989 and 1991, the same years during which the securities scam started brewing up in the background. That bares the truth about the close involvement of the ministers, politicians, political parties and bureaucrats, corporate and brokers as part of the efforts to amass money that was direly needed for use in those elections. Elections without money mean a body without flesh.

That lead to peeping into what was going on in the backyard of the government system sooner the MOF came to know about the huge surplus funds lying with the PSUs that had built up in 1986-1991 during which period, besides the financial resources mobilized by the PSUs by issue of public sector bonds to make up their resource gap, also created availability of additional financial resources when some of the PSUs especially the PSUs in oil sector raised funds from the multilateral financing agencies at the instance of the government considering the precarious financial position that was prevailing in 1990-91. The allegations made against the former Prime Minister opened the sidewalk space for his ministers and bureaucrats to go a bit further to explore the scope through the commercial banks and brokers combined and exploit the opportunities for investment of the large surplus funds through a new channel. Chandra Swami, a reference about whom has been made before who was close to the former Prime Minister as also had close links with the stock market activities, became handy to the ministers and the bureaucrats.

The policy changes in investment of surplus funds with PSUs that followed in 1987 and 1988 read with the fresh instructions issued by the RBI to the commercial banks on their investment portfolio in 1987 created an environment that facilitated the financial market to take different turn where by the government instructions opened up the doors for PSUs for investment of their surplus funds in the government securities and the public sector bonds through the secondary market being operated between the commercial banks and the brokers. So the temptation suddenly came up among the commercial banks and, naturally among the broking community. PSUs lacked knowledge in operation of the secondary market having not entered into that area any time in the past, considered it appropriate to route their surplus funds through the commercial banks. RBI was aware of this and the critical question that confronted the commercial banks was shuffling and reshuffling of the securities held physically within the interbank operations permitted by the RBI in its fresh instructions stated before through the medium of their official brokers.

This hurdle stated to be brought to the notice of the RBI. So far as the government securities were concerned, the system already existed for purchase and sale of the government securities through Subsidiary Ledger Account [SLA] mode that provided for filling up the prescribed form regarding the interbank purchase and sale and filing it with PDO in the RBI which made record of such transactions in the SLA. The real problem was with respect to the public sector bonds for which the commercial banks were looking for advice from the RBI. The BR concept having already been introduced between the two nationalized banks stated before, though it was considered irregular during inspection by the RBI officers but allowed to continue its operation when RBI did not stop its recurrence. This facility did not necessitate physical transfer of the interbank purchase and sale of public sector bonds through the brokers.

Thus, the BR became as part of the system followed by the commercial banks and brokers, however, in the meanwhile, RBI seems to have sounded the Indian Banks Association [IBR] to work out the standard format of the

BR and the rules that govern the BR. This was done by the IBA in May, 1991 and circulated the BR Format together with rules governing it that enabled the commercial banks to uniformly adopt and operate the investment deals. The buyers of the securities that consisted most of the PSUs having surplus funds were to be searched out by the brokers and brought together with the commercial banks for effecting the sale through the BR basis. This became a routine operational process among the commercial banks, brokers and the buyers that offered scope for the brokers to take their own position in place of the commercial banks and convincing the PSUs that they were operating as official brokers of the commercial banks and had the authority to deal with the PSUs direct in finalization of the investments deals. PSUs also got it confirmed orally or in writing from the concerned commercial banks.

This enabled the brokers to collect also the cheques made and issued by the PSUs for investment of their surplus funds for which BRs were received by the PSUs within next couple of days duly completed and signed by the two authorized signatories of the concerned commercial bank. The cheques were drawn in favour of the investment bank crossed as A/c Payee and were to be credited in their accounts. The brokers having taken official position and having collected the cheques from the investing PSUs deposited the cheques in their local banks, most of whom were foreign banks having latest transfer facility of the funds to the banks located outside Delhi in whose name the cheques were issued. The brokers requested these banks to credit the cheque in their accounts with some agreed terms of understanding and considered such credits as part of their banking operations according to their own internal rules and system. This is where the scam struck. The amount of the cheques in some cases was transferred to the bank in whose name it was issued crossed as A/c Payee was also credited into the brokers account in their bank under their own understanding, the fact of which was not known to the PSUs. The investment operations went likewise and the reality came to light when the scam broke out. It was then that the government ordered the investigating agency to immediately start investigation. The subsequent events became known to the individual investors as the matter entered the public domain.

The financial scam of 1992 was a daylight loot scam when the fraudulent acts and deeds were done before the eyes and under the nose of the authorities who remained silent all through whereas they had the knowledge of what was going on among the commercial banks and the brokers in the secondary market and the stock exchange but did not act upon at the right time and, if that would have been done, not only the further damage would have been controlled, the mischiefs of the miscreants would have been exposed much earlier than awaiting till 1992. That was the right opportunity which was crossed over due to inaction on the part of the authorities concerned. There were thus two occasions, the first in 1986 and later much before 1992 to have prevented the scam but the same were overlooked.

The Bank Receipt [BR] which was found to be real culprit in the entire scam was known to the RBI in 1986 when RBI could have swung into action to check the status prevailing in other commercial banks. There was no control over the foreign banks who were the creators of the scam with openly defying the policy guidelines issued by the RBI on the plea that those were not in consonance with the banking practice they understood and followed. This thinking had already spread among the nationalized commercial banks who tied up with their brokers for operation of the public sector bonds in the secondary market which was officially permitted. The modus operandi was kept secret between the commercial banks and the brokers that denied any knowledge of such happening to the PSUs who remained dormant and continued to comply with the government instructions on the investment of surplus funds. Such dealings were considered by the investigating agency which was also aware of the instructions issued by the Ministry of Finance to PSUs as conspiracy.

Could it be said that the procedure so followed by the PSUs was illegal and, if that was illegal, then the entire process followed by the commercial banks duly permitted by the RBI was also illegal. PSUs acted in accordance with the instructions of the MOF on investment of surplus funds and there was hardly any need for them to ascertain the legality aspects of the BR, the investment transactions being done through the commercial banks.

Those who had actually misused the BRs in the commercial banks in collusion with their brokers did commit criminal offence. Those from whom the investigating agencies made recoveries during its raids also committed criminal offence. Also, those who caused financial loss to the organization on that account also committed criminal offence. But those from whom no recoveries were made during the raids nor those who did not cause any financial loss to the organization they were serving, they did not commit any criminal offence that were also considered by the investigating agency as having committed offence. I am submitting all these matters not as arguments before the Court of Law but in this book to make understand the entire reality of the securities scam.

The Janakiraman Committee Report was a post mortem report but in that it had pointed out lapses on the part of the commercial banks and the foreign banks but not on lapses of the RBI which constituted the Committee. That is self-explanatory.

The JPC did go into the depth of the scam and its process of examination of the all the relevant documents, information and material as well as the very questioning of the high profiles as accused in its capacity as Court was admirable. That process did bring out the exposure of the high profiles, few of them, having been subjected to close examination. The findings of the JPC also included the serious lapses on the part of the MOF and the RBI which, combined together, also suggests about something having went wrong somewhere officially that lead to the scam. The brokers had obliged them, the details in respect of which understood to have been recorded in the floppies and magnetic tapes maintained by the brokers which were immediately seized by the investigating agency the moment the scam was broke out. That is also self-explanatory.

All the circumstances submitted before in this book point to the fact that the scam occurred not in the ordinary course but in an extraordinary course where the lapses on the part of the authorities were dominant but action was dormant. Those who were indicted by the JPC in its verdict were singled out by the investigating agency from the criminal proceedings. The JPC having authority to give its findings and make recommendations to stop such scams in future did not have powers to take the action against the indicted persons that are vested in the government.

The investigating agency seems to have considered the selectivity is more important for it than the sensitivity to act against those who were involved in the scam. There is nothing wrong with law in this respect but the law is in the hands of its enforcing authorities and what they consider appropriate is right. They pounce upon the ordinary citizens and pause over the high profiles whenever there is breach of law committed by both. This is the inherent weakness of the investigating and law enforcement agencies in our country. We are subjugated people since centuries, for reason of which the law enforcing authorities have learnt to be discriminative in every walk of life and the citizens as subjugates have become used to such kind of treatment. Questioning such treatment involves approaching the courts of law which is time consuming and financially dragging. There is no system in our country that assures the citizens relief within a reasonable time limit.

Fate is never fair. You are caught in a current much stronger than you are; struggle against it and you'll drown not just yourself but those who try to save you. Swim with it. and you'll survive." – Cassandra Clare

REFERENCES

1. JPC yet to start questioning any of securities scam accused – INDIA TODAY - ZAFAR AGHA - ISSUE DATE: Sep 15, 1992 | UPDATED: Aug 1, 2013 13:38 IST.
2. JPC grapples to uncover country's biggest financial scam – INDIA TODAY - W.P.S Sidhu - ISSUE DATE: Sep 30, 1992 | UPDATED: Aug 21, 2013 12:38 IST.
3. Securities scam: Manmohan Singh emerges from JPC crisis with stronger backing for reforms – INDIA TODAY - ZAFAR AGHA, Yubaraj Ghimire - ISSUE DATE: Jan 15, 1994 | UPDATED: Jul 2, 2013 15:03 IST.
4. JPC probe on securities scam: Secretariat prepares messy draft report – INDIA TODAY - SHEFALI BHIMAL - ISSUE DATE: May 15, 1993 | UPDATED: Aug 8, 2013 19:25 IST.
5. Securities scam: Top government functionaries also accused by JPC – INDIA TODAY - SHEFALI BHIMAL, DAKSESH PARIKH - ISSUE DATE: Jan 15, 1994 | UPDATED: Jul 2, 2013 14:50 IST.
6. In Harshad Mehta's wake – Frontline - Published : Jan 19, 2002 00:00 IST - PRAVEEN SWAMI IN MUMBAI.
7. Stocks scam: Bankers p[lay the blame game – INDIA TODAY - RAHUL PATHAK - ISSUE DATE: Oct 31, 1992 | UPDATED: Aug 16, 2013 18:51 IST.

8. RAJYA SABHA (1992) Point of privilege Attempt to influence some members of a Joint Parliamentary Committee by a Minister and a Government official.
9. Securities scam: Manmohan Singh pleads 'not guilty' to all charges made by JPC – INDIA TODAY - ALAM SRINIVAS - ISSUE DATE: Jan 15, 1994 | UPDATED: Jul 2, 2013 14:46 IST.
10. More ministers involved in securities scam as JPC extracts more confessions – INDIA TODAY - W.P.S Sidhu - ISSUE DATE: Nov 15, 1992 | UPDATED: Aug 14, 2013 16:19 IST.
11. Government of India Ministry of Finance - 27th PROGRESS REPORT ON THE ACTION TAKEN PURSUANT TO THE RECOMMENDATIONS OF THE JOINT PARLIAMENTARY COMMITTEE ON STOCK MARKET SCAM AND MATTERS RELATING THERETO December, 2016.
12. Government of India Ministry of Finance - PROGRESS OF OGRESS OF OGRESS OF THE ACTION TAKEN PURSUANT TO THE RECOMMENDATIONS OF TIONS OF JOINT P JOINT PARLIAMENT ARLIAMENTARY COMMITTEE ON STOCK MARKET SCAM AND MATTERS RELATING THERETO December 2003 December 2003.
13. Government of India Ministry of Finance 11TH PROGRESS REPORT ON THE ACTION TAKEN PURSUANT TO THE RECOMMENDATIONS OF THE JOINT PARLIAMENTARY COMMITTEE ON STOCK MARKET SCAM AND MATTERS RELATING THERETO December, 2008.

14. Government of India Ministry of Finance 12TH PROGRESS REPORT ON THE ACTION TAKEN PURSUANT TO THE RECOMMENDATIONS OF THE JOINT PARLIAMENTARY COMMITTEE ON STOCK MARKET SCAM AND MATTERS RELATING THERETO June, 2009.
15. The Securities Scam- In document The Insider's View - Memoirs of a Public Servant - Javid Chowdhury (Page 81-90) – 1Library Website.
16. Government of India Ministry of Finance 12TH PROGRESS REPORT ON THE ACTION TAKEN PURSUANT TO THE RECOMMENDATIONS OF THE JOINT PARLIAMENTARY COMMITTEE ON STOCK MARKET SCAM AND MATTERS RELATING THERETO June, 2009.
17. Government of India Ministry of Finance 30th PROGRESS REPORT ON THE ACTION TAKEN PURSUANT TO THE RECOMMENDATIONS OF THE JOINT PARLIAMENTARY COMMITTEE ON STOCK MARKET SCAM AND MATTERS RELATING THERETO July, 2018.
18. Government of India Ministry of Finance SEVENTH PROGRESS REPORT ON THE ACTION TAKEN PURSUANT TO THE RECOMMENDATIONS OF THE JOINT PARLIAMENTARY COMMITTEE ON STOCK MARKET SCAM AND MATTERS RELATING THERETO December 2006.
19. Government of India Ministry of Finance 8TH PROGRESS REPORT ON THE ACTION TAKEN PURSUANT TO THE RECOMMENDATIONS OF THE JOINT PARLIAMENTARY COMMITTEE ON

STOCK MARKET SCAM AND MATTERS RELATING THERETO May 2007.
20. Government of India Ministry of Finance SIXTH PROGRESS REPORT ON THE ACTION TAKEN PURSUANT TO THE RECOMMENDATIONS OF THE JOINT PARLIAMENTARY COMMITTEE ON STOCK MARKET SCAM AND MATTERS RELATING THERETO May 2006.
21. Government of India Ministry of Finance 9TH PROGRESS REPORT ON THE ACTION TAKEN PURSUANT TO THE RECOMMENDATIONS OF THE JOINT PARLIAMENTARY COMMITTEE ON STOCK MARKET SCAM AND MATTERS RELATING THERETO December, 2007.
22. Government of India Ministry of Finance FOURTH PROGRESS REPORT ON THE ACTION TAKEN PURSUANT TO THE RECOMMENDATIONS OF THE JOINT PARLIAMENTARY COMMITTEE ON STOCK MARKET SCAM AND MATTERS RELATING THERETO July 2005.
23. Government of India Ministry of Finance THIRD PROGRESS REPORT ON THE ACTION TAKEN PURSUANT TO THE RECOMMENDATIONS OF THE JOINT PARLIAMENTARY COMMITTEE ON STOCK MARKET SCAM AND MATTERS RELATING THERETO December 2004.
24. The scam economy – INDIA TODAY - Sudeep Chakravarti - ISSUE DATE: Dec 21, 2015 | UPDATED: Dec 11, 2015 13:34 IST.
25. The RBI Act, 1934.
26. The Banking Regulations Act, 1949.

27. Janakiraman report makes alarming revelations about modus operandi of foreign banks – INDIA TODAY - DAKSESH PARIKH - ISSUE DATE: Sep 30, 1992 | UPDATED: Aug 21, 2013 13:59 IST.
28. Securities Scam: Genesis, Mechanics and Impact Samir K. Barua & Jayanth R. Varma Indian Institute of Management Ahmedabad, India 380 015 Reproduced with the permission of Vikalpa, the journal of the Indian Institute of Management, Ahmedabad, in which the paper was first published (January-March 1993, 18(1), 3-12).
29. Bhatia, Sanjay (1993) "Securities Scam-A legal Perspective," National Law School of India Review: Vol. 5: Iss. 1, Article 9.
30. 'Mystery' deaths in scandals – The Telegraph Online – Our Correspondent - Published 16.03.11, 06:30 PM/Friday, 26 May 2023.
31. Playing the game: Scams & Frauds – Summary Reads – Follow – November 14, 2020.
32. In fact: RBI head and crisis manager during 1991 BOP turmoil – The Indian Express - Written by Shaji Vikraman - Updated: April 5, 2017 18:07 IST.
33. Scam 1992 Explained: How Harshad Mehta, brokers and banks gamed the system – CNBC TV18 - By Santosh Nair   Mar 25, 2022 10:37:17 AM IST (Updated).
34. CBI closes in on Harshad Mehta, securities scam likely to net bureaucrats and politicians – INDIA TODAY - DAKSESH PARIKH - ISSUE DATE: Jun 15, 1992 | UPDATED: Aug 26, 2013 17:53 IST.
35. 1991 Indian economic crisis – Wikipedia.

36. https://in.search.yahoo.com/search?fr=mcafee&type=E211IN1494G0&p=RBI+Notifications+on+Janakiraman+Committee+Recommendations.
37. The Psychology of Scapegoating - Neel Burton, MD – Psychology Today – December 21, 2013.
38. https://in.search.yahoo.com/search?fr=mcafee&type=E211IN1494G0&p=RS%3D0c+%5BAnnexure+VI+issued+by+RBI%5D+SGL+and+BR
39. Legal Structures for Voluntary and Community Groups - 1 Jul 2013 Denise Copeland Last updated: 6 Jul 2022.
40. CAN A PUBLIC INTEREST WRIT PETITION UNDER ARTICLE 226 OF THE COI BE MAINTAINED BY AN UNREGISTERED ASSOCIATION? – Shivam Goel, Founder Partner at Lex Unified; Senior Editor at Legal Maxim – June26, 2020.
41. Indian Stock Market Scam 1992 – 13angle Website.
42. IBA - Association Without Any Accountability & Responsibility - by S, Ramachandran - AllBankingSolutions.com - 3rd September, 2015 – Letter to Union Finance Minister.
43. "Rules framed by IBA for BR provided that the security was deliverable later as soon as possible preferably within 90 days extendable by fresh issue of BR against old BR." - INDIAN BANKS' ASS I' ION - No. OPR.C/52-20/1039 6th May. 1991. Chief Executives of All Member Banks [Format of BR not attached though mentioned therein].
44. Have no authority over banks: IBA – The Times of India - TNN / Oct 7, 2019, 04:00 IST.
45. Unincorporated association – Wikipedia.

46. Tax Guru – Indian Banks Association is a public authority under RTI Act, 2005 - 13 November, 2017.
47. What Is an Unincorporated Non-profit Association (UNA)? – Legal Match Website.
48. Why is Indian Banks' Association not under RTI? – Business Line - Updated - February 25, 2021 at 09:28 PM.
49. Fairgrowth Financial's executives own up to company's involvement in securities scam – INDIA TODAY - UPDATED: Aug 23, 2013 16:43 IST.
50. www.taxguru.in Complaint No. CIC/MP/C/2015/000044 Complaint No. CIC/MP/C/2016/00123 - Shri R K Jain V/S Indian Bank Association (IBA) Ms. Ita Bose V/S Indian Bank Association (IBA).
51. Letter dated December, 1987 from Secretary Expenditure, Ministry of Finance regarding investment of surplus funds of PSUs.
52. Letter dated February, 1988 from the Additional Secretary Expenditure, Ministry of Finance regarding further instructions on investment of surplus funds PSUs.
53. Indian Banks Association and RTI – IAS Parliament – February 21, 2017.
54. Of Truth by Francis Bacon | Summary, Analysis, Explanations - August 13, 2021 by Somnath Sarkar – e-Literature.
55. What Is a Bank Receipt? - *K. Kinsella* - Last Modified Date: May 15, 2023 – Smart Capital Mind Website.
56. CIC Order on Complaint No. CIC/MP/C/2015/000044 Complaint No. CIC/MP/C/2016/00123 - Shri R K Jain

V/S Indian Bank Association (IBA) Ms. Ita Bose V/S Indian Bank Association (IBA].
57. Legal concept of association of persons – Financial Express - Written by HP Ranina
October 12, 2008 01:54 IST.
58. Harshad Mehta – Wikipedia.
59. Investopedia - Modus Operandi: Meaning and Understanding a Business' M.O - By WILL KENTON - Updated September 12, 2022 - Reviewed by KHADIJA KHARTIT - Fact checked by KATRINA MUNICHIELLO.
60. Decoding The Harshad Mehta Stock Market Scam of 1992 – Research & Ranking Website.
61. Policy, Organisation and Society - : Bill Damachis (1994) The Bombay Securities Scam of 1992: The Systemic and Structural Origins, Policy, Organisation and Society, 7:1, 40-45, DOI: 10.1080/10349952.1994.11876795.
62. 1992 Indian Stock Market Scam – Wikipedia.
63. The Worst Financial Scam in Indian History.
64. Munich Personal RePEc Archive [MPRA] - Financial Market Regulation-Security Scams In India with historical evidence and the role of corporate governance Narayanan, Supreena Madras School Of Economics 22 April 2004 –
65. Harshad Mehta Scam CA Manish K Dhoot (CA, B. Com, NCFM, CPCM) (5015 Points) 15 August 2010.
66. April, Scam, and the Big Bull: Have Regulators Learnt From Harshad Mehta's Case? –The Quint - YASHWANT DESHMUKHSUTANU GURU - Published: 25 Apr 2023, 6:00 PM IST.

67. Science Arena Publications International journal of Business Management [SCI] -
68. Impact of Securities and Financial Scams on Regulatory Framework Ms. Pooja Sharma Assistant, professor, Lovely Professional University, Jalandhar.
69. Securities scam: No info about our governor of that time, says RBI – DNA - | Edited By: |Source: PTI |Updated: Mar 17, 2018, 05:47 AM IST.
70. Who is Swamiji in scam 1992? - https://thetradebond.com/swamiji-in-scam-1992-harshad-mehta/
71. Trade Brains - Harshad Mehta Scam- How one man deceived entire Dalal Street? - by Aron Almeida | Mar 5, 2023 | Market, News
72. Indian Economy - What is Board for Financial Supervision (BFS)? - tojo jose - January 7, 2017.
73. Press Information Bureau - Government of India - Ministry of Finance - Powers of Reserve Bank of India (RBI) - 08 JAN 2019 5:24PM by PIB Delhi.
74. The Harshad Mehta Scam of 1992.- Marketfeed Team - Oct 13.
75. CBI is nothing more than its political master's slave – Deccan Herald - Josy Joseph, OCT 28 2018, 00:28 ISTUPDATED: OCT 28 2018, 02:20 IST.
76. Securities scandal: Harshad Mehta being put behind bars, millions lose their fortune – INDIA TODAY - DAKSESH PARIKH, ARUN KATIYAR - ISSUE DATE: Jun 30, 1992 | UPDATED: Aug 23, 2013 16:34 IST.
77. India Before 1991.in – 1991 Crisis.

78. Repetition makes a fact seem more true, regardless of whether it is or not. Understanding this effect can help you avoid falling for propaganda, says psychologist Tom Stafford.
79. Scapegoat, the weight of other people's guilt.
80. BBC News - RBI: What is the Indian central bank's conflict with the government?
Published 1 November 2018.
81. What they said and what actually happened how they reacted – INDIA TODAY - UPDATED: Jan 8, 2013 12:29 IST.
82. List of Indian general elections – Wikipedia.
83. Scapegoating – Wikipedia.
84. IE Pedia - Difference Between Natural and Man Made Disaster - June 23, 2016 - by Hasa.
85. Excuses and Character: Personal and Social Implications of Excuses
86. Barry R. Schlenker, Beth A. Pontari, and Andrew N. ChristopherView all authors and affiliations – SAGE journals - Volume 5, Issue 1.
87. 26 Years Later, the 1992 Scam Trials Linger, Show No Signs of Ending
Sucheta Dalal 03 August 2018 - Money Life.
88. 10 biggest Indian political scams – IPleaders - May 21, 2022 – 4056
89. Systems failure is a significant business risk - pwc
90. Why we should accept blame when we are wrong! - May 5, 2019, 11:28 AM IST Vinita Dawra Nangia in O-zone, Lifestyle, TOI.
91. Supreme Court rulings on delay in investigation of a crime - -Kartar Singh v. State of Punjab, reported in (1994) 3 SCC 569 – posted on the KANOON Website.

ABOUT THE AUTHOR

Graduate in Commerce 1961. Completed short Vigilance Course organized by the Institute of Secretariat Training & Management and in Parliamentary Procedures and Practices organized by the Bureau of Parliamentary Studies & Training, Ten days on job training in World Bank (1990), Washington and was a Team Member of the World Bank and ADB Teams for Project Appraisal and Special Studies. Was a member of the Loan Negotiation Team of the Government of India for ADB Loan for power projects.

Served Rural Electrification Corporation Limited {REC} for 18 years and Power Finance Corporation Limited {PFC} for 12 years, overall 30 years.

While I was working in Rural Electrification Corporation Limited (REC) as Deputy Secretary, my services were sought by the erstwhile Ministry of Energy for drafting MOA and AOA, other related documents and for incorporating PFC. PFC was incorporated on 16 July, 1986 under the Companies Act, 1956 after due approvals and as per the procedure prescribed under company law. My services were again sought by the Ministry on immediate basis in the first week of September, 1987. Joined PFC on 17th September, 1987 on deputation for one year, from REC for raising Rs. 100 Cr. from the financial market including its utilization for critical power projects selected by the erstwhile Planning Commission before 31st March, 1988, as per the mandate to the Ministry from the MOF/PMO. CMD was yet to be appointed. I was reporting to Joint Secretary (F) in the Ministry.

CMD assumed office on 14th January, 1988. The entire amount mobilized was utilized for the projects stated before the mandated date after due approvals and loan documentation. Awarded honorarium and commendation letter. Absorbed in the services of PFC after one year as per the desire of the CMD as Employee Number One (001) of PFC.

As my moral duty, I wish to state that at fag end of my service in PFC, I was implicated in a politically motivated criminal case when the security scam broke out in 1992, in connection with investment transactions of around Rs. 419 Cr. made with a UCO Bank, Hamam Street, Mumbai, even though the fact being that the investment transactions related to 1988-90 and had no relationship with security scam.

PFC did not file any complaint with the CBI. CBI registered the case suomoto.

The then CMD appeared before the Joint Parliamentary Committee (JPC) in connection with investment of Rs. 300 Cr in March, 1992 made by him, the period covered under Securities Scam.

Due to tremendous political pressure, soon thereafter, I was placed under suspension in November 1992. On appeal in the Hon'ble High Court of Delhi and the orders passed by the Hon'ble High Court, the suspension order was revoked in May; 1996.

The charge sheet doesn't mention a word about any allegation against me of corruption or recovery from me or any of my relatives or of any financial loss to PFC.

Even though PFC did not file complaint with CBI as stated before, sanction for prosecution was accorded by the then CMD which was suggestive of bias, if not malicious. The Statutory Auditor's Report incorporated in the Annual Report of PFC for 1992-93 {P 39, Para 1. Page 40 Para 11.6 and Page 41 Para 4, 5, 9 Point 26.1} regarding investment of Rs. 300 Cr. stated above supports the malafide intention of the then CMD. PFC suffered financial loss of Rs.15 Cr under the above investment. After due process of inquiry, the amount is stated to have been written off in the books of accounts while there was no financial loss whatsoever in the transactions made by me with the approval of the then CMD. There was no criminal or departmental action against those who caused financial loss of Rs. 15 cr. which was rather written off?

PFC then being newly established company; there was no procedure on investment of surplus funds laid down by the Board of Directors (BOD). A procedure was established by me with the approval of the CMD who had the powers on all matters of investment of funds as per delegated powers by the BOD. All the transactions of investment of surplus funds were accordingly made with the approval of CMD. PFC did not deal investment transactions with any Broker's firm as a matter of policy though its Articles permitted to deal with brokers.

The New Delhi Main Branch of the UCO Bank, Hamam Street, Mumbai which was approached to offer the quotes for investment of surplus funds advised PFC to approach their Branch at Hamam Street, Mumbai which was said to be solely dealing in securities transactions through its Official Brokers under the instructions of its Head Office. On the mandate of the Nationalized Bank at Mumbai with whom the investment transactions were done, PFC obtained quotes from the Representative of their Official Broker's firm in New Delhi and all the investments, were based on merits of rate and absorbing capacity, duly approved by the then CMD were made in the name of UCO Bank, Hamam Street, Mumbai.

All the investment transactions with the aforesaid Bank were made by RBI Cheques (Banker's Cheques) crossed A/c Payee initially through the New Delhi Main Branch and later, as mandated by the UCO Bank Branch at Hamam Street, Mumbai. The investments were routed through a designated foreign Bank (ANZ Grindlays Bank, Parliament Street, New Delhi stated before) which had the online money transfer facility (SWIFT facility) since investment amount was to be transferred on the same day as the interest thereon was to start from the date of the cheque.

PFC had given specific written mandate in the form of letters along with the Banker's Cheque crossed A/c Payee to the said foreign Bank with copy to the Hamam Street Brach of UCO Bank at Mumbai for transfer of money to the invested Bank at Mumbai. The designated foreign bank for transfer, as per the Charge Sheet, credited the proceeds of the banker's cheque to the account of the Broker's firm. It is also stated in the Charge Sheet the forwarding letters and the banker's cheques were handed over by the concerned Officers in PFC to the local representative of the broker's firm. The practice followed was to handover to the letters and cheques to the duly authorized representatives of the banks and the same procedure was followed as per such authorization letter given by the UCO Bank, Hamam Street at Mumbai to PFC. PFC had also received such mandates from five to six other banks.

I was not aware of crediting the banker's cheque proceeds to the account of Broker's firm by the said foreign bank since all the monies invested together with interest due and payable were received back by PFC on due dates with no loss of funds, thus leaving no scope for suspicion on misuse. The charge is undue favour to the Broker's Firm when, as stated before, no investment transaction was done with that Broker's Firm or any other Broker's Firm by PFC. As stated before, there was no recovery from me or any of my relatives as per the Search Report of CBI which I submitted to the then CMD of PFC. Under these circumstances, there was no undue favour to the Broker's firm, whatsoever.

The then CMD ordered special audit of the investment transactions of the value stated before. The special audit report contains the complete procedure followed by the investment department with no adverse comments or qualifications, thus authenticated the investment procedure followed with the approval of the then CMD. The special audit report also specifically confirmed in Part III to the specific queries of CMD to the effect there were no deviations in the investment procedure followed with the said UCO Bank and the transactions had the approval of the competent authority i.e. the then CMD.

This report was considered by the Central Vigilance Commission (CVC) which requested the Ministry of Energy to forward it to the Director of CBI for taking into consideration while investigating the case. This was accordingly done by the Ministry of Energy (now Power). CBI, except attaching a copy of the same with Charge Sheet as part of the documents (D23), did not mention a single word about the same in the Charge Sheet, thus had not taken the report into consideration during the investigation. The report would have bared the allegations made in the Charge Sheet had CBI taken same into consideration during investigation and had dealt it also in the Charge Sheet. This was biased and prejudicial on the part of the CBI.

I was under depression for about six months after the suspension. I made written submissions to the CMD, PFC, then Secretary in the Ministry and the Hon'ble Minister of Energy but there was no response from any one. My wife developed hypertension in 1993 which could not be controlled despite best medical treatment. She suffered brain stroke 12th May, 2005 midnight, admitted to the hospital, remained in coma for 28 days. On regaining on the 29th day, the Doctors found her having completely paralyzed right side and loss of speech. She remained bed ridden for eight years and passed away on 7th Dec 2013. I and my family came under social stigma and the social standing of the family was ruined.

The case was transferred to Special Court in Mumbai on the petitions filed by some of the accused persons residing in Mumbai sometime in 2017. On appeal by CBI in Hon'ble Court of Delhi, in 2017, the transfer of case was stayed. Final Order is still awaited. The regular trial at the Trial Court is yet to commence. The case has thus been pending for the last 30 years. I have been struggling in managing the legal and travel expenses. I have been living since then with loss of face, reputation and integrity built over 30 years of my service both in REC and PFC.

I was due for retirement on 31st December, 1996; my service was extended up to 31st July, 1997, the date on which I retired from the services of PFC. There being no Pension Scheme in PFC at that time, I served as Consultant in Multinational Consultancy Organizations for 18 years post retirement to financially support myself and my family. PFC engaged me as consultant in May, 2006 on policy, procedural and compliance matters of SPVs set up by PFC under Ultra Mega Power Projects, an Initiative launched by the GOI/MOP in 2005-06, served PFC in that position for two years on contract basis. In June, 2008 joined another multinational subsidiary company (a Subsidiary of German based Parent Company) as Senior Advisor [Finance, Commercial and Regulatory Affairs] Best Professional Employee and Special Contribution Awards were given while working in this company.

I am now aged 87 years old and, on that ground and there being no allegation of any recovery nor financial loss to PFC, filed petition for discharge in the Hon'ble High Court of Delhi permissible under the law which, though appreciated the facts, dismissed the petition as not a fit case on the ground that other accused had not filed any such petition. Among the accused persons in the case, I was the only person eldest of all others.

On completion of the contract in 2018, I took up writing of books. So far, I have authored 15 books on various subjects. "Time We Change for a Better India"(Jan 2017), "A Wake up Call for Every Indian"(Oct 2019) and "Jammu & Kashmir – The Truth of The Matter" (Nov. 2019), "The Living God on Earth" (Jan 2020), "Sounds of Silences in India's Constitution – Dangers Ahead" (December, 2020), "COVID-19 not a Natural Calamity –

An analysis of its Origin and the Fallout" (January, 2021), "India's Political Blunders Bleeding Its Borders {May, 2021), "Socialist, Secular and Religion in India – The Misconceptions" (June, 2021), "India's Stressed Assets Conundrum-Suggested Way-Out" (Oct, 2021), "Anyone who can tell where did Covid-19 come from that killed millions humans in the world-Is silence an answer" (Nov 2021), "Indian Parliament Monsoon Session {2021} Ruckus – Time to think about course of action" (Dec 2021), "About the correctness of certain Tariff decisions under the Electricity Act, 2003 – in retrospect" 2021, India's Futuristic Democracy – Threats of Constitutional Gaps and Digital Era [2022],India's Freebies, and Welfare Schemes – A Fiscal Disaster [2023], Aeolian Sound against the Doctrine of Basic Structure [2023] and We are One India One People [2023].